Books by Susan Allen Toth

Blooming: A Small-Town Girlhood
Ivy Days: Making My Way Out East

Ivy Days ❧

SUSAN ALLEN TOTH

Ivy Days

Making My Way Out East

LITTLE, BROWN AND COMPANY
Boston – Toronto

FIRST EDITION

Grateful acknowledgment to the Loft and to the McKnight
Foundation for a Loft-McKnight Grant, which helped provide the time to write this book.

All of the incidents in this book are true although many of the
names have been changed.

LIBRARY OF CONGRESS CATALOGING IN PUBLICATION DATA.

Toth, Susan Allen.
  Ivy days.

  1. Toth, Susan Allen.   2. Smith College—Alumnae—
Biography.   I. Title.
LD7152.9.T67   1984   378.744′23′0924   84–2912
ISBN 0–316–85078–0

MV

Designed by Patricia Girvin Dunbar

Published simultaneously in Canada
by Little, Brown & Company (Canada) Limited

PRINTED IN THE UNITED STATES OF AMERICA

Contents

For Jennifer and James,
who continued my education

Ivy Days 🌿

IT WAS HOT under the lights. Trying to keep my hands quiet, I wiped them surreptitiously on my best skirt and hoped they wouldn't leave a noticeable stain. My cheeks burned as I stared into the darkness, trying to pick out a special friend who had promised to wave encouragingly. When I had agreed to appear on this panel, months before, it had sounded easy and innocuous. "The program called 'Choices' is part of a nationwide Smith campaign," the committee chairwoman had explained. "Distinguished alumnae talking about the choices in their lives. Maybe fifteen minutes or so each, then questions. It will be so interesting. We're all excited!" It did sound sort of interesting, I thought. I always liked to hear people talking about their lives. Yes, of course, I told the chairwoman, I'd be glad to. I was flattered to be asked. In January, May was a long time away.

But in January I had been a different person. During the winter just past, I had suddenly been seized by violent anxieties. They had forced me to examine many aspects of my life and to try to decide what, at forty, I might want, or be able, to change. Just another midlife crisis, several onlookers had told me, not unsympathetically. Maybe. To me, the geysers that kept exploding unexpectedly under my feet made me fearful of exploring unknown paths and even, for a time, threatened my ordinary routes. I didn't want to leave my house for long, venture too far, or drive any distance on a freeway. Although those fears eventually passed, now, in May, I was still shaky. And in the midst of this tumult, I was going to have to consider, publicly, my choices in life: what had they been, how had they formed me, and what were they now?

Glancing down the row of precisely aligned chairs, I took quick stock of my four fellow witnesses. As I fidgeted, they were chatting with each other, relaxed and confident. Smith women, I thought, always looked ready to chair a meeting: skirts carefully covering crossed knees, makeup smooth, self-esteem as firmly in place as a gavel. I was in no mood to be generous. I knew something about the other panelists. All were married, none had jobs on which they were dependent for financial support, their children were older or grown. I was a single parent, and my nine-year-old daughter was home with a bad cold. Although tomorrow I might reasonably remember that they had problems like anyone else, tonight they seemed enviably settled and secure.

As the President of the college gracefully bent forward into the microphone, and began to introduce the program and panelists, I leaned back, testing the kinks in my neck, and tried to estimate the size of the audience. I was surprised at how large it was. Why had they come? I wondered. None of us on stage was a celebrity, or even much known beyond the confines of the Twin Cities. But we were under the lights, I supposed, because we had been judged to have made something of our lives. That was a phrase that had always intrigued me. "Magda, now there's a woman who has made something of her life," a male friend had recently said to me about a mutual acquaintance. I had wanted to picture exactly what shape Magda had given to her five decades, what identifiable object her life now resembled. A mountain, an altar, a perfect Chinese vase? Try as I might, I could not see my own life as having any shape at all. It bulged in unseemly places, sank like an empty ice bag in others, sometimes grew like a fungus in the night. On a few rare days it soared aloft, a handful of colorful helium balloons, tugging at restraining strings. But when a balloon eventually deflates, what shape does it have?

Perhaps, I surmised as I looked out at the audience, that is why they have come. They are not certain what their lives look like either, and they think ours may have more coherence. But why, simply because we have noticeable careers or community status, should our lives necessarily have more shape than theirs? I knew one or two women, sitting beyond these bright lights, who probably lived in much more tranquillity than some of us here on stage. Typical of Smith, I muttered to myself in that mixture of pride and irritation with which I often regarded the college that had so influenced my life. We're here to celebrate visible achievement. But does anyone ever ask what that achievement costs? Whether it is worth the price?

As I listened to the first panelists describe their lives, and choices, I became more agitated. No one mentioned self-doubt. No one mentioned difficulties. No one mentioned regrets, hesitations, or qualifications. It all sounded, I thought, far too easy. Leave aside the fact, which no one noted, that, being white, upper-middle-class, and well educated, we were among the lucky few to have choices at all. What was the difference between their stories and mine? Husbands, presumably helping with home and parenting? Lack of economic pressure? Determinedly optimistic outlooks? By the time my turn came, I was more than fidgety, I was angry. Angry with myself for being so confused and uncertain, angry with the others that they weren't.

Although I was clutching a few scribbled notes, I suddenly decided to begin instead with a story about my daughter. Earlier that day, when she had come home from third grade, she had found me lying on my bed, bathrobe tucked around my knees and shades drawn. It was only four o'clock, but the day, like so many days recently, had overwhelmed me. I wanted to rest for a while before cooking dinner, cleaning the kitchen, dressing, and driving to the evening program. Usually when Jennie scampered through the back door, I was just home from school myself, busy opening mail, answering the phone, emptying the cat box, starting the laundry, or tidying the living room. Today, as she stood by my bed, she was worried.

"Why are you lying down, Mommy? Are you sick?" she asked.

"No, honey, I'm just tired," I said reassuringly. "I have to go out tonight, and I wanted to rest awhile." I'd like to rest for days, *I felt like adding. Have a sleep cure. A rest home in the country. A chalet in the Swiss Alps, guarded by Dobermans.*

"I don't know, Mommy," Jennie went on, unsatisfied. "You've been resting a lot lately." She paused, then added accusingly, "I think something's wrong. Mommies aren't supposed *to rest."*

Sputtering, I shooed her out of my room. I wasn't bothered by her acuteness in noticing that I was feeling depressed, but by her assumption that mothers had to be in constant motion. What kind of model had I given her? Did she think life always had to be lived at high speed? Didn't she think it was all right to stop occasionally? Had she ever really seen me *stop? When did either of us take time out? Did she equate achievement with exhaustion? Did I?*

When my turn on the panel arrived, I told my story. "What are we teaching our children about choices?" I asked, more to myself than to the audience. "Do we ever have time to stop and smell the flowers?" This image, I later realized, had emerged from one of Jennie's favorite childhood stories. Ferdinand, a pacifist Spanish bull, had turned his back on a glorious career in the ring because he preferred to spend his gentle life at pasture, simply sniffing the flowers. I had read this tale myself as a child. I had always liked Ferdinand, reluctant hero that he was, but never before had I considered envying him. When I finished my wandering remarks, winding down in somewhat a complaining voice, my fellow panelists had a chance to respond. They clearly wanted to help. One recommended periodic weekend trips with one's husband, and another spoke with obvious sincerity of the support given her by religious faith. A third asked equally fervently, "Have you tried jogging?"

No one, I thought with amazement, seemed to think there might be a darker side to a life of public achievement, or even any possible shadows behind the relentless heat of those spotlights fixing us on stage. Perhaps Smith was supposed to prepare us for life under lights. Indeed, life there had begun for me in a brilliant glare, the humiliating beams of our physical-education Posture Pictures, snapped of each naked, shivering freshman in her first few days of orientation. Afterward I had returned, gratefully, to the comforting darkness of my fourth-floor room, where I could shut the door and hold this new and frightening world safely at bay. From one small window, if I stretched far to the left, I could just glimpse the lowering top of one of the Holyoke mountains. Looking at its shape, massive against the sky, I knew I was in the East. Here were mountains I had to climb.

I felt little drops of perspiration form on my forehead from the stage lights. Returning to the present, I focused again on the discussion around me. Soon it would be my turn to answer questions from the audience. I hoped no one would ask me to assess, once and for all, the net effect of Smith on my later life. Could I make my responses sound sufficiently positive? Why should I? How did I really feel: grateful, angry, or both? How soon could I leave the stage and go home to bed?

Two years later, with much work behind me, happier and more settled in my life, I returned to Smith for a special reunion. I had not attended my fifth, tenth, fifteenth, or twentieth reunions, but this one was different. Carolyn, an old friend from Lawrence House, had decided to organize a meeting of women who had over a six-year period lived in our dormitory, both when it was a scholarship cooperative house and later when it had been more or less integrated. Carolyn and I agreed that our Smith experience had been special. After twenty years or so, what would other Lawrence women remember? How had we turned out? Once both warmly and irritatingly close, how would we feel about each other now? About the college?

At first I was too beguiled by the Northampton spring to think clearly. As I had left home, a sprinkling of snow had dusted Minnesota with the last of winter. There it was cold and muddy. Here, my jacket over my arm, I walked over the campus with the incredulity of a new freshman, admiring the close-cropped green grass and lavish flowerbeds. How could I have forgotten how brightly the sun shone? How the clusters of magnolia blossoms and mountain laurel hung over doorways, perfumed the air, spilled white petals on the walks? Had I ever noticed the lovingly tended rock garden outside the conservatory, with its coral primroses, blue and violet iris, and wildflowers I couldn't name? Why had I never followed this landscaped trail, less than a block from the back door of Lawrence House? Had the old brick buildings always glowed like this under the tangled ivy?

Inside the new art building, I was awed by its generous spaces, the well-lit slide library so much larger and more efficient than the crowded one I remembered. Other new buildings, a center for performing arts, a gymnasium, an addition to the main library, demanded my attention too. Whether one wanted to dance or study the stars, everything was available to make it not only possible but enticing. My own college, where I had taught for fifteen years and felt completely at home, was not much smaller than Smith and well endowed. But we could never dream of a Faculty Center like the one I walked into now, a spacious modern building cantilevered over Paradise Pond, with an outdoor terrace for fair-weather dining and indoor meeting rooms for private conferences.

Resting that first afternoon on my assigned dormitory bed in a large, well-lit, tall-ceilinged room — far more attractive than Lawrence's dark cubicles — I was assailed by a nagging guilt. For a time I forgot my memories of tension and pressure, scholarship grade-points and House Council inspections, raised voices and doors slamming. Somehow, I thought, I had never responded as I should have to the opportunities I now saw around me. Why hadn't I always loved it here? Why had I forgone the once-in-a-lifetime chance to become an expert in Greek classical archaeology? Why hadn't I mastered French, instead of dropping my language after the second year? Why hadn't I taken full advantage of my geology labs, or tennis instruction, or the chance to learn everything about seventeenth-century prose? Why had I not swept along the path by John M. Greene Hall with the careless, swinging stride of the girl I could see this moment from my window, who looked confident and in charge of her world? Why weren't time and life arranged so that I could do it all over again, now that I knew better, and this time do it right?

Something familiar about that voice stopped me from listening to it any longer. Enough, I thought. I had done the best I could. Instead I thought ahead to the Lawrence House cocktail party in a few hours. I wasn't sure I was going to enjoy this reunion. Only two of my own class of Lawrence graduating seniors had returned, the others demurring with excuses or not bothering to answer Carolyn's persistent inquiries at all. No one from the class ahead of us had come back. I remembered little of the younger girls in Lawrence, who had seemed to my upperclassman's eyes rather silly, frivolous, lacking in experience. What would we have to say to each other?

Lots, I discovered, to my surprise. As circles broke and reformed around the table of wine and cheese, conversation altered slightly but always returned to the same topics. With intense attention, women in their late thirties and early forties listened to each other tell what they were doing with their lives. We spoke of marriages, hard-won successes and some failures; children, wonderful and difficult; careers in transition; friends not here and new friends, women's friendships in general, the ways friends had helped us survive. We spoke of coping and small triumphs. One woman, whose husband was slowly dying of a rare incurable cancer, told of their camping trip in the Sierras a few months ago. Another described, amidst much sympathetic laughter, her first date as a divorcée at the age of forty. We asked each other about men and causes, politics and houses, travels and life in different cities. Most of us had energy and hope; almost no one wanted to be twenty again.

What struck me about these conversations was how open and honest everyone seemed to be. As if we were seated on each other's rumpled beds, or were sharing cigarettes between classes, or talking earnestly over a last cup of coffee at the Lawrence breakfast table, no one tried to impress anyone else. I never learned, nor did I want to, how much money any of us made. Except when someone mentioned the painful pleasure of renovating an old house, or adjusting to a cramped apartment, I did not know or care in what style anyone lived. That was not our common bond. Instead, one woman said to another, "What have you done about the drug problem? Isn't it incredible that we both have teen-age daughters?"

As the weekend progressed, conversations continued in dormitory rooms and over shared meals. Now, as one woman spoke about her years in therapy, another joined in. Someone who had been quiet and reticent at the first reunion meeting suddenly began to talk about her unhappy marriage and to ask others what kind of help and future she might hope for. When someone mentioned alcoholism and how it was now openly discussed in a way unthinkable when we'd been at Smith, a cheery, spiffily dressed woman stared into her coffee cup.

Her face clouded over. "I haven't told anyone at home about this," she said, looking up, "but my husband is an alcoholic. I don't know what to do." An hour later, with exchanged addresses of chemical dependency centers tucked into her purse, she rose from the table with a determined grimace. "I don't know why I can talk about these things with all of you, but not at home," she said regretfully. "It's so much easier here."

As I sat, exhausted but pleased, in the plane going home, I thought I knew why we had been easy with each other. Part, of course, was due to the peculiar rootlessness of reunions. I had even had to sneak occasional glimpses at pictures of Jennifer and James to remind myself that yes, I did have another, grown-up life back home in Minnesota. For a brief time we had been able just to be single women together. Fed and housed by someone else, we had no responsibility for others. We had had that indulgence college students seldom recognize, to focus without guilt only on ourselves and our own concerns.

But beyond those obvious external conditions, I thought that our years at Smith had given us some lasting gifts. We had long ago been trained to ask questions and to push for answers. We had believed that we needed to look for truth and to value it highly. Most of all, we had learned to take ourselves seriously as women and as human beings.

The sunshine streaming through the airplane window was so bright I had to pull the shade down so I could try to take a nap. As I did, my own inner vision darkened. Yes, Smith had helped turn the women I'd met this weekend into special people, ones I'd want as friends if they lived nearby. But that wasn't the whole picture I was taking home. On the last day of the reunion, I'd slipped away to Lawrence House, now empty of most students and alumnae. Climbing to the third floor, I had quietly knocked on the door of my old upperclassman's room to see if it was empty. No one answered. Pushing open the door, I found myself in a space so familiar and yet so alien I felt disoriented. Stripped of all but furniture, linens neatly folded on the bare bed, it was smaller than I'd remembered. The one window let in even less light. The warm air was stuffy, the corners of the room shadowed. Turning, feeling for a moment a kind of claustrophobic panic, I stared at the blank walls. They were covered with a dingy beige wallpaper, one that seemed identical to that of twenty-some years ago. How could I have survived so long in a space like this? Outside, in the hall, even though I'd closed the door behind me, I could hear someone's heels tapping down the corridor. Long-ago noises flooded into the room with me, voices, phones ringing, doors slamming. I caught my breath and fled.

Which was the real picture? I asked myself on the homeward trip as I closed my eyes and let those images float past me. The confident girl I'd seen, her books under her arm, briskly walking the magnolia-strewn path by John M. Greene Hall? Or the small dark room which still carried an aura of depression? How did either or both of these pictures lead to one of the lunch table where Lawrence House alumnae openly talked about their most private hopes and fears and gathered strength from each other's stories? Or to my sense that I had just spent a weekend among significant, if in no way famous, women?

"Are you glad you went to Smith?" people sometimes ask me. I never know what to say. Yes, and no. Yes, but. Of course, but on the other hand. My college years changed me in ways I am still trying to understand. Somewhere else would have shaped me differently, but how? Better or worse? How can I be sorry I went to Smith, if I'm not sorry I became who I am? How can I be entirely glad, if I wish I had been able to do some things otherwise? Keep asking yourself questions, I tell my students who are writing essays, until you know what you really think. Don't give up too quickly. Don't settle for easy answers. I don't always tell them how long one has to continue asking.

Ivy Days

Out East 🌿

"ALL RIGHT, Allen, drop the sheet," said a brisk voice. Though blinded by two glowing spotlights, I tried to meet for a reassuring moment the matter-of-fact eyes of the gym teacher who stood next to the photographer. I blinked, couldn't focus, and gave up. Taking a deep breath, I sucked in my stomach, straightened stiffly, and dropped the white percale sheet I'd modestly wound like a disinfected sarong around my nude body. Though my feet tingled with cold from the tile floor, the heat of the lights assaulted my bare skin. Behind the camera the photographer pressed a button with a loud click. "Turn sideways, please," she said, sounding bored. Another click. "All right. That's all. That will do it. Pick up your sheet. Out the door on your left." The gym teacher strode toward the other door, where a long line of girls, anonymously white-sheeted, waited. "Next, please. Hurry up, please. Name?" she called, not wanting to see if I had yet made my exit. Hurriedly wrapping the sheet around me again, its ends flapping and dragging, I scurried out of the small stuffy room toward the lockers. Now I could get dressed and go back to the House. I hadn't yet learned to call it home.

Posture Pictures were a mesmerizing highlight of Smith's Orientation Week. All freshmen were required to take Basic Motor Skills, where they would learn proper body movement, and these pictures were a diagnostic tool. Each girl's body, carefully studied in black-and-white by the physical education staff, its flaws, faults, and misalignments noted, was graded A to F. In an individual conference, a phys. ed. instructor would inform a freshman of her possibilities for improving this grade. You could not graduate from Smith until your body was at least a C, and many seniors, we were warned, spent a humiliating spring semester trying to expand their chests and tuck in their tailbones.

Although Posture Pictures were taken within the first few days, I knew none of us freshmen would see them for several weeks. Meanwhile rumors flourished, most of which, my Big Sister, Dulie, comforted me, were total fabrications. No, no, it wasn't true that Amherst men sometimes broke into the gym offices, raided the files, and stole the whole sheaf of pictures. And then posted them on telephone poles with names attached. At least, she'd heard it maybe had happened *once*, but only once, and that was a long time ago. Don't worry, Sue, don't worry.

Somehow I had not expected to be so cleanly stripped in my first week at Smith. Whenever I thought of entering life in the East, opening the door that stood invisibly somewhere in eastern Pennsylvania, and stepping into a world of old ivy-covered brick buildings, white Colonial houses, and rock-strewn farms, I saw myself as suitably clothed. When I passed through that door, I would be transformed, a transcendent hope like that in Handel's *Messiah* when the bass triumphantly trumpets forth, "And we shall be changed." No longer swathed in white triple-rolled socks and billowing crinolined skirts, I would suddenly be adorned in whatever sleek, sophisticated robes they were currently wearing "out East." Some days, when I felt more confident, I called it "back East." Though my Erickson ancestors had come from the Old Country, the Allen side proudly traced itself back to Ethan Allen, the Green Mountain Boys, and Vermont. Back East. "Out East," though, felt more accurate: a far-off land, unknown, frightening.

My idea of the East was drawn from many disparate images. Some had sunk visually into my mind from years of staring at the large Currier & Ives calendars the Travelers' Insurance agent, from whom we never bought insurance, hopefully sent my mother each December: horse-drawn carriages dashing through snow, hunters shouldering newly shot turkeys, fields tidied by stone walls and villages crowned by white steeples. Others had filtered through poetry and prose in high-school American literature class: Hawthorne, Melville, Whittier, Longfellow, Amy Lowell, Sara Teasdale, and a touch of Edna St. Vincent Millay. From Hawthorne I envisioned crumbling manses, dark gloomy rooms, lurking Puritans; from Whittier, happy snowbound families that nonetheless had shipwrecks in their background.

New England men wrote about sin, sorrow, and the sea; the few women, about love and music. Sara Teasdale promised life had loveliness to sell: that sounded more like life in the East than in Iowa. I knew Amy Lowell was a "bluestocking," an image which had little to do with legs in my mind, but rather with short, cropped hair (there was a picture of Amy in our book) and a mannish, aggressive attitude toward life. Women in the East were obviously individualists. Edna St. Vincent Millay climbed rocks at dawn, lay stretched out listening to the surf just as I listened to the waves on the shore at Lake Carlos, and burned her candle, illogically but wonderfully, at both ends.

I wasn't exactly sure how Edna St. Vincent Millay, whom I admired so furiously I always accorded her the dignity of her full name, dressed. I wanted to know because, wondering what people were like out East, I thought I would find them less foreign if I knew what they wore. Clothes were a language I understood. I knew what Eastern college girls looked like. I had seen them all in the August issue of *Mademoiselle.* During high school, I studied that bulging catalog of fashions, "The College Issue," as if I were a medical student poring over Gray's *Anatomy,* memorizing each twist of sinew or articulation of bone. Since I had never visited any Eastern college campus, I searched for clues to manners and mores in the backgrounds of pictures as well as in the foreground models. I could never differentiate among the brick administration buildings, ivy-covered dormitories, and sidewalks crowded with bicycles. The University of Pennsylvania, as displayed in *Mademoiselle,* did not stand out from Simmons, or Vassar, or Middlebury. Even Agnes Scott (down South) and Stanford (out West) seemed discouragingly similar to the hallowed halls back East. And the girls, to my surprise, all looked much the same, no matter where they were from: slender figures, glossy caps of hair, triumphant smiles.

The Eastern look, I eventually decided, was meant to accommodate the two main Eastern activities, sports and parties. Girls in Ames didn't have many athletic opportunities: we swam, played volleyball at picnics, hit badminton birds in each other's backyards, and occasionally bowled a few lines. Two or three girls whose parents belonged to the Country Club golfed, though not seriously. But if the pictures in my magazines and college catalogs told the truth, Eastern girls played lots of sports: they canoed, wielded field-hockey sticks, skiied in nearby mountains. They had swim meets and tennis ladders, outing clubs and crew teams, horseback-riding and lacrosse. For all these activities, they had special costumes, white tennis skirts, riding jodhpurs, ski sweaters. Even their everyday clothes seemed sporty to me — brisk, crisp, and no-nonsense; blazers, kneesocks, kilts, and Bermuda shorts all had a kind of truncated efficiency.

When Eastern girls weren't racing across an athletic field or tennis court, they were liable, I gathered, to be at parties. Ames only had two kinds of parties when I was in high school: casual "record hops," at school or at someone's house, where one wore one's best skirt and sweater; or "formals," the big social events like the Junior-Senior Prom or the Christmas Dance, which one attended in strapless bodice and layers of tulle. But social life in the East looked much more complicated. Catalogs and brochures showed varying glimpses of "mixers," football games, house dances, fraternity costume parties, and informal "dates" that seemed to involve standing around outside, and smiling broadly, under a large tree or on the banks of a small pond.

The kind of party that worried me most, though, was the "cocktail party," which everyone I knew in Ames agreed was liable to take a lot of my time in the East. Since I didn't drink yet, except an occasional sip of sherry, I was uneasy at this idea. But primarily I wasn't sure what I would be supposed to wear. No one in Ames High had any use for a "cocktail dress," and I did considerable research, pondering racks of what we called "party dresses," as well as magazine layouts, before I decided what a cocktail dress was. Girls in my Eastern pictures definitely wore them a lot: tight black dresses, with perhaps a knee-high slit in the back, three-quarter sleeves, a V-neckline in front. When the time arrived for me to make my fateful purchase — I could only afford one — I faltered, fearing bulges, and chose a conservative, high-necked, princess-style dress, double-breasted with shiny buttons. Though the dress was expensive, I reassured myself that I could wear it "other places" — maybe to a fancy restaurant or funerals, of neither of which at age seventeen I had much experience.

After agonies of observation, conclusions, and final selection, I arrived with trunk and suitcases at Smith only to find that I was both overprepared and still, inexplicably, shut out of Eastern fashion. When I got off the train in Northampton, hot and sweaty in my homemade tweed suit and little hat, I could see immediately that the older girls, the real "Smithies" who met us freshmen at the station, as well as some more savvy newcomers, were not dressed quite as *Mademoiselle* had promised me. No spiffy knickers, linen jackets, certainly no suits. At first the "Smithies" looked sloppy: button-down shirts with tails hanging out over jeans or slacks, faded madras Bermuda shorts, sweaters and plaid skirts whose colors didn't always match. But soon I found how hard it was to emulate this look, not only because I didn't own most of those items, but also because, when I tried them, they just did not feel right. Wool crew-neck sweaters itched at the back of my neck; knee socks slowly crept to my ankles and collapsed; pleated skirts pulled over my hips. They didn't belong to me. The girls I envied obviously did not *think* about their clothes; they simply got up in the morning, pulled on what they'd been comfortable in for years, and headed out to face the day.

Although I tried to revise my expectations, and achieve the faded, woolly look I saw around me, I was seldom satisfied. Because I had little spending money left for clothes, I shopped the sale racks. As a result, I ended up with a plaid skirt that wasn't really a kilt; an Orlon sweater rather than wool; a corduroy vest instead of a tweed blazer. After only a few days on campus, I knew where to look for the genuine articles, but I quickly found I couldn't afford them. All along Green Street, a commercial block just a few feet from Lawrence House, small, exclusive shops offered tempting window displays of skirts, sweaters, Bermudas, blazers, ribbon belts, and chintz knitting bags. One store, I discovered, didn't even have much stock inside. Instead, with a rack of only a few choice coats and suits, the management subtly suggested that a serious shopper, one worthy of their attention, would sit in one of the velvet-upholstered, gilt-backed chairs and let Madame Laletti bring an appropriate selection from the back room. Once I mistakenly wandered inside; caught, I pretended I was "just browsing," fingering intently the two or three available coats before escaping.

The presence of Green Street, its shops glittering with gold circle pins and flowering with Liberty of London blouses, was a constant reminder of a kind of schizophrenia I dimly sensed at Smith. On the one hand, much to my surprise, dress was very democratic. During the week everyone was casual, sloppy, even determinedly grubby. Many of us wore jeans, safety-pinned skirts, old baggy sweaters, and sometimes spent all day in our gym outfits, coarse cotton tunics over matching bright jersey bloomers. Without closely examining the original fabric on which the dirt flourished, one couldn't distinguish a DuPont or Rockefeller in a smudged pair of slacks from Mary O'Connor, Jane Doe, or Sue Allen from Ames, Iowa. No one tried to impress anyone else. Until, at least, the weekend. On Friday, as hordes of girls left the campus for weekend dates, they blossomed in pea jackets, tams, cashmere polo coats, and even short, snappy Peck and Peck suits, and they carried suitcases whose bulging sides suggested outfits *Mademoiselle* would have approved. Although dates appeared on Fridays through Sundays, popping up on lawns, porches, and living-room carpets like rare and short-lived jack-in-the-pulpits, those of us left on campus pretended not to notice. "Studying this weekend," we determinedly remained as we were, wrinkled and defiantly grungy in our everyday skirts and stained cardigans.

Although in my four years at Smith, I never really felt I had the right wardrobe — or was sure I could successfully wear it if I did — I was eventually able to achieve the rumpled, dirty look that I thought was my only alternative to Green Street. Late in my junior year, I found a trenchcoat on sale in downtown Northampton. Although it was not just like everyone else's in style and color — too creamy white, no epaulets — it was my first trenchcoat, and I loved it. Soon it acquired a patina of smudges, smears, and studied neglect. With it I wore my "tennies," also gradually soiled to a satisfactory gray.

On the sunny spring morning of my senior year when I knew I might receive an award at honors chapel — I had read about one for which I was a logical candidate — I deliberately dressed in jeans, sweatshirt, gray tennies, and my battered trenchcoat. Hands jammed casually in my pockets, belt looped around my waist, collar turned up, I strode happily up the stage stairs to accept the certificate for the Victoria Louise Schrager Prize from the outstretched hand of President Mendenhall. It was for a senior who had made an outstanding contribution in academics and extracurricular activities, and it meant to me that at last I had made it. Yet I was almost as proud of how I looked: not beautiful, not striking, but absolutely authentic. I remember wiggling my bare toes in my threadbare sneakers, secure in the knowledge that my stark ankles (though rubbed rawish red at the back) looked much more sophisticated than if I'd worn socks. For a brief while at Smith we had a word, plain but oddly transformed, that meant "with it," "cool," or "neat." That low-keyed and powerful word was "shoe." For those moments on the stage, I felt "shoe." Finally I was dressed right.

A few months later, packing my clothes for home, I folded my black cocktail dress and placed it in the Christian Charities giveaway box on the Lawrence House landing. It had never been worn. I was a litle sad, thinking of the uninformed girl who had once sewn herself a tweed suit in order to travel "out East."

One reason I was so obsessed with clothes as a key to the East was my inability to make much sense of its landscape. Not until I was long gone from Smith, well into my thirties and traveling by car through upper New England, did I begin to see how its patchy fields and big cities, endless suburbs and isolated villages, worn mountains and rocky seacoast, fitted together. So I used Bermuda shorts, Shetland sweaters, and camel's hair coats as a way to get hold of the East and hang on.

What I saw looked very different from Iowa. Stepping off the train in Northampton that hot September day in 1957, I was still trying to assimilate fast-moving images from our clacking rush through western Massachusetts: wooded hills, mills, sooty industrial towns. For the next few months, what I mainly saw of New England was the Smith campus, the half-mile walk that led from my dormitory to Northampton's Main Street, and the seven-mile drive between Smith and Amherst. On the drive I noticed tobacco fields with workers stooping beneath gauze nets, narrow highways busy with traffic, small towns with old white clapboard houses. In Northampton I studied Main Street, with its massive hotel containing Wiggins Tavern, patterned after a Colonial inn, with open hearth, exposed rafters, low ceiling. I registered impressions of an ancient opera house, the Academy of Music, now showing movies; the Hampshire Bookshop, Tudor-timbered on the outside and inside piled high with books like a library. I ignored anything ordinary, an ugly marble bank, Woolworth's, a pizza parlor, or whatever else we had back home.

What did I make of these selective snapshots? I pasted them together into a mental album, "The East," something I could authoritatively show to my friends and family back in Iowa. The East, I could tell them, was very old. Columns, faded brick, widows' walks. None of the new ramblers and bungalows we had on the outskirts of Ames. Even stores often had white Colonial fronts and pasted-on pillars, so they looked vaguely historic. I thought of the low ceilings in Wiggins Tavern and the Tudor front of the Hampshire Bookshop, and yes, I thought, I could honestly tell everyone that the East was indeed quaint. Did they know that Jonathan Edwards had once preached in a Congregational church in Northampton? In American Lit. we had had to read an excerpt from one of his sermons, about sinners being spiders held over the fire by an angry God; some of my friends might remember and be impressed. Though I never actually went inside his Northampton church, *I* was.

Maybe mentioning Jonathan Edwards would make my point about culture and the East. I didn't want to hurt anyone's feelings back in Ames, but it was clear to me, after just a few months, that they had more culture than we did. Jenny Lind herself had christened the college's little lake, "Paradise Pond." Besides Jonathan Edwards, Emily Dickinson had lived nearby in Amherst. Boston was only a few hours away: Oliver Wendell Holmes, Amy Lowell, and all those others. I couldn't help comparing the Hampshire

Bookshop to the businesslike Iowa State Bookstore, with its stacks of engineering texts towering above the waxed linoleum aisles; the Academy of Music, rotund and majestic, to the square, uninspired New Ames Theatre; Wiggins, with its waitresses in pinafores and mobcaps, to the Solar Inn, the ramshackle steak house where Ames couples went on their wedding anniversaries.

Part of my seduction by the East was undoubtedly its siren song of money. Smith was a well-endowed institution, with a lavishly maintained campus and with a tradition of what the housemothers, and the administration, often called "gracious living." Later, reading Fitzgerald, I knew what he meant by the sound of money in Daisy Buchanan's voice. That was what I heard when someone talked of "gracious living." Though sometimes I bicycled to a professor's house or to a nearby city park, I really never saw the working side of Northampton, with its factories, commercial developments, and modest residential areas. If I saw, I didn't notice. For me, the East was typified by Smith. Years later, returning for the first time to the college, I was appalled at my ignorance of the town that enclosed it. I didn't even know what streets to take or how far Northampton extended. It was bigger, and less unusual, than I'd ever realized.

I think I fell in love with the East the first time I saw the College Boathouse on a bright September afternoon. As a sophomore guide ended her orientation tour for us freshmen, she stopped at Paradise Pond, Smith's pride and pictured in every brochure. It was beautiful, a small lake surrounded by wooded paths, with a tiny island in the center, a waterfall at one end, and a gentle long slope leading down to the water. I thought of Lake La Verne, Iowa State's famous landmark. Despite its melodic name, it was a stagnant, shallow pond, with water so murky that it was laughingly called "Lake La Mud." Ames's main highway, U.S. 30, ran just a few feet from Lake La Verne, and the lake was only thinly cushioned from noisy traffic by a few trees. Paradise Pond was undisturbed, just the faint sound of the waterfall breaking the silence, and its grassy banks were velvety green, carefully tended and landscaped.

Walking briskly along, our guide soon brought us to the College Boathouse, nestled snugly into the bank. Boathouses I'd seen before were only plain sheds to hold motorboats, rickety and weather-beaten garages stuck over the water of Minnesota lakes. The College Boathouse, shining with fresh dark green paint, was different. More spacious than many houses in Ames, it was swabbed and sparkling clean inside, like a well-scrubbed ship, boasting racks of canoes and sculls with gleaming wood and polished trim. Along one wall hung paddles and oars, also freshly varnished, and their glossy wood reminded me, incongruously, of our maple dining-room table at home. Most boats I knew were old, peeling, wooden rowboats; the canoes here were like expensive furniture. As I ran my hand gingerly along the edge of a scull, admiring the way it was ingeniously suspended just above the quiet water seeping in from Paradise Pond, I was struck by the offhand largesse of an institution that could provide such boats, such *numbers* of boats, such a *house* for such numbers of boats. Why hadn't the college advertised this boathouse, or even mentioned it, in any of its admissions leaflets? Obviously accustomed to such things, people here took it for granted. I would not only have to learn how to use a facility like this, confidently, as if I owned it, but I would also have to learn not to be impressed — perhaps, finally, not to notice it at all.

At first I was so overwhelmed by the Smith campus itself that I did not much wonder what lay beyond it. I concentrated on learning the campus pathways, exploring the labyrinth of the library, finding my gym locker and the geology lab. I tried to make myself as much at home as possible. In some ways, I succeeded. But I never fully conquered, or even understood, a kind of constriction, a tightness in my chest, that only eased for a time when I took the train home to Iowa at Christmas. Even then I wasn't sure what the feeling was. For four years, I now believe, I lived with a kind of deep claustrophobia, a sense of being closed in. It was part of the price I paid for going "out East."

The town I grew up in was not large. By the time I was a teenager, I knew almost all its streets and connections, its stores and parks and schools. Bicycling everywhere or cruising in cars with my friends, I had the security of moving freely in a wholly known world. More important, I knew what lay beyond the town. Iowa's peaceful countryside, open fields, and sweeping skies were part of my unconscious landscape, lying in the back of my mind like a stage setting no one ever changed. Although I never lived in the actual country, it was the context in which Ames existed, the sea in which our small town was an important island. Smaller towns were smaller islands, Des Moines a large one. But the land surrounded them all. Driving Highway 30, straight through Ames, one left the endless fields of corn for perhaps ten minutes of houses, gas stations, and stores, and then plunged into the ocean of corn again.

In winter and early spring, stubbled fields revealed the contours of the land, rippling toward the horizon in broken rhythms of bent brown cornstalks or ridged black furrows. By summer, all one saw was waves of green. The corn stood so tall on either side of the highway that it was as if Moses had struck his staff on the sunbaked ground and the green sea had opened a narrow path.

Even when I couldn't see beyond the first few rows of giant stalks, I knew the fields rolled on for miles. Whatever direction we drove from Ames, we passed through the same landscape, black earth, plowed fields, and large clean skies. The farms themselves were tidy dots of house, barn, and sheds, far enough from the road to seem more like Monopoly buildings than real homes with real people. My Iowa landscape was mostly earth and air, plants and sky. Seven miles to the Nevada liquor store, fifteen miles to the park in Boone, thirty miles to shop in Des Moines, fifty or sixty miles to basketball or football games in Newton, Grinnell, Marshalltown: everywhere my mother drove me I absorbed the same sense of space. Outside the towns was a reassuring repetition of fields and farm, fields and farm.

That unconscious assumption of space was part of what made my confinement in Northampton difficult. I didn't have time, or awareness, to ask myself why I sometimes felt almost smothered in Lawrence House, with its fifty-seven girls; why a walk around the artfully landscaped campus didn't always make me feel better; why I spent so much time lying on my bed looking out my small window at a patch of sky.

But I did instinctively know that I longed each year for Mountain Day. Mountain Day was a special Smith holiday, set aside so that students could admire the New England fall foliage. No one ever knew exactly when Mountain Day would fall, but early one crisp October morning, the loud ringing of the carillon signaled the cancellation of all classes. A few determined students remained on campus to study, some fled on buses to see their boyfriends an hour or two away, but most of us scurried about to find bicycles and food for picnic lunches. Soon a flood of girls streamed on their bicycles down the main street of Northampton, like a fall parade, heading to the highways out of town.

All Mountain Days blend into my first one that fall of my freshman year. I was curious about whether I could indeed find a mountain close to this Eastern campus. Another freshman across the hall, Meg, who lived in nearby Greenfield, said sure, we could bike to Mount Tom, easily, it wasn't very far, and so, with our roommates, we started off. I am amazed now that we made it. Flabby, out of condition, but high-spirited, we donned sweatshirts, mounted our secondhand, one-speed bikes, and headed for the mountain. On we bicycled, singing loudly, along the edge of a well-traveled highway, through straggling towns that seemed almost continuous, past occasional tobacco fields and vegetable stands. Ahead and behind us, we could see other lines of Smith girls, sometimes waving to us, passing us, or turning onto the Amherst exit.

The sun was high, warming our backs until we had to take off our sweatshirts and tie them around our waists. I looked at everything as hard as I could, every peeling farmhouse, heap of squash, white board fence, to see if I could discern a pattern. It was nice to see people going about ordinary tasks, shopping, working in gardens, trimming hedges. Closed in since my arrival at Smith, I felt miraculously released. The first few miles I scarcely noticed the heaviness of my bike or the unaccustomed strain on my muscles. Stopping occasionally to rest, we plugged onward, puffing and laughing, until finally in early afternoon we found the turnoff to the Mount Tom Lookout Tower. After we climbed the tower ladder, we sank gratefully onto the plank floor in the hot midday sun and decided to go no farther.

Though I recall few details about the surrounding countryside, I know I gasped at the view. We were high above the ground, looking out on a panorama of hills, with fiery masses of leaves everywhere. The fall colors seemed more profuse and vivid than ours at home, probably because my part of Iowa had few hills to provide this sweep of reds, yellows, and golds. "This is it," I thought to myself, with an assurance I hadn't had before. "This is New England, just like the pictures." I had foresightedly brought my Brownie, and I took my own pictures. Turning the pages of my photograph album today, I can see us still, rumpled but happy, with the hills behind us, sweatshirts tied around our waists, Coke bottles on the plank floor, and victorious grins on our faces. That afternoon, while we picnicked and talked and napped for a while on the rough boards, happiness flooded over me with the warm sunshine.

The distance to Mount Tom had been much farther than we'd imagined, or than Meg remembered, and so we didn't dare stay too long. After an hour or so, Meg looked at her watch and warned us we'd have to start back. Pedaling home, we were all tired. We didn't talk much, and we didn't want to sing. My roommate, Alice, who'd been doing ski exercises, tried to start "One Hundred Bottles of Beer on the Wall," but no one joined in. My bottom was blistered, and my muscles ached. I began to think of tomorrow, lessons undone, art slides unstudied.

When we dragged in the front door, it was almost time for dinner. As I hurried upstairs to change into a skirt, I brushed by Lee Anderson, an ambitious, competitive girl who was in my Art History class. "Boy, did you get sunburned," she said, stopping to stare. "We went to Mount Tom," I said proudly. "We bicycled all the way. Where did you go?"

"I decided to stay here," Lee said, with more than a trace of self-satisfaction. "It was just great. There was absolutely no one in the art library, so I had yesterday's slides all to myself. I just got caught up a few minutes ago, and am I relieved. Yesterday's lecture was really important, didn't you think?" I didn't answer, except with a kind of grunt. I hurried past Lee toward my room. At least, I thought to myself, now I have seen New England.

Although I did not have much opportunity to decipher the topography of New England, I was kept amply busy trying to make some sense of the immediate life around me. Some codes were fairly simple to decipher, like the language of scarves. Many girls wore six-foot scarves, striped according to the different school colors of the men's colleges. Scarves were given, not purchased; you acquired one only when a man endowed you with it as a token of conquest. It was usually a sign of going steady. Someone who always wore a royal-blue-and-white scarf was obviously involved with a Yale man; but a girl who sometimes wore a purple-and-white scarf (Amherst), sometimes green-and-white (Dartmouth), and sometimes crimson-and-white (Harvard) was indulging in some boasting.

It was also easy to learn the cachet of carrying a Harvard bookbag, especially if it was faded and worn. It was all right to buy one's own bookbag, but preferably from the Harvard Coop itself (I soon learned to pronounce this abbreviation of the Harvard Cooperative Society like "chicken coop"). Knitting was important, too. Knitting while listening to a lecture made one look unconcerned, though one had to put down the needles occasionally to take notes. Most girls knitted sweaters in complicated Fair Isle patterns, like the crew-neck Shetlands I so admired on Green Street. Since I had never done any handwork except hemming skirts, this code took longer to unravel. I didn't begin until my junior year. Then, with lessons from Jane, a helpful friend in Lawrence, who went over each morning's work after lunch and painstakingly fixed all my dropped stitches, I began a plain scarf for my new stepfather. Gray yarn was on sale at the yarn shop, so gray it was. All fall I knitted and purled, purled and knitted in a stitch that Jane told me was simplicity itself. I dragged the scarf around with me from class to class. As the scarf slowly stretched out, foot by foot, its width stretched too, loosening as my stitches grew more confident. By the time I was almost finished, the scarf looked as if it had a strange wobble. When I ran out of yarn, I could not match the gray, so I had to settle for a large set of loud orange stripes at one end. Though my stepfather claimed he loved it, and dutifully wore it in my presence, I always felt a little badly that I hadn't produced a Fair Isle sweater instead.

I didn't learn everything as easily as knitting. I did not, for example, ever learn how to gallop. Although I saw occasional girls heading to the pool or the hockey field, I knew that not every Smith girl canoed or crewed or played lacrosse. Sports were foreign dialects I didn't think I had to acquire. But I knew I had to master

Basic Motor Skills. All freshmen had to take a year of this course, and from the first day, when I was told my Posture Picture had only been a mediocre C−, I felt doomed to failure. Though I listened carefully, so I could learn to walk gracefully, lift my suitcase to an overhead train rack with correct motions, and lower myself properly to a chair, I could never follow directions with my body as well as I could with my mind. Calisthenics and stretching exercises were even worse. Grunting and straining, I lay embarrassed on my workout mat as the teacher slid her hand beneath my back to show the class how to tell when one's spine wasn't really flat.

The unit I hated most was Rhythm and Movement. The whole class, thirty-odd girls, assembled in the dance studio. Miss Street, lean, leathery, and muscled, called out the exercises: "Circle, dip, sway, two steps forward, three back; do you have it, girls?" One bleak day she announced, "This time, girls, we'll finish with something really simple. I just want you to gallop in time to the music. Nice, large steps, please, in a big circle around the room. Do you have it, girls? Everybody ready? All right, now, ONE, TWO, THREE." I opened and closed my mouth in the brief space after her questions, but I did not have the courage to speak. Everyone else seemed to understand what was happening. I had absolutely no idea how to gallop.

On the count of THREE I began to move, trying to merge with the rest of the girls, hanging close behind someone tall, half-skipping and half-walking, with a desperate energy that did not disguise the fact that I was obviously out of synch. "STOP," Miss Street called, and we all halted. "A few of you girls seem to be having a little trouble," she said kindly. "Now, watch me." She galloped a few steps. It looked easy, a kind of shuffling motion like the two-step. "All right? Everyone ready? ONE, TWO, THREE." It looked easy all right, but it wasn't. I couldn't seem to get my feet to move together. I kept hopping and skipping instead. "STOP!" Miss Street looked at me. "All right, that's enough for today," she waved her hand in dismissal to the class, "but I'd like *you*" — and she pointed to me — "to stay after class."

The rest of the girls ran for the showers, a few looking back at me curiously. My face burning, I slowly walked across the wide polished floor to Miss Street. For ten minutes she worked with me, patiently directing, watching my feet, shaking her head. Then she had to admit I'd be late to my next class, and, looking defeated, she waved me off to the showers with the others.

Athletics were clearly out. But I wasn't quite sure what else one did at Smith — that is, what actual activities one joined — in order to belong. At Freshman Orientation, posters announced, "Everyone sings at Smith!", urging us all to audition for the two freshman choirs. I liked the idea of being part of "everyone," and wearing a pretty long white dress, but I had to be realistic. My voice, while fairly tuneful, had a range of only an octave, and I always mouthed the higher notes in "The Star-Spangled Banner." Once, by a fluke, I had been selected for eighth-grade Octet, as an alleged mezzo-soprano, and I had been forced to act my heart out, with vigorous facial expressions but no actual noise, whenever our songs took me above middle "G." I couldn't let that happen again. Sophie, a new friend across the hall, was devoutly religious and immediately joined a Methodist church group, but I wasn't going to pretend about that either.

That left my old high-school standbys, theatre and journalism. In high school, lots of us worked on plays or the weekly paper, and talent wasn't much of an issue. At Smith, I found I was intimidated by the intense dedication required for both the *Sophian* and dramatic productions. I was equally wary of the theatre crowd, with their long straight hair, black tights, and capes, and the newspaper gang, plainer and tougher, who lived all day at the noisy, crowded paper office.

I wasn't sure where to find my friends. I'd been warned in Iowa about "preppies," whose money and sophistication would make me feel provincial, and I had expected to be daunted by girls from Foxcroft, St. Timothy's, or Emma Willard. But buoyed by Lawrence House's reverse snobbery, our certainty that scholarship girls were morally superior, I found I was less impressed by the boarding-school types than I'd feared. Classifying girls into "types" was one way I dealt with differences at Smith. I assumed that the Shetland-sweatered, scarf-swathed girls in camel's-hair coats who taxied each weekend to New Haven or Hanover were all alike. Superficial and irritatingly smug. They shared some secrets of background and breeding I might never know, I told myself, but

I didn't care. I had better things to do. Years later, one of my closest friends in the city where I now live turned out to be a girl I'd
once dismissed as "a typical Smithie"; to me, she'd *looked* like one
of them, and that had been enough to make me think she wasn't a
serious person. We sometimes wonder if we could have met on any
common ground, on some patch of that campus, twenty-five years
ago. Neither of us, remembering our defensive and uncertain
younger selves, is confident.

Although Lawrence House held few "Smithies," we divided into
other small groups. I was one of the "straight" and studious girls,
who included Alice, a Unitarian minister's daughter; Sophie, who
wanted to marry a minister; Meg, who hiked and skiied; and a few
others. We saw ourselves differentiated from the rebellious ones,
girls who stuck together as tightly as we did. They played avid
bridge, shrieked at private jokes in the dining room, and occupied
the musty "smoker" as if it were a fort under siege. They openly
flaunted their resistance to Lawrence House rules, though they
stopped short of anything that might bring serious trouble. They
were reckless, we thought, and vaguely immoral. They all dated
frequently. Once one of their dates, tipsy but daring, bicycled
through the front door and managed to circle the living room on
his wheels before Mrs. Stevens, sputtering like a volcano, chased
him outside. Though my friends and I deprecated such drunken
antics, I think we all wished we had been there to watch.

The parties the wild girls went to always sounded lurid, especially since I drew my conclusions mainly from snatches of conversation overheard Monday mornings. In the winter of my senior
year, I sat late at breakfast one Monday, drinking an extra cup of
coffee. Next to me Penny Davis was telling Lolly Turnbull about
her weekend in New York. There Penny had met one of last year's
seniors, Madge Kettle, a special friend to the wild bunch, who had
always been weird herself, swooping suddenly through a room with
a whinnying laugh, or lurking in the smoker all night and emerg-
ing, red-eyed and pale, but humming part of a Bach cantata, just
in time for the breakfast bell. Madge had evidently gone last weekend to a party at the cousin's apartment where Penny was staying,
and Penny was giggling so hard she could scarcely tell Lolly what
had happened.

"It was *hysterical,*" Penny said, poking Lolly for emphasis. "See, my cousin had just cleaned her apartment, rushing around like mad before the party, and she threw out an old vase of flowers this guy had sent her for Valentine's. Really gorgeous gardenias, but they'd gotten all wilted. So she flushed them down the toilet, to get rid of all that smelly water in the vase. But she rushed right out of the bathroom, I guess, and one big white gardenia stuck in the bowl. Well, when Madge came, she was half potted already. So she went right away into the bathroom to use the toilet. And you should have seen her face when she came out!" Penny snorted.

"She came back into the living room looking real funny," Penny went on. "She grabbed my arm real hard, like she was pinching it to see if it was real" — Penny pinched Lolly, who said, with a smile, "Hey!" and pulled her arm away — "and then she whispered to me, in a real low voice" — and as I strained to hear, Penny lowered her voice in a husky imitation — "Pensy, tell me straight. And I mean, I want to *know,* so be honest. I guess I'm a little high. But would you please go into the bathroom? And look in the toilet? I want to know if you think there's a gardenia in there." Penny and Lolly laughed together, while Penny quickly glanced once at me to see if I was joining in. I wanted to, but I wasn't sure I was supposed to have heard. And I was somehow shaken by the picture I had in my mind. I poured the lukewarm coffee from my saucer back into the cup and wondered what it would be like to walk into a bathroom and find a gardenia in the toilet. It was the kind of thing one would have to expect at a party in New York, I felt, the kind of Eastern party I had never attended.

Although I was sure I had properly classified the iconoclasts in Lawrence, in fact I probably knew as little about what they really thought and felt as they did about me. I think now about Lolly Turnbull, who was the most elusive of them all. We should have been friends, but though we were both scholarship girls, English majors, class of '61 and members of Lawrence House, we never seemed to have anything in common. Lolly, who had grown up in North Carolina, was my idea of a Southern belle, midcentury style: unbelievably pretty, a perfect heart-shaped face with dark framing curls, a trace of a languorous accent. She was fast on the hockey field, rode horseback, and partied as hard as she played hockey.

Somehow she got her work done, probably late at night when I was sound asleep, but I never saw her studying. She always managed to make Dean's List, but she evidently aspired no higher. Though she called herself a Southerner, I always thought of Lolly as being part of the real East. Once, on a Saturday night, I saw her in a black cocktail dress, tight and low-cut. It looked just right on her.

By the time we were seniors, I pictured Lolly's life, with a mixture of envy and disapproval, as one of unimaginable sophistication and decadence, the opposite of my own. Rumors drifted about her love life; in a secret poll we seniors took, thirty percent of us were no longer virgins, and we in the seventy percent thought we knew who the others were. Every weekend, whether or not a paper was due or an exam pending, Lolly packed her bags for a trip to Yale or Princeton, or gaily tripped down the stairs to meet a new beau from Amherst, her light laughter rising up the stairwell as I trudged toward my room, laden with books. She had a striped scarf from every man's college. In the hall outside my door, a freshman answering the phone always seemed to bellow, "Turnbull! Lol-ly Turnbull! Turnbull, it's for you!" When I read in my English classes about Circe, Morgan Le Fay, or La Belle Dame Sans Merci, I sometimes thought of Lolly's heart-shaped face. Once, when I reverently passed an admired professor's office, just daring to peek inside, I saw her seated easily in a chair a few inches from his desk, her legs crossed, as she chatted with him. She blew cigarette smoke just past his nose as he leaned forward, attentive.

As we neared graduation, I was curious about what Lolly was going to do. I didn't foresee any ordinary career for her, and she talked carelessly, as if she had no particular ambitions, of possibly trying the foreign service, or law school in Washington, or maybe just renting an apartment in New York. After four years of all this crap, she said, she was going to live a little. As we hauled our suitcases down the stairs on Commencement Day, she said with an exaggerated drawl, "Come and see me in New York, you-all, and maybe we can have a drink together."

I didn't think I would ever see Lolly again. Remembering the dark circles under her eyes on Monday mornings, her murmurs about Southern Comfort and sloe gin fizzes, I couldn't quite picture her in a working world. Over the years, thinking of my college past and acquaintances, I occasionally wondered what had happened to Lolly. She was probably a foreign correspondent in a place like Casablanca, I decided, having seen my share of Bogart movies. I saw her in a nightclub there, a fan whirring overhead, someone at the piano, Lolly drinking sloe gin fizzes. By now, though still beautiful, she was probably world-weary, even more cynical. Sleeping around. Maybe on drugs. Her youth gone. Terribly alone. By now I was myself divorced and uncertain about my future.

We met, Lolly and I, fifteen years after graduation, at a women's studies conference in New York. She tapped me on the arm and said, "Aren't you Sue Allen?" I would not have recognized her. Then in her mid-thirties, Lolly was a little plump, no longer the nymphlike creature I remembered. Her black curly hair was longer, controlled, and rather dignified. She had a few noticeable wrinkles under her eyes. She was warm and friendly, genuinely glad to see me, inquisitive in a nice way about what I was doing. Over lunch, we talked about our lives. She had been to graduate school, taught, married quite late — just three years ago — and had twin baby girls. She and her husband lived on an old farm in Pennsylvania, where they raised golden retrievers, but she still commuted every day to her job as dean of humanities at a community college. She seemed very happy. She was surprised and sorry to hear about my failed marriage.

Over coffee, waiting for Lolly to light up a Gauloise with her old practiced flick, I asked her if she had given up smoking. "Oh, yes," she said, surprised. "Of course. Years ago. Who could smoke these days, knowing what we do about cancer?" I nodded. Before we parted, I hesitated, then impulsively told Lolly I'd always imagined she'd have ended up in Casablanca. She looked puzzled, but laughed. Picking up her trim leather briefcase, she gave me a quick hug, said affectionately, "Keep in touch, now, Sue," and plunged back into the convention crowd. As I watched her go, I wondered whether I had wholly invented that other Lolly Turnbull.

Not knowing who was who, or what was what, I clung to anything in my new life that provided order and security. In those years Smith had a reassuringly rigid structure of rules. Together with a set of commandments about social behavior, the academic

Honor System neatly and thoroughly fenced off the straight and narrow path. It was hardly possible to go wrong. Quickly I learned where to smoke (downstairs in Lawrence House, on the library steps, in the basement of Seelye Hall), where to drink (only off-campus), how to dress for meals (skirts at night and Sunday noon, no pajamas at breakfast), how long to wait for a late professor (twenty minutes for a full professor, fifteen for an associate, ten for an instructor). I went without demur to Wednesday morning chapel, which required a verbal excuse in advance, issued by the student-body president, for any absence. I was not the only one to take this stricture seriously. During my senior year, when I shared a tiny suite with the current president, Sophie's phone rang constantly on Wednesday mornings. "Yes, that's OK, you're excused," she said over and over, trying to pull up her socks and button her shirt. "OK, OK, I understand. Thank you. OK."

The Honor System had a mystique of its own, reverently discussed in a long letter to incoming freshmen and then reinforced by deans in orientation pep talks. I never questioned this elaborate code, which provided moral guidance for exams without proctors, forbade the use of translations in foreign-language classes, and sternly warned against failing to check out library books. Seniors made sure we freshmen heard about the girl who'd been caught with four library books in her room, not properly checked out, and who'd been summarily expelled. Another girl in her house, obeying the dictates of the code, had turned her in. When I heard two Lawrence House girls muttering about the requirement of signing an attendance sheet at the classes held the last morning before Christmas vacation, I left the living room. I feared that one of them was about to agree to sign the sheet for the other, and I didn't want the responsibility of knowing about it.

Lawrence House had its own versions of campus rules, like House Inspection and Quiet Hours. As a scholarship house, priding itself on appearances, the House Council authorized weekly tours to each room by selected council members, who checked the dust and mess, took off points for violations, and if necessary issued warning tags or a fifty-cent ticket. Fifty cents was a lot of money to someone on a twenty-five-dollar-a-month allowance. So Thursday afternoons, between three and four o'clock, when inspection started, my roommate and I swept, dusted, made beds, straightened books, and tried to anticipate the council's vagaries. When Mona Bragdon, an edgy and sharp-tongued junior, inspected, she always ran her finger over the most unlikely spots. Once, but not twice, she caught us with dust on the top of our closet door; another time, on the door paneling; yet another, around the light bulb on the floor lamp. Mona, who loved to issue fines, ripped the judgment off her notepad with a decidedly malevolent smile.

Although I resented House Inspection, I wholeheartedly supported Quiet Hours. Not that it was ever very noisy in Lawrence House. Other campus dorms might be able to afford occasional rowdiness, loud parties in the rooms, and midnight carousing; but Lawrence girls, all on scholarship, had to study. It was eerily quiet most of the time in Lawrence. Doors sometimes opened and shut, the hall telephone rang, footsteps skittered up and down the stairs, but otherwise, all you could hear in the hall was the sound of a toilet flushing behind the bathroom door at the end of the corridor. Quiet Hours were decreed for all day, until just before dinner, and for most of the evening, with a break from ten to ten-thirty P.M., when girls gathered in each other's rooms for a pot of tea or a little music on a portable phonograph, and voices broke the silence of the halls. After this brief outburst of life, everyone retired again.

For my first two years, Quiet Hours were sternly enforced on my floor by Olive Standish, a senior History major whose acknowledged genius was augmented by her constant studying. Snappish and short-tempered, Olive seldom smiled, and, under dark twisted eyebrows, her frown was formidable. If a voice was raised in our hall before ten or after ten-thirty, Olive opened her door and glared the length of the hall to see if she could spot the offenders. Then she yelled in an angry, deep voice, "Quiet Hours!" and slammed her door. If she had to open it again, she merely called, "SECOND NOTICE!" But that was enough, because we knew that Olive would report any further noisemakers to House Council. That meant an appearance before the next council meeting, a humiliating lecture from the house president, and a fine. Olive kept the fourth floor quiet.

Although I continued to respect Quiet Hours long after Olive had graduated and gone, Lawrence House began to change. After my sophomore year, when the scholarship houses were abolished, and nonscholarship girls integrated into them, the new students in Lawrence didn't care about what we older girls thought was Lawrence's superior reputation. No one worried as much about dining-room etiquette or House Inspection, and House Council met less and fined almost no one for anything. On the fourth floor, trouble began to brew. As a dedicated studier and early sleeper, I tried to assume the post Olive had so successfully maintained as guardian of the peace. Peering up and down the hall after ten-thirty, I shouted as loudly as I dared, "Quiet Hours!", but I lacked Olive's ringing authority. The underclassmen knew I would never report them, and worse, that the House Council wouldn't do much if I did. I was the only girl on the floor who didn't stay up late. Everyone else perked along with coffee, No-Doz, and gab sessions until after midnight.

Determined to end my constant harassment, the late-nighters took an ingenious revenge. Knowing that I always got up during the night to stumble sleepily down the hall to the bathroom, they prepared a surprise for me. One night, after yelling in vain for quiet and eventually collapsing into a deep sleep, I rose at midnight. In the hall, I registered dimly that the night-lights were out, the hall darker than usual — in fact, impenetrably black. However, I knew the way, and, semiconscious, padded blindly along. Suddenly something wet and awful struck me in the face. I gasped and then screamed. From behind a nearby door I heard tumultuous giggles as someone called out, in a voice choked by laughter, "Quiet Hours!" Frightened and furious, I ran to the hall door and flicked on the lights. There, suspended by a long string from the ceiling, hung a disembodied, slimy sheep's eye, a relic from someone's zoology lab. Attached to it was a placard with large black letters: "IF THINE EYE OFFEND THEE, PLUCK IT OUT." Eventually, though it took a while, I joined the laughter.

I had gotten the message. Next day I bought some wax earstopples at the corner drugstore. Some mornings I'd have to retrieve them from under my bed, small flesh-pink wads, fingerprinted into odd shapes where I'd jammed them into my ears, and covered with dust from the floor. My roommate said they looked obscene. I thought she was right, but I also saw them as a reminder of a faintly sensed failure, my own failure to fit in. Somewhere, somehow, although I had learned and followed the rules, they had let me down.

No matter how hard I tried to tell myself that I belonged at Smith, it was still a long way from home. During my freshman fall, I looked ahead to Christmas vacation with longing that alternated with fear it would never come. In my mind I retraced my recent journey, now in reverse: taxi to the station, two-car commuter train to Springfield; New York Central, with its Pullman cars and coaches, to Albany, Buffalo, Cleveland, Chicago; change to the LaSalle Street Station, find the rickety Chicago & Northwestern cars that would carry me across Illinois to the Mississippi, Iowa, and home. Iowa lay on the other side of two days and nights of rattling, blurring travel. Behind such a barrier, Ames seemed like an enchanted country, waiting for me to return and break through the briars. Day by day I crossed the dates off my calendar: September, first hour exam, Freshman English essay due, October, a weekend in Boston, slide test in Art History, hour exam, November. The X's on the calendar slowly began to outnumber the unmarked days.

And day by day I wrote my mother. I told myself I was mainly worried about her, not me; she was alone in our house for the first time in her life. My sister had left for college last year, but I had been home. How would she manage now? I had tried, anxiously, to talk with a few of her close friends who lived nearby: do keep an eye on Mother, I said as one grown-up to another, she may be lonely when I'm gone. Of course she'll keep busy, she always does, but even her full-time teaching job, concerts, dinner parties, the A.A.U.P., always gave her plenty of time at home with us. I don't want her to get depressed.

For my part, I assured Mother, I would write a letter every day. Don't overextend yourself, she said, and suggested postcards instead. Every morning, after breakfast if I could, or else during stolen moments of a slow lecture, I painstakingly transcribed my news of the day: the weather, my courses, my friends. I was careful not to sound too bleak, and most of the cards, when I read them today, are determinedly cheerful, with staccato exclamation marks and breathless dashes. On Sundays I wrote real letters, tapping them out on my baby-blue Smith-Corona, Mother's gift at my high-school graduation.

Although I told myself these daily bulletins were for Mother's sake, not mine, I should have known better. Writing those daily postcards was a way I could pretend to myself that my mother shared my life, that she understood everything that was happening, that she was still right there with me. I didn't want to leave her out, but I was also afraid of what might happen to me if I did. I had no experience in being away from my mother. A few times I had spent a week at Camp Fire Girls' camp, forty miles away; as an eight-year-old Blue Bird, I had broken down in homesick sobs the first night in the dining hall, and had been comforted by a counselor on the hall steps. I had survived and gone on to enjoy the rest of my week. Perhaps I had imagined going away to college would be like that. What did I know about complex emotional bonds?

When my own daughter, at ten, worried about whether she could last a month at *her* camp without me, I assured her she could. "You've been away many times for two weeks," I reminded her, "and besides, you're used to sleeping alone."

"What do you mean?" she asked, puzzled.

Gently, for I am sad for both my mother and myself when I remember this, I told Jennie how, sometime after my father's death when I was seven, I began to sleep in the big double bed with my mother. We each had our own side, plenty of room, no crowding. It seemed very natural. Except when friends slept over and Mother moved to the studio couch in the study, that was where I stayed until I went away to college. Your grandma and I were very dependent on each other. "Huh," said Jennie, thoughtfully.

As I struggled to find my way through the forest of that freshman fall, I wished my mother was near. I missed her so much it is still a pain I do not want to recall, as though I were reliving an amputation without anesthetic. Amputees, I'm told, sometimes have the sensation that the missing limb is still there; that was how I often felt about my mother, to whom I talked in my postcards, letters, a few long-distance calls, and, most of all, my imagination. Every day I daydreamed my way back home, picturing the morning light streaming through our dining-room window, the dented aluminum coffeepot perking on the stove, Mother putting on her blue Lucite reading glasses to study the front page of the morning paper. I saw golden oak leaves littering the sparse grass in our front yard, Mother hurriedly gathering remnants of zucchini and parsley before the first frost, myself excused from dishes so I could savor the last warmth of the sun on a long walk along Lincoln Way. Sometimes I found myself back in our old red-brick Presbyterian church, with familiar faces singing or yawning in the choir stalls; in Ames High, where new seniors — still too young — were taking our places at pep assemblies and Friday-night dances; on Main Street, with stores I could have wandered into, eyes closed, and known exactly at what counter I'd find jeans, records, or candy. Although I kept very busy, as my mother had taught me, I was homesick in its root meaning, with a lump in my stomach that never entirely disappeared, an ache that throbbed whenever I thought of Christmas.

For weeks I did not know how homesick I was. Proud of my independence, working hard to succeed, I did not want to admit that I was not making what was called "a good adjustment." I carried the weight, I thought, of many expectations: my own, my mother's, my friends', relatives', teachers', and well-wishers'. No one from Ames had ever been to Smith before, and I was a standard-bearer. How could I confess I was scared? How dare I be homesick? Finally my body spoke up for me, loudly and unmistakably. At first I thought I had Hong Kong flu. An ominous rumor had swept the campus in midfall of my freshman year, warning about a wave of an exotic disease that was slowly sweeping over the East Coast. Its very name evoked the frightening mystery of the Far East, introduced to us by the recent Korean War, which had alerted everyone to the Yellow Peril, and had illustrated it with movies like *The Manchurian Candidate.* Hong Kong flu was clearly no ordinary bacteria. Its effects were devastating, I was told, with fever, terrible fatigue, and weakness. It lasted for weeks, with no cure except long and continuous bed rest. Since I was barely keeping up with my classes now, I knew that once I had Hong Kong flu, it would all be over. I'd never be able to retrieve myself. I'd have to leave Smith, go home, and maybe never come back. That possibility lurked in the hidden dark corners of my mind.

Soon two girls on the floor below me in Lawrence House were diagnosed as having The Flu and dispatched immediately to the

Infirmary. The beast, I felt, was insidiously moving closer. I was not surprised to wake one day and find my throat a touch sore, my head aching, and my stomach unpleasantly churning. I felt so awful I did not think I could even get out of bed. I asked my roommate to get Mrs. Stevens.

Getting sick in Lawrence House had its own set of rules. Mrs. Stevens was guardian of the sickroom supplies, mainly a thermometer, aspirin, Bromo-Seltzer, and a few carefully guarded sleeping pills, which were dispensed only after Mrs. Stevens had probed deeply into the conditions of their use. Mrs. Stevens liked to take temperatures. If she found a low fever, she advised attending classes, but taking two aspirin and going to bed early. In extreme cases, she sent her patient, reluctantly, to the College Doctor's Office. Nobody really wanted to go there anyway, since the doctors, we thought, were an overworked handful of rejects, all aging, or foreign, or old. One had a strange squint, so that she peered askew down one's throat in a most disconcerting manner. Another, who was from some Central European country no longer in existence, spoke with such a guttural accent that her diagnoses and instructions were unintelligible. The third, far past retirement, though gruffly kind, was also deaf and forgetful, so one had to shout one's symptoms, several times, with embarrassing loudness. Most tellingly, the Smith doctors were all women; though ourselves students at a woman's college, we knew that a woman doctor, especially one who could do no better than our Doctor's Office, was not much to write home about. The best the D.O. could offer was a trip to the College Infirmary, a sunny, spacious, modern building on the far shores of Paradise Pond, where rumor temptingly whispered that the food was cooked to individual order and the nurses were great. It was almost as hard to get into the Infirmary as into heaven. When Mrs. Stevens took a temperature, though, there was a chance a path might open from the housemother's suite to the Infirmary door.

That freshman morning when Mrs. Stevens entered my room, she was puffing slightly and looking just discernibly irritated. She had had to climb three flights of stairs. Ordinarily, we all knew, we were supposed when sick to knock at the door of her suite. Bedside visits were reserved for emergencies. But I felt so ill I had had no qualms. I told her about my headache, my upset stomach, my dizziness. Lying back on my pillow, I sucked on the thermometer, imagining the mercury shooting upward, its dangerous red tongue pointing without doubt to the infirmary. I still remember my shock when Mrs. Stevens, removing the thermometer, looked at me with an artificial smile and said, chirpily, "Normal." She sounded so definite I raised myself from my pillow as if I had been attacked by her aggressive cheerfulness.

"Normal? Are you sure?" I asked incredulously. How could it be normal? Had she made a mistake? I knew I was burning up. I was sick, I was in fact, *very* sick, I needed to be taken care of, and the only mother substitute around looked as if she were going to back out the door.

"Oh, yes. Just a hair over 99. I think you can get dressed and go to class, dear," Mrs. Stevens said. She actually took a step toward the hall. I couldn't believe she was so unfeeling.

"But I feel terrible," I said. "I know I'm sick." My roommate, Alice, perched on the edge of her bed, looked at my closely. She was taking Zoology and planning on medical school. My head ached fiercely, and I longed to pull the covers over my head and turn my face to the wall. "I feel terrible," I said again, this time with a kind of groan, heartfelt, but, I was sure, not overdone.

Mrs. Stevens turned back. She walked close to the bed again and peered down at me, studying my case. She obviously sensed something might indeed be wrong, and she probably was wondering if it might, as I'd heard her pronounce with verbal capitals, "Be Mental." Mrs. Stevens liked to diagnose Something Mental in her girls. Usually she felt she was quite competent to cure Something Mental with a friendly chat, or even, in difficult instances, with a private dinner served on trays in her suite. She pulled out my desk chair and sat down next to my bed. "Sue," she said, "perhaps we'd better have a little talk." I looked dumbly at her. I had already told her I was sick. What else was there to talk about? "Tell me," she went on, her tiny eyes blinking quickly, "is anything bothering you?" My roommate on the opposite bed crossed her legs and tried to look as if she weren't listening.

"I don't think so," I said faintly. "I just feel sick. My head hurts, and my stomach. I wonder if maybe I ought to go to the Infirmary."

"Now, now," Mrs. Stevens went on, even more firmly. "I don't think there will be any need of that." Just then there was a tap on my door. Sophie, my friend across the hall, stood tentatively on the threshhold, waving a white envelope.

"Mail's here," Sophie said. "Sue, there's a letter for you. I brought it up." She held it out. Mrs. Stevens walked over, took it, and handed it to me.

I glanced at the familiar handwriting. "It's from my mother," I said unnecessarily, and was horrified to hear my voice quaver.

"Your mother? How nice. I've heard you mention her. How *is* your mother, dear?" Mrs. Stevens inquired, leaning forward slightly. She was almost visibly snuffling on the trail.

Although I thought I was going to answer her, instead I began to cry. The sobs astonished me with their force, exploding like shock waves from some deep geologic disturbance. Once I started, I couldn't stop. I was ashamed to be so out of control and tried to muffle my face in my pillow. But to my glancing surprise, in the midst of the tumult, I felt somehow released. The hard rock in my stomach had finally begun to move.

That was how I met Patricia Poynton. The door from Mrs. Stevens' suite led, it turned out, not to the shelter of the infirmary but to the fearsome office of the Student Counselor. It was fearsome mainly because I knew so little about it. None of my friends had ever been to the Student Counselor, and if Miss Poynton had been introduced to us during Freshman Orientation, I didn't remember. She sounded frightening, though, simply because of her profession. A counselor was related somehow to a psychologist, I knew, who was related to a psychiatrist. The whole field was alarming. No one I knew in Ames had ever seen a psychiatrist; at least, if someone had, I had never heard about it. One would have had to drive all the way to Des Moines or Iowa City for such a consultation. As a voracious reader, I knew something about psychiatrists, though, who seemed a peculiarly Eastern breed, flourishing mainly in New York City. They were called "shrinks," they were balding men with glinting eyeglasses, and they were absorbed by secrets, hidden compulsions, and, above all, sex. The thought of going to see Miss Poynton made me very uncomfortable.

But I didn't have much choice. Although Mrs. Stevens had

asked me to come to her suite twice for after-supper chats, I was not responding well. Each morning she sought me out in the living room, lowering her voice solicitously, to ask, "And how are we feeling this morning, Sue?" I had to tell her I was not, in fact, feeling much better. The rock in my stomach had moved, but it was still there. After a week or so, Mrs. Stevens beckoned to me after breakfast. Seated on her small chaise longue, I folded my hands tightly in my lap as she explained what she had done on my behalf. "I've talked to Miss Bailey, dear," she said, invoking the name of the Supreme Being for scholarship girls, the Head of Scholarships and Student Aid. "We both think it would be a good idea if you saw Miss Poynton, our Student Counselor. Miss Bailey has already called her. So all you have to do is drop by her office sometime today and make an appointment." Feeling the rock grow heavier, I nodded.

Two days later I walked slowly up three flights of stairs in an office building I seldom entered. Miss Poynton's hideaway seemed deliberately remote, as if the college wanted to help those of us with Something Mental hide our problems from public view. I had taken the precaution of looking up Miss Poynton in the back of our catalog, where degrees and dates of appointment were listed, to see what I could learn about her. I figured from the dates she was somewhere in her thirties, and not married, still a Miss Poynton. She hadn't been such a success herself. She had a master's degree in social work, which didn't seem very impressive either. Perhaps I was so disturbed only a real psychiatrist, the kind with an M.D., could help.

In years of reading and teaching modern novels, I can now identify a certain kind of story in which a psychiatrist or analyst functions as a central character, probing, cleansing, and then healing hidden wounds. This character, often personally mysterious, wields great power. If my life had been a novel in the 1950s, Miss Poynton might have transformed the narrative. But it wasn't, and she didn't. Pleasant, attractive, though certainly in her thirties and a touch graying, she smiled kindly as she asked me how I liked Smith, where I was from, had I made any friends. As I told her how I missed my mother, I quavered a little, but the horrendous sobs that had seized me in front of Mrs. Stevens were mercifully absent. I explained I wanted to do well at Smith, and I was worried about keeping my scholarship. Yes, I liked Smith, but it was a little frightening. Yes, I had friends, especially Sophie across the hall. Lots of friends, really. Everyone had been very nice to me. She nodded understandingly. Then there was a silence. I was sorry I had nothing interesting to tell her.

After a few more questions, and earnest responses, our interview was over. She asked me to see her again after my first few hour exams, and I agreed. She hadn't been scary after all, and, in fact, I felt as though our meeting had been almost anticlimactic. It would be all right to come back, just once. Most important, I felt I had made a good impression. I didn't want a dire report to make its way to Miss Bailey.

A month or so later, when I visited Miss Poynton again, I said I was feeling better, and indeed I was. My exams had been OK, I knew I wasn't going to flunk out, soon I would be home for Christmas. We agreed I didn't need to come again. Later that year Miss Poynton and I passed each other on campus, as I was hurrying to class with several friends. She greeted me by name, and I answered her, wishing I didn't have to. I was afraid that everyone would realize why she knew me. For four years, when I saw her at concerts or on the street or in the library, I felt discomfited. She reminded me of a stone on which I had badly stumbled and almost fallen.

As my freshman fall moved into December, I could hardly bear the excitement that swept over me whenever I thought of going home. Only the rigors of papers, tests, and assignments kept my feet firmly planted on the path to the library. Every day in December my spirits rose higher, irrepressibly ballooning to the cold gray skies. I even welcomed the snow, a dazzling white promise that confirmed the imminence of Christmas. I began to assemble my luggage, anxious not to forget anything. I took more clothes than I could wear in a month, including my new Smith sweatshirt. It was embossed with the Smith motto in Greek, which said either "Virtue Through Knowledge" or "Knowledge Through Virtue," I was never sure which. It was not a bad way to show people where you went to school, I thought, if they didn't already know; a sweatshirt wasn't like showing off. I wished I had a six-foot scarf from a man's college to take home.

After I made my train reservations, I sent letters to my closest friends to tell them exactly what hour and what day I would arrive. I promised everyone that we would catch up on everything soon, we would have lots to talk about, we would party every night. I thought of my best friend from high school, Peggy O'Reilly, who was miserable at a Catholic convent college; I would be able to comfort her. I thought of another friend, Patsy Jones, who was trying to decide whether to go steady with her old beau, Tim Melgaard, even though they were at different schools; I would hear all the pros and cons. I had so much to find out about everyone. And what about Joe, Charlie, Bob, and the other boys? Had they changed? What were they doing? Somehow there would have to be time for them, too. I knew I wanted to take most of my books home, since Smith held its final exams in January. But I'd surely be able to do lots of studying. Two weeks in Ames seemed like forever.

When the morning of Christmas vacation arrived, with its promise of a noon dismissal, our whole house was in an uproar. Suitcases were piled in the downstairs hall, boots and books jumbled in heaps, coats stacked on living-room chairs for quick getaways. Taxis, booked weeks in advance, would be waiting outside Seelye Hall for the girls who had tight travel connections. Luckily, I had arranged to share a cab, snatching an offered space from a girl in my History class. A whir of excitement, rare in Lawrence House, filled the halls, as we tacitly abandoned any pretense at Quiet Hours and slammed doors, yelled farewells, laughed and jostled each other down the stairs with our suitcases.

Right after breakfast, those of us who were traveling any distance gathered in the dining room to make our bag lunches. The cooks put out a large glass bowl of peanut butter, another of tuna-fish-and-mayonnaise, and a third of egg salad, next to an institutional-sized loaf of slightly stale white bread. In an even larger bowl were oranges, bananas, and a few shiny red apples. The apples looked so appealing they went fast, as I learned when I quickly snatched the last two. Imagining two impoverished days on trains, I slathered half a dozen sandwiches together. I tried not to remind myself I didn't like either egg salad or mayonnaise. For four years, vacation after vacation, Christmas and Easter and summer, the fare on the dining-room table never changed. Peanut butter, tuna fish, egg salad. Telling myself it was free, I always packed twice as much as I could eat. After only a few hours on a warm, crowded train, the egg salad got soggy, the tuna fish smelled funny, the bananas turned brown, and most of all, the sweetish apples were soft and mealy. The smell of apple permeated everything. Even when I tried tinfoil or plastic bags, the apples seemed to tinge every other bit of food. Even today when I think of trains, I still smell the slightly sickening, cidery aroma of softening apples. Yet, seeing those bright red apples in the bowl, year after year, I could never resist them. They signified something about health, vacation, and freedom.

That first Christmas vacation I was too excited to eat right away. When I finally passed the hurdle of changing trains in Springfield, walked down the tunnel to the right track, and found my seat on the New York Central's New England States, I settled back with a great sigh of relief for the overnight trip to Chicago. I watched the changing scenery in a daze of relaxation and happiness. No longer did I need to crane my neck and watch like a tourist for new sights. I had been this way before. The country didn't exactly look familiar, perhaps because I'd passed much of it before during the night, but I didn't care. I didn't need to study the landscape. At one end was Northampton. At the other end was home.

Though I had of course packed my textbooks, I left them in my bag. Somehow Smith seemed to disappear as soon as we left the station in Springfield. I was blissfully alone, able to measure out the miles by watching, daydreaming and dozing between cities. Consulting my timetable, I checked each stop, numbering them like beads, moving them onto another side of an abacus I'd invented. That was Syracuse, Syracuse is gone, no more Syracuse. Now Buffalo, Buffalo in two hours, after Buffalo I'll try to sleep. All that will be left then is Cleveland; after Cleveland, Chicago; and then I'm practically home.

When the hours grew long, I read. Every vacation I packed special paperback books for my train trips, buying them weeks in advance and savoring their possibilities as they lay, untouched, on my shelf. I only chose books I couldn't justify reading otherwise, books that I'd never find in Freshman English or Creative Writing or Introduction to the Novel. One year it was Agatha Christie, another *The Silver Chalice,* once — as a senior — *Love without Fear.* As if my own emotional state weren't pitched high enough, I plunged deep into those feverish worlds, vibrating to passions that drifted on as endlessly as the miles, pausing now and then to look out the window and muse about romance, sex, mystery. To keep myself company during meals, I continued to read. Through rape, regret, and salvation, I munched absentmindedly on stale sandwiches, trying to forget the smell of apples. Underneath it all, I always heard the comforting sound of the wheels, carrying me home.

When I reached Chicago, everything speeded up. As soon as I'd left the New York Central, I was back in country that I knew. The few Smith girls I'd recognized on the New England States got off by Chicago, heading to unknown destinations. I went alone to the LaSalle Street Station to catch the Chicago and Northwestern.

Before long we crossed the Mississippi into Iowa. Crawling through the Chicago suburbs, then Rock Island–Moline–Davenport, the train was stuck in urban grime, a harsh industrial landscape that didn't look so different from Cleveland or Buffalo. The Midwest hadn't had much snow that Christmas, and everything seemed grayish-brown and dirty. Looking out the window, I didn't think I had much to celebrate. But soon the wheels of the train sounded more encouraging, as they hurried faster and faster, covering ground with exuberant speed. Now the towns disappeared, and mostly I saw fields, farms, and the gentle curve of an infinite horizon. Smoke and soot evaporated, and the world looked clean again.

I no longer tried to read. During the last hour of the trip, I pulled my wool cap tightly over my ears, buttoned my coat, and stood outside the cars on a swaying metal platform. After two days in stale coaches, the fresh air, cold and crisp, felt wonderful. Below my feet, the deafening sound of metal on metal told me what was happening was real. I blinked and stared, my eyes watering with cold and excitement. Right there, so close I could almost touch them, were silos and fences and snow-sprinkled stubble, grazing black cattle and old-fashioned corncribs and rows of Butler storage bins. I was practically home.

Most of all, I breathed in lungfuls of space, taking huge breaths as if I'd come from a dark submarine into a world of bright skies.

In later years, when I sometimes traveled on night tra
loneliness about that Midwestern space, as I watche
lights of distant farms flutter and disappear in the
even then, with a sadness I could not explain, I wa⸱
stretched so far. Out there, in the country where I
all the room I felt I would ever need.

Soon we were passing through towns whose basketball teams ı
had booed, whose cheerleaders I might recognize, whose Presbyterian youth fellowships had attended our synod conferences. I even
welcomed the swinging signposts at the tiny stations we whipped
past, because they bore names I recognized: Mechanicsville, Belle
Plaine, Tama, State Center. As our train meandered through the
center of larger towns, I saw people on the streets who looked like
people in Ames, doing their shopping, driving their cars, or standing at corners. Most of them didn't notice us, and I was aware how
removed they were from the excitement I felt. Of course, they
couldn't know I was going home. I was glad to see the store signs,
Sears, Super Valu, Our Own Hardware; I liked the new developments with their tract ramblers dotting the edges of town; I wanted
to wave at an old brick school that looked just like Louise Craw-
ford Elementary, back in Ames.

It was late afternoon when the train slowed for its arrival in
Ames. Hugging myself and stamping my feet, I leaned as far over
the platform as I dared to catch my first glimpse of the station.
Suddenly I saw them: a huddled group, my best friend, Peggy
O'Reilly and five or six others, with my mother standing just to the
side. They began waving and screaming as soon as they saw me,
and I waved and screamed back. Then the train stopped, I was in
the midst of hugs and laughter, registering startled impressions of
different haircuts and new winter coats, talking with everyone at
once. My mother cleared her throat. "Don't I get a hug too?" she
said with a smile. Unlike my friends, she had not run or pushed, so
they had reached me first. I felt an awful pang. How long I had anticipated the moment when I would first see her! But she was smiling, and I put my guilt aside.

That moment at the train station, when I plunged into the welcoming circle of my old friends, was the highlight of my Christmas
vacation. Happy as I was to pull into our driveway, plop my bags

37 ❧

ʌn in my old room, and sink into my chair at the kitchen table,
. was somehow more relieved than ecstatic. I wasn't sure why I felt
faintly let down. Everything was just as I'd remembered, though
perhaps a little more cluttered, just a bit smaller. I noticed a worn
spot on the rug and a heap of Mother's magazines on my bookcase.
So much had happened to me, so much had changed, I thought,
and yet I wasn't sure how I could even begin to explain. I made an
effort, told a few stories about Smith that sounded flat out of context, and realized sometime that first evening that I probably
couldn't find the words — or the time — to describe what it was
like for me out East.

Though I told my mother what I thought she might want to
hear, I had less success with my friends. We found we were not
nearly as interested in listening to each other as when we'd promised in our letters, "I'll tell you all about it when I see you." When
my old friend Christy described the giant papier-mâché panda the
Pi Phis had built for Northwestern's Homecoming, my mind
began to wander. As I tried to evoke our exciting bicycle trip on
Mountain Day, Christy interrupted, politely, with a bit of news
about the Northwestern marching band. Though Peggy O'Reilly
and I shared details about our college roommates, I think both of
us felt surprisingly estranged. After only a few months, our new
worlds had swallowed us up.

But we had little time for introspection. Every hour the phone
rang, till Mother sighed in exasperation, as if I were thirteen again.
People dropped in all through the day, family friends, neighbors,
younger friends still in high school. At night the old gang gathered
for party after party, mostly informal get-togethers in someone's
living room or in the booths of the Rainbow Cafe or at round
tables in the Oak Grill. A few of my former boyfriends called for
private dates, a movie or ice-skating or just "going out." Somewhere in the midst of all the commotion was Christmas, a short
lull, with the usual stockings, turkey dinner, and visiting relatives.
On the night of the Christmas Formal, an annual high-school
event, three or four of us decided, for a lark, to visit the Great Hall
of the Iowa State Union, where it was always held. Once we'd gone
to the Christmas Dance as eager participants, nervous, anticipat-
ing the night for weeks. Now, dressed in ordinary coats and boots,

we shuffled outside the door for a few minutes, watching the new sophomores, juniors, and seniors whirling and dipping inside in their tulles and tuxedos. A few kids recognized us and waved, but we didn't try to go into the hall. Feeling subdued, and old, we left the Union and headed downtown to see if we could spot anyone coming out of the Sportsman's Lounge.

After Christmas, I began to feel scared. The days had gone so quickly. In less than a week, I would have to go down to the train station again, to leave Ames once more and return to Smith. I had done almost none of my backlogged work for midyear exams. My mother said she'd hardly seen me. I had promised Bob we'd go out once more, and Peggy said we still needed to have a good long talk. As I looked ahead to January, I could not imagine surviving the rigors of five three-hour exams. I had never taken any essay test longer than an hour. I was sure I wouldn't know enough to fill all that time and all those bluebooks. I was three weeks behind in Ancient History, four chapters in Geology. I didn't know the French subjunctive, and I'd been conning my way through class discussions about Henry James. What would happen to me?

One night I broke down in front of my mother and cried. I didn't want to go back, I said. She listened sympathetically, her face creased with concern. "Well, I didn't dream you felt this way," she finally said. "You don't have to stay there, you know. Perhaps you should come home and go to Iowa State, or transfer somewhere else at the end of the year." Those did not seem to me like possible solutions. I knew I had to go back. I tried to recover; I didn't want Mother to worry. "No, of course it's not really that bad," I said. "It's a great school. I know that. I wouldn't think of not going back."

Getting on the train on that cold January morning was one of the hardest things I have ever done. Most of my friends had already left, and only my mother, sister, and Peggy came down to the station to see me off. Mother had packed a special lunch bag, with brownies, home-made bread, and an apple she said wouldn't smell. As I hugged my mother good-bye, I wished I had spent more time at home with her. I promised Peggy I would write soon. I knew she hated going back to the convent, and I felt bad for her too. When the train pulled out, I stood on the outside platform, waving, tears welling up, with that recognizable rock in my stomach, until the station had faded from sight. Inside the coach I cried for a while, blowing hard into a handful of Kleenex, hoping no one would notice. I didn't think I could ever be more miserable.

But within a few hours, I began to feel better. I was an old hand at train travel now, and I knew where we were going. After a while I opened my Ancient History book to begin some cramming. It was going to be a long, dull trip, and I might as well make some use of it. I could look forward to Mother's lunch, and maybe tonight I'd eat in the dining car with some money she'd given me. At least I was going to get the exams over with.

When the taxi stopped in front of Lawrence House two days later, I was astonished to find that I felt excited. I hurried up the stairs. When I checked my box, I found some mail waiting. A new calendar had been posted, listing the upcoming foreign films, chapel talks, and lectures. The wooden floors in Lawrence, waxed in our absence, gleamed as bright as they had in September. A fresh linen napkin was rolled in my napkin box. Someone's *New York Times* had been tossed on a chair. I grabbed it, realizing I hadn't seen one for two weeks. On the landing, I studied the week's menus, written in Mrs. Stevens' elegant script, and was pleased to see two of my favorites coming soon, cherry crisp and sticky buns. Upstairs in my hall I saw a sheet of paper tacked to the door of my room. Sophie had written a poem to welcome me back. "I'm here already, so come see me right away," she had penciled on the bottom.

As I read Sophie's poem, I grinned at her funny verses. She had decorated the note with little stick figures. I was so glad she was already here. I dumped my bags in my room, glancing at the furniture to see that nothing had changed. Then I dashed across the hall to see if Sophie and I could go together to Friendly's Ice Cream Parlor for supper. I wanted to have a Big Beef, rare ground sirloin dripping with juice on soppy buttered toast. We didn't have anything quite like that in Ames. Although I didn't want to admit it to Sophie, who knew how homesick I'd been all fall, I was oddly relieved to be back in Lawrence. This, I guessed, was where I belonged now. Somehow, I felt I had come home.

Learning to Live with Women 🌿

"I THINK I'm going to have a slumber party," my friend Julie said hopefully. This would not sound unusual, except Julie is thirty-eight. "I'm going to rent a cabin on the St. Croix and invite you, Laurie, and Jill to sleep over on Saturday night. We'll have a real party, lots of food, stay up late and talk. Just us. No men." It sounded nice, I thought, but also a little strange. Most of my women friends and I snatch time for each other on the phone, at lunch, or during hurried visits after we drop our children in other parts of town. A slumber party seemed so formal, so planned, so definitive.

That wasn't all that seemed strange to me about a slumber party. For days after Julie's invitation I thought about it. Partly I was remembering the exhausting marathons we girls endured in our early adolescence. Am I your best friend, and will you sleep next to me? Why are you spending so much time with Betsy, after you told me you liked me better? Don't you think Jane's shower cap looks dumb?

Yet the memories of those long-ago, intimate slumber parties were not entirely negative. Maybe I felt a little sad that Julie's party could not possibly be such an intense celebration of female friendship. We were all too grown-up, too distanced from those early passionate ties. Though I liked Laurie and Jill, I didn't really know much about them; would any of us be able to let down our guards? My women friends and I usually saw each other in pairs. Though then we talked freely, how would all of us manage in a group? Still, I wanted to find out. I wanted to try to recapture that closeness we girls felt when, snuggled beneath our blankets, we shared jokes and secrets.

But on the other hand, I wasn't sure I really wanted to go. Would I like spending a night in a cabin full of women? Would I feel self-conscious about getting up two or three times, as I often did at home, to go to the bathroom? I was used to sleeping alone in a room. What about listening to all that breathing, tossing and turning, and oh God, perhaps loud snoring? As I began to fret, I remembered when I'd had these ambivalent feelings about women and closeness before. They flooded me at college House Meetings, when we girls crowded together into our dormitory living room. I warmed toward girls I ordinarily disliked when I saw them in fuzzy slippers and chenille robes, like members of the same primitive tribe. And yet we were gathered in that living room to work out the problems we all had living together. We argued and voted, tabled and amended, and concluded, grumbling, with unsatisfying compromises.

Those House Meetings were where we most openly faced the difficulties of living with women, I thought to myself. We wanted to be close to each other, but we wanted our privacy and independence too. We were wary of what we might do to each other tomorrow: who would hog the washing machine, not take her turn in the kitchen, unfairly enforce room inspection, answer the phone rudely if our boyfriends called. We did not, in the end, trust each other.

Did men have House Meetings? I couldn't picture the boys I knew then in pajamas or bathrobes, leaning companionably against each other's knees, listening to lectures about bathtub rings or uncollected cups after Friday-afternoon tea. Did I imagine they had had more important issues to discuss, like nuclear disarmament or the causes of the American Civil War? Or did I think they simply didn't irritate each other with the daily details of domestic life?

Perhaps I couldn't conjure up this scene effectively because I couldn't see a contrast between those boys in the daytime, at ease in cords and button-down shirts and sweaters, and boys at a House Meeting. They did not unfrock, take off their stage makeup, and let their hair down. They did not have two separate selves, public and private, costumed and unmasked, as girls in those days did. Perhaps, I thought further, that's why men don't have slumber parties. They don't have the shared intimacy of a secret. Our secret as women was the knowledge that we led two different lives, one in relation to the public world, another in relation to each other. For most women, the public world then implied men; in some ways, it still does. Women have an implicitly acknowledged bond, so at some protected times, like House Meeting and slumber parties, we can let down our guards and "be ourselves." (In pre-feminist days, we didn't ask each other who we were when we weren't "being ourselves.")

We cherish those times and still as grown women seek them out, whether in consciousness-raising groups, bridge clubs, or slimnastics classes. But I couldn't imagine Julie's friend Vic trying to assemble three or four adult males for a weekend on the St. Croix, unless the party had a specific purpose, like fishing or skiing. What would it mean to Vic and his friends to "be themselves"? Why did grown women still have "girlfriends," even if we felt a bit sheepish about the term, but grown men never referred to each other as "boyfriends"? If we had all the intimacy, did that mean we also had all the ruffled sensibilities? Would any of Vic's male friends worry about whether his pajamas were too cute, or what to do if someone snored, or how to sleep comfortably in a crowded room? Were women more, or less, comfortable with each other than men? I did not know, nor had I known during four years at Smith, the answers to these questions.

When I was packing my suitcases for Smith, an old friend of my mother's dropped in to visit. As she watched me fold my sweaters and roll my socks, she asked questions about what lay ahead in the unknown world of an Eastern women's college. Like many of my mother's friends, she was puzzled by my refusal to stay at home and attend the state university. None of my answers really satisfied her, but at the end of our visit, she rose and took her leave with a determinedly gracious gesture. Hugging me, she said, "Oh, well, Susan, you may be doing the right thing. You're going to spend most of your life with women. Men just aren't around much. You're going to have to depend on women. You might as well learn to live with them."

Many times during the next four years I thought about her remark. As I elbowed among the girls charging into the dining room; as I waited up till midnight with two or three other friends to hear whether someone had had a good time with her blind date; as I pulled someone's damp underwear from the basement washing machine, I knew that I was probably learning to live with women. What exactly I was learning, though, I wasn't sure.

Learning to live with women was learning to live in small, dark, enclosed spaces. When, years later, I sat on an alumnae panel in a hot darkened auditorium, under the unrelenting glare of overhead lights, I felt that the setting was peculiarly right. Blanketing darkness, suffocating closeness, artificial light: once we had all been hothouse flowers, blooming under pressure. I remember my college years as a succession of indoor rooms. The library, of course, with its tiny fluorescent-lit carrels and crowded reading rooms; drafty, echoing classrooms; Lawrence House, with its stuffy "smoker," airless dining room, and my own cubicle, so dark and claustrophobic that I pushed my bed under the window.

Learning to live with women was descending the basement stairs every Sunday morning to the Lawrence House laundry room, where two battered machines, a washer and a dryer, shook precariously on the uneven cement floor. Aside from my own room, the laundry room was the only spot in the house where I had a chance to be alone. Though I brought a book to read, I usually felt my energy smothered by the warm, humid breath that hovered over the machines. Lulled by the clunks of the old washer, or hypnotized by the tossing dryer, I sat on an upended wooden crate and gave in to the luxury of feeling separated from the fifty-six other girls in the house above.

I had to stay to guard my laundry. On weekends everyone wanted to wash clothes, but since no one ever thought of a sign-up sheet, we jostled for place with the same determination we felt lining up before the closed doors of the dining room. Doing laundry did not bring out a cooperative spirit. Sometimes an aggressive girl heaped her mildewed gym clothes, yellowed blouses, and soiled underpants on the floor next to the busy washer, hoping to claim next place by intimidating anyone who got there first. Usually I furtively kicked the pile with my foot, pushing it away from the washer and back toward the wall.

It was never safe to leave newly washed clothes in the dryer and vanish upstairs until the dryer stopped. Though the basement was empty when I returned, as if a sneak thief had silently slipped in and out, my wash was unceremoniously heaped in a corner, still damp. An impatient girl had obviously pulled my clothes out in order to put hers in. Furious, I nevertheless restrained myself from opening the dryer in *my* turn and throwing *her* pile of clothes on the floor where she'd tossed *mine*. It wasn't that I didn't want to, but I was afraid whoever it was might know who *I* was. Sometimes I pawed through the offender's laundry, looking for an identifying label or familiar blouse so I could stare at her that noon with hate in my heart.

Despite such shadowboxing in the laundry room, I rather liked my Sunday morning time there because it was a domestic break from studying. Doing laundry reminded me of another self, someone who used to live in a real house with real people. Even girls who had been glad to leave home, who said they couldn't stand their mothers, who argued long-distance with their fathers about allowances, showed occasional signs of missing the outside world. When a history professor came to dinner one night with her only child, so young he needed a dictionary to sit on, we all stared surreptitiously at him. Several of us sidled up after dessert to exchange a few inane words, and remind ourselves what a child sounded like. Girls with faculty baby-sitting jobs bounced off importantly on weekends to houses with dens, television sets, and families. "It was nice to be in a home again," sighed my roommate after one such Saturday-night assignment. She didn't have to explain what she meant.

As freshmen, we needed to make new homes for ourselves, coping with the anonymous spaces into which we had been transplanted. We began with our rooms. Though issued the same regulation furniture — wooden desk, square dresser, and narrow bed — most of us struggled to make our rooms distinctive. But no one in Lawrence House had much money to spend on interior decorating. When I arrived at Smith, Lawrence had been for many years one of the three cooperative houses on campus. For a reduction in room and board — in 1957, $250 from a bill of perhaps $1,000 — the girls in Lawrence performed certain housekeeping chores that in other houses were done by maids, like washing dishes, cleaning bathrooms, or vacuuming the housemother's suite. Most Lawrence girls had other forms of financial aid, too; we were all "on scholarship," a phrase that now sounds as if we were gratefully floating through Smith supported only by a spar of the college's generosity.

With fifty-seven scholarship girls in one house, Lawrence developed its own ethos, evident even in room decoration. Freshmen were advised to haunt the Furniture Exchange, a fall sale sponsored by one of Smith's charitable organizations; upperclassmen posted lists of used items they were willing to part with, for a price; a few girls borrowed the house sewing machine to make cheap curtains. Although one Northampton shop specialized in fancy spreads, drapes, and other accessories, Lawrence House decorated itself with burlap, India prints, corkboards, and stamped tin from Woolworth's.

Though severely limited on how much we could transform each cubicle, still, we achieved differences. Lawrence felt strongly about individuality. Olivia's stark and studious room, with brick-and-board bookcases lining all the walls, no clothes in sight, and a navy-blue corduroy spread neatly covering her bed, was a world apart from Lolly's, whose ragged collection of old teddy bears lay heaped on a rumpled, unmade bed, beneath a wall covered with tacked-up college banners, near a closet so jammed with clothes its door wouldn't shut. I argued with my own roommate, who preferred dark plaids, about bright pink chintz curtains and a purple wastebasket; I wanted our room to be different, too. Diana, who kept to herself, never let anyone into her room, as far as I could tell; but when I once peeked through her door, left uncharacteristically ajar, the room looked exactly the same, and as empty, as when we had first arrived in September. Except for a few books stacked precisely perpendicular to the edges of the desk, there were no visible signs of Diana anywhere. Her closet door was securely closed, and her dresser top was bare. No shoes sticking out from under the bed, no gym suit tossed on a chair, no coffee cup on a table or sill. Not even a calendar hung on her wall. Something about Diana's room frightened me, and I shut the door before moving on down the hall.

I am not so certain now what my own room — or rather, my three different but similar rooms over a period of four years — looked like. Although I can remember dashes of color, like the pink curtains, my rooms still fade in my mind into one indistinguishable drab cell. Over forty years I can visualize most of the interiors of places I have lived, watching my shadowy self sit or stand or move across many rooms. But all I can see at Smith is my narrow bed, covered with Aunt Ted's quilt.

In that hot, muggy June when I graduated from high school, Aunt Ted's congratulatory present seemed at first rather heavy and a little old-fashioned. Between two pieces of sprigged cotton in a pink-and-gray paisley pattern, she had hand-tufted a fluffy wool batting, tying each tuft with a piece of soft pink wool. Although I didn't find room for it in my trunk and suitcases that first fall, when I returned home for Christmas I took my quilt back to Smith with me. Sturdy but soft, plain and unpretentiously Midwestern, it lay folded for the rest of my college years on the foot of my bed. On cool afternoons I snuggled beneath it as I lay propped on my bed reading. As the wind whistled through the leaky windowpane in winter, I pulled the quilt around my ears at night and slept snugly. When I was sad or lonely, I burrowed under my quilt like an animal seeking shelter in a dark cave.

Aunt Ted's quilt became a totem as much as a furnishing. Sometime during my first year, I began to suffer from occasional insomnia. It came and went, like a tropical malady that would burst into a sudden visible outbreak, and then subside for an unpredictable time. Usually I waited more or less helplessly for it to disappear, drank soothing tea at bedtime, counted sheep, and walked back and forth to the bathroom. But during one bad patch I nightly took my quilt to the maid's room. Although Lawrence House didn't have any maids, we had a small spare room at the end of the hall that had once been provided for them. Empty except for a broken wooden chair and a dirty mattress on an iron bedstead, it was like a barren attic chamber, with slanted ceilings and a tiny window tucked under the eaves. During the day, we took occasional turns using it as a study refuge, but at night it was deserted. Sometimes when the terrors of not sleeping turned into waking nightmares, I jumped out, grabbed my quilt, and sneaked into the maid's room, glancing shamefacedly around me to make sure I was unnoticed. There I wrapped myself in my quilt like a sleeping bag and curled up on the bare mattress. As though the heavy pressures back in my room had remained there, here the air was peaceful and soothing. Inside my quilt I felt safe at last. Usually after a short while I fell asleep and only woke when I heard girls thundering down the hall toward breakfast.

No matter how tired I was, I always got up for breakfast. Food mattered. I was not the only girl who attentively studied the menus, handwritten by Mrs. Stevens and posted weekly on the house notice board. We gave the menus almost the same attention as the posted exam schedules. As we freshmen floundered in our new independence, many of us clung desperately to food. Nobody had access to kitchen facilities, and few could afford more than an occasional hamburger or grilled-cheese sandwich at the small cafes on Green Street. All we had to satisfy the sharp pangs of homesickness or timidity or fear that masqueraded as hunger were those three meals a day in the Lawrence House dining room.

For me, food was not only a rare sensual pleasure, but it also offered a reassuringly predictable future. No matter how grim the week, I could always look forward to Friday-night "sticky buns," pecan-studded rolls with a brown-sugar glaze the texture of glue; a Sunday dinner of beef and Yorkshire pudding, sloshed with gravy; and Thursday-morning French toast afloat in weak maple syrup. Not long ago, reminiscing with an old college friend, I found she too could mentally reproduce menus from twenty-five years ago. She relished the memory of crusty "cheese strata," a soufflé thick with stringy cheddar and melted butter, and she even felt nostalgic about "veal birds," anonymous meat patties that bore little resemblance to veal and whose bland breaded taste we could both easily evoke.

Neither of us thinks we cared so much about food until we left home. But in the intervening years, we have both armed ourselves, successively, with blenders, wire whisks, Crock Pots, and woks; like many women of our generation, we learned to study Craig Claiborne, cherish Julia Child, and trade Weight Watchers' recipes. Was this partly the result of our comforting ourselves with pecan rolls and cheese soufflé? Was learning to care passionately about food part of learning to live with women?

I wish Melanie Greer were here to talk about tapioca pudding. As a freshman, I was told that Melanie, one of the smartest juniors in the formidable field of classics, was sure to make Junior Phi Bete, maybe even Summa. Pale, wispy, and bespectacled, she seemed otherworldly to me, and I studied her from a distance, noting the mannerisms that made her distinctive, the huge mohair sweaters dropping on her timy frame, the nearsighted blink of her soft blue eyes, her gleeful squeak. I mostly heard her squeak on the night we had tapioca pudding.

Everyone somehow knew that shy Melanie, who never asserted other visible tastes, adored tapioca pudding. "Tapioca pudding tonight!" a girl would call out from the landing as she read the day's menu. "Someone tell Melanie!" Even Mrs. Stevens, who affected not to comment unduly on food, would smile at Head Table and chide us all, "Don't let's be greedy about seconds. We must remember our Melanie!" After everyone else had left the dining room, Melanie quietly assembled all the serving bowls and sat down at an empty table. Peeking through the door, I could see Melanie all alone, eating quickly so the dishwashers could finish, spooning down mouthful after mouthful of white, jellied, lumpy pudding. Ethereal though she was, she ate with a ravenous intensity that ill matched that pale nursery food. It was the same passion, I thought, with which she probably devoured ancient Greek.

Our thoughtfulness toward Melanie was unusual, probably because no one else cared much about tapioca pudding. Otherwise, when it came to food, it was each girl for herself. Our generosity dissolved with the first warm whiffs of tomato-and-bread casserole or the whispered rumors of apple pie, never enough for everyone to have seconds. Though our meals were surrounded with an elaborate pretense of etiquette, nowhere was the illusion of family life stretched as thin as it was in the Lawrence dining room. When the dining room filled with the clatter of dishes, clinking of glasses, and scraping of silverware, those harsh, metallic sounds were an echo of our communal life.

Dinner in Lawrence House was an event, one whose details sometimes still waft back to me in a hot, steamy blast, as though, suddenly returned, I am sitting a few inches from the kitchen doors, now swung open as the Dinner Squad enters with their large metal trays. Platters of hot meat, potatoes, and peas surge by me, and odors of food mingle with the faint ammonia stench of the kitchen beyond.

We all waited for dinner with anticipation, crowding just outside the dining room, nudging our way toward the doors. When the captain of Dinner Squad rang the gong and opened the doors, we rushed inside. The first girls got to choose their own seats at the scattered round tables; not only did we want to sit with particular friends, but we also wanted to avoid the last counterclockwise chair at each table for eight. When the girl who was waitress brought a tray of leftover seconds, by rule she had to begin with the head of the table and work her way around it in order. If you sat in the last seat, your chances of an additional pork chop depended entirely on the magnanimity of the girl who sat just ahead of you. None of us was particularly magnanimous.

Having elbowed and stamped our way to the tables and seats with a last rush, like the end of musical chairs, we slid to a stop at attention until Mrs. Stevens delivered her well-articulated grace, followed by a bright, searching glance around the room so she could see who had not come in to dinner. Those of us who had been too slow in entering the dining room slid sulkily into the empty seats at Mrs. Stevens' table, where conversation was strained and carefully monitored.

Dinner always moved slowly. By rule, none of us could leave the dining room until Mrs. Stevens had risen, smoothly slid her chair under the table, and sailed into the living room to pour coffee from the silver urn. Since she ate decorously and very deliberately, many of us finished before she did. Darting impatient glances at Head Table, a few bold girls coughed and clinked their spoons on empty dessert plates. Mrs. Stevens remained impervious, continuing to smile, making polite inquiries of the girls at her table, and setting her fork between bites just so, crosswise on the right side of her plate.

On the nights when I served on Dinner Squad, dinner was not merely slow; it was interminable. Nowhere did I feel quite as foreign at Smith as I did standing stiffly by the sideboard, watching my table, waiting to serve the next course. Part of Lawrence House tradition was that just because we were scholarship girls, and therefore had no maid service, we did not skimp on ceremony. We scrupulously observed many niceties that other, less punctilious houses could afford to let lapse. Didn't we have maids? We would be better maids than any they had in Dewey or Parsons. A co-op house? We could show those snobs in the Quad something about gracious living. In dining room service, Lawrence House pride came close to megalomania.

"Keep your trays UP and look straight AHEAD!" hissed Molly O'Brien, looking back over her shoulder at us seven freshmen who were trying to balance the heavy round metal trays on our unsteady shoulders. Lined up in the kitchen, we waited for Molly's signal to follow her into the dining room. Molly, an experienced sophomore and captain of Dinner Squad, checked us over quickly:

aprons clean, trays properly loaded, giggling and talking hushed in case noise filtered under the door during Mrs. Stevens' grace. Outside the dining room, Molly was friendly and pleasant. But when on duty, she was instantly transformed, snapping a reprimand to any slougher.

During the first meeting of Dinner Squad, which rotated among freshmen and sophomores on a weekly basis, Molly had explained the strict house rules while we beginners gobbled our early dinners. Don't talk unnecessarily with the girls at the table you're serving; offer the tray with your left hand under it, at the diner's left side, and keep your right arm neatly crossed behind your waist; clear from the right, left hand held behind; but be sure not to clear until Mrs. Stevens signals everyone has finished. While waiting, stand straight by your sideboard or tray table. No slumping. No talking then, either. The same rules applied at lunch, also served formally.

Something about the rules bothered me. It was not that I had a lot to say to the girls I was serving, especially when I was concentrating on balancing my tray and not burning my fingers on the hot silver-plate dishes. But somehow, marching stiffly around the table, I felt demeaned. As Mona Bragdon fingered the silver tongs, picking among the roast potatoes or flipping the roast beef for a rare slice, I wanted to slam the tray on her hands. Instead I would offer Mona another chance at the fried chicken. Just before I'd brought it in, the whole platter had fallen onto the kitchen floor, pieces of chicken sliding under the dusty stove. Sweeping down, Mrs. Ryan, the cook, had flicked off a few particles of dirt and genially patted the pieces back on the plate. I wished I could tell Mona after she had eaten it.

But food nourished friendships as well. If I remember the Lawrence dining room with some undigested anger, I can counter with memories of evening tea in Molly O'Brien's room. As one of the few upperclassmen on the fourth floor, Molly had a special status, enhanced by her quiet dignity, her refusal to take sides in acrimonious house disputes, and her sense of privacy. She was the kind of person of whom one did not dare to ask an uncomfortably personal question, partly from respect, and partly from fear of the cool impassive stare that could spread over her face like ice swiftly sealing a clear, deep lake. Despite her aloofness, she had a glancing, keen humor that escaped in startling peals of laughter, as if an Irish leprechaun lurked somewhere, restrained and muffled by Molly's sheer will power. When Molly befriended my roommate Sophie and me in our sophomore year, I was delighted.

The most important mark of Molly's esteem was her occasional invitation to tea, issued between 10 and 10:30 P.M., when we had all returned from the library, but just before nighttime Quiet Hours. Knocking at Sophie's and my door, Molly would incline her head through the opening, and ask, "Anybody want some tea?" with an air of gently conferring grace. We grabbed our stained mugs from our desks and walked as quietly as we could down the hall. We didn't want the girls who hadn't been asked to feel bad.

From books, movies, and perhaps snatches of conversation with girls at Iowa State, I had envisioned college as an effervescent brew of academic work lightened by social frolics. I pictured loud, cheery dormitory "gab sessions," enhanced by cookies from home, bouncy music on someone's stereo, and perhaps pillow fights. Probably what I thought I would find was a cross between a continuous slumber party, *Little Women,* and an advanced section of Camp Fire Camp. What I got instead was tea in Molly O'Brien's room.

Serene and dimly lit, Molly's room with its few but carefully arranged possessions seemed like a monastic cell. Sitting cross-legged on Molly's Indian felt rug, embroidered with enchantingly colored animals, I sipped weak Lipton's and nibbled on vanilla wafers. In the background I could hear flutes and violins playing unidentifiable melodies; after taking Introduction to Music her freshman year, Molly had been converted to Schubert and Mozart, she'd told us, and at her tea parties she played only chamber music on an old record player, softly, so we couldn't disturb anyone in the hall. I admired the record jackets of her classical collection with the same inchoate yearning I directed at the Piranesi print on her wall; Sophie and I listened to Sinatra, Chris Connor, and sometimes Rachmaninoff's "Variations on a Theme by Paganini," and we both felt artistically advanced when we eventually agreed to replace Van Gogh's "Sunflowers" with a Modigliani.

Part of my picture of Happy College Life, enhanced by the

Smith brochures that showed photographs of girls allegedly engaged in deep intellectual discussion, included myself in earnest conversation about Life, Death, Philosophy, Art, and Literature. Even at Molly's tea parties, however, esthetic as they seemed to me, I never got there. Molly and I usually exchanged a few tentative comparisons about how much we'd understood, or studied, in Art History that week. We aired views about next semester's courses, weekend possibilities, and vacation plans. Sometimes we all simmered and sniped about Robin, down the hall, who had filled the one bathtub with chlorine to soak her underwear overnight, or about Olive, across the hall, who had just reported another miserable freshman for an infraction of Quiet Hours. After a few such commiserations, however, Molly would frown and noticeably change the subject. Personal nastiness, she let us feel, had no place in this room. Rebuked, we sipped our tea. Soon Molly put her cup down, lifted the phonograph needle, and said politely, "Well, it's back to work for me, I'm afraid." We picked up our mugs and shuffled out. Trudging back to my room, I felt I had attended, however briefly, some kind of salon.

Social life in Lawrence came closest to my fantasies on Sunday mornings. Since many of us had Saturday-morning classes, Sunday was the only day for safely sleeping late. It was also the only time when a formal meal was not served in the Lawrence dining room. Instead, a special Sunday squad brought breakfast trays to each floor. There early risers could find orange juice in a large pitcher, strong coffee, and large, dry, but heavily iced sweet rolls in a cellophane-wrapped package. Loading up, I wandered from room to room, listening for sounds of friends who might also be up and stirring. Usually, at least by midmorning, a few of us assembled in someone's double room, crammed ourselves onto the two twin beds and the floor, and picnicked together, sprinkling crumbs and slurping coffee with a happy abandon we didn't have in the dining room downstairs.

Sunday morning was a special time in Lawrence House. No one studied. The library wasn't open until 1 P.M.; the living room was filled with the comforting rustle of the Sunday *New York Times.* Upstairs in Carolyn's and Griffie's room, four or five of us eagerly compared notes on last night's Bergman movie, sighed over the gorgeousness of Paul Newman in his latest film, or begged for details about someone's date. We asked each other, was he cute? Was he nice? Was he fun? Did you have a good time? What did you do? What did he talk about? Will you see him again? Do you *want* to see him again? Like trained sociologists, we posed a standard questionnaire. Under the guarded answers we could usually detect each other's real responses.

"Yes, he was all right, but not very bright"; Betty hadn't had a very good time, and she had probably frightened away another man with her anxious, intelligent air. We worried about Betty and her glooms. "I thought he was absolutely adorable, but he didn't say anything about seeing me again. We had a wonderful time. I just hope he calls." Lisa, who was shy, was feeling rejected once more. We all hoped he *would* call; most of us knew what it was like to wait in uncertainty as the week lengthened and Saturday night loomed vacantly ahead. "Oh, we just went back to Bart's room and listened to music and talked. He knows so much about philosophy and he's thought so much about *life*," said Sophie in her turn. She was the social success on our floor, having met her ideal man, Bart, the very first Sunday of her freshman fall, at an Amherst church group. Cozily settled into going steady, she seemed destined to acquire an engagement ring in the far future. Her Saturday-night summaries varied between domestic bliss and black romantic quarrels; we listened with respect and a little awe, as if a traveler from a distantly glimpsed, cloud-covered country were describing a mountain fastness we all planned to reach but hadn't yet set out for. Sophie, we agreed, was the only one of us who really knew about love. When, a year later, after a series of tumultuous battles, Sophie broke up with Bart, we were all shocked and a little chastened.

As the morning wore on, as the coffee in our cups grew colder and was replenished by flat instant, heated by someone's plug-in coil, and as our stale cinnamon rolls disappeared, our spirits began to droop. One girl after another slipped from the room, to do laundry or write a letter home or type up lab notes. Occasionally I left with Sophie for a chapel service, snuggled back into bed to read, or scavenged in the living room downstairs for an abandoned, crumpled *Times*. But by noon, when the dinner gong rang, I began to sink into a lethargy that gradually deepened into depression toward evening. Lawrence House was not a happy place on late Sunday afternoons. Slamming doors and dragging suitcases, tired girls returned from their weekends away, sometimes with discouraged faces that told of unsuccessful dates, sometimes satisfied with the weekend but sorry that the date had been left far behind. At Sunday-night supper we did not have to wear skirts; slopping into the dining room, we sat dully together in jeans or unpressed skirts. Spare time that had seemed so deliciously ample on early Sunday morning had unaccountably evaporated, and we faced a week of unrelenting classes, study, tests, papers. Since the cooks had Sunday night off, we were confronted with gray slices of leftover meat, Velveeta, bologna, fruit Jell-O. Sunday nights always seemed peculiarly cheerless, cold and congealed like the food we ate.

Except for Sunday breakfast, all our meals were communal ones. Yet the food I remember most vividly as a symbol of my life in Lawrence House is not veal birds, or sticky buns, or tapioca pudding. What I still taste, rolling it on my tongue with a mixture of appetite and gagging, is the peculiar chalky flatness of chocolate Metrecal. To me, Metrecal is a magic name of the 1950s, like Canasta. I seized on both of them as examples of improvements to the quality of life. Thinking of Metrecal, I realize how eagerly at Smith I tried to improve — and nurture myself at the same time — with whatever I was offered.

When I heard about Metrecal, it seemed like a miracle: a chocolate malt that would make me thin. As I steadily gained weight that freshman year, my guilt rose in almost geometric progression with my pounds. At five pounds over my entering weight, which I had honed all summer after high school like a prizefighter preparing for a title bout, my best dress grew tight over the hips. At ten pounds, I could no longer zip my comfortable plaid skirt quite to the top. At fifteen pounds, I wore my blouses outside my jeans, hung most of my new clothes in the back of my closet, and despaired. Metrecal gave me hope. Three premeasured cans a day: it seemed so simple. Expensive, since my tightly stretched budget barely covered coffee and occasional English muffins at Gino's, but absolutely worth every penny, I told myself, if it helped restore my buried self-respect.

Armed with what I was sure was a combination of sturdy fortitude and virtue, I periodically spent my week's pocket money on a six-pack of chocolate Metrecal and took it to my room. Trying to convince myself that I was gaining at least an hour of study time, as well as losing unwanted calories, I determinedly stayed upstairs when the lunch gong rang. Everyone else pounded down the stairs; the house shook with a hundred feet, then settled into quiet as the dining-room door opened and shut again. A hush I never heard at any other time fell over the hall outside my room. Alone on my bed, I felt absolutely deserted. Pretending that what I felt was not an echoing abyss but, instead, peace and quiet, I poured my Metrecal into a small glass to make it last longer. Sip by sip, it disappeared with alarming quickness, and left me a little queasy, but still hungry. Sometimes I added a few Ry-Krisp crackers as a bonus, but they didn't take very long to eat either, and they soaked up the taste of Metrecal so all I had on my tongue was dry cracker crumbs.

Three floors below me, I could picture Lunch Squad heaving through the swinging kitchen doors with their trays of noodle soup, hot dogs, buns, and creamed corn. For dessert they were having cherry crisp. My friends would all be sitting at a table together, laughing and talking. Maybe Billie would be telling one of her funny stories, or Joyce would hint about her weekend in New York with Samuel. When I finally walked downstairs and past the dining room on my way to the library, the scraping and clinking that often irritated me now signaled a kind of fellowship I had chosen to ignore. After a long afternoon, in which I tried not to think of food, or nibbled on an apple, or drank more coffee than I really wanted, I usually returned to Lawrence at dinnertime with my resolution dissolved. Sometimes, with a second infusion of Metrecal, I lasted until bedtime, but I never could rise the next morning and face another six-ounce can with equanimity. Breakfast beckoned. Juice, eggs, toast, jam, coffee. It was irresistible. Feeling I had let down not only my hopes but also Metrecal and its inventor, I promised myself to try again tomorrow, or the next day. I wouldn't get on the scales until Sunday. Maybe on Sunday, I'd be thinner; maybe I'd feel stronger; maybe I could go back on Metrecal then. Sunday was always very far away.

Sitting alone in my room, drinking Metrecal, and hearing unaccustomed silence in the vacant rooms around me, was the only time I can remember Lawrence House empty of life. Though never noisy, Lawrence vibrated to doors slamming, voices seeping over transoms and under thresholds, phones ringing and toilets flushing, while on the main floor one could always hear the slap of bridge cards, books thudding onto chairs or tables, and the clacking of typewriters in the smokers' lounge. Even at the bleakest hours of the night, when I went down the hall to the bathroom, I could see a light on in someone's room or hear faint scratchings behind someone's door. Sometimes this constant hum seemed comforting, but sometimes it grated on my nerves. There were so many of us, living so closely together. On alternate Thursday nights the hum rose louder and louder, into an orchestra of dissonance, at House Meeting.

When the housemother, House Council, or house president decided we needed to meet together, the president posted a notice on the first-floor newel post: "House Meeting Tonight."

Promptly at ten our house president rang the dinner gong, and a stream of girls poured down the stairs, flopping in slippers, tugging bags of knitting, snatching ashtrays, bumming cigarettes, and waving wild hand-signals to early arrivals to find choice seats. We all wanted to be near good friends so we could vent our feelings at outrageous opinions with a meaningful poke. Seniors were allowed seats of honor on the few living-room chairs; the rest of us scrunched on the floor, crammed together, breathing each other's shampoo, hand lotion, and cigarette smoke.

As a freshman, I sneaked incredulous glances at the suddenly vulnerable juniors and seniors who seemed so smoothly put together in the daytime. Without her familiar red plaid kilt, Shetland sweater, and matching knee socks, Moira Manning looked like a stranger in her worn pale-pink flannel pajamas. I wondered what beautiful Dee Dee Boylston's boyfriend, the legendary Tad of Harvard, would say if he saw her now, her smooth blonde pageboy turned into ugly metal curlers, her face white with cold cream, her brow wrinkled as she bent over knitting. I never said anything to Dee Dee in the daytime, but now I thought I could.

Although our House Meetings were supposed to be enlightened models of democracy, I remember them instead as seething stewpots. They were perhaps not such a bad introduction, though I didn't think so then, to the realities of political life. Our house president presided, tapping a silver-handled gavel. Chosen each spring for a one-year term, the president was always a girl whom everyone respected and liked, someone who had no enemies, someone who was nice, responsible, and perhaps a little bland. We had to believe our house president was above pettiness, made of slightly finer stuff than we ourselves, someone we could trust to defend each of us against the other.

Not an issue of any lasting importance that I can now remember ever arose in House Meeting. Should we relax the standards for weekly House Inspection? How should we make the girl who was supposed to Sit On Bells, answering phones and the front door, show up regularly? Who had taken the hot plate from the third-floor bathroom? Was it a violation of the Honor System to steal a hot plate? Should that person report herself? Did anyone else who knew about it have the responsibility to report her? Should she just return the hot plate and be given another chance? Would that destroy the Honor System?

Although afterward I was astonished at the acrimonious debate on what seemed in retrospect trivial points, at the time I too was always drawn in. Every week something came up that involved even the most obscure corner of the living room; somebody really *cared* whether or not we should be required to wear skirts for Sunday dinner, or whether we needed to raise the house dues by fifty cents. Someone took offense at something someone else had said, voices rose, a third party intervened, and then, authoritatively, the house president gaveled, and reminded us how late it was. The smoke in the hot, stuffy room grew thicker and thicker. When Mona Bragdon raised her hand, we all groaned, for Mona had a gift for introducing side issues, unforeseen complications, or an entanglement that would delay adjournment for at least another half hour.

Even when the president dismissed us at last, and we pulled ourselves off the floor and dragged sleepily upstairs, the night was not always over. Mona Bragdon was also fire warden, required to hold three drills a year. Sometimes she decided — in the house's best interest, she assured us — that we needed more. Mona loved fire drills. She preferred to pick a late night after House Meeting. Soon after we'd collapsed in our beds, a terrifying clang sounded in the hall, a fire alarm loud enough to waken all the exhausted ghosts in Lawrence House. Our instructions were clear and simple; Mona read them aloud to House Meeting several times a year. Grab a pillow and a blanket or towel, presumably to beat out flames; wear shoes or slippers; shut the door to your room; hit the sidewalk in three minutes flat.

Huddled together for warmth in the cold outside, clutching our blankets, we listened for Mona, stopwatch in hand, to finish calling the roll. Sometimes, after Mona had clicked her stopwatch and turned off the clanging bell, a lone straggler trailed shamefacedly onto the porch. She was greeted with a chorus of boos, since if we didn't all make the drill under three minutes, we had to do it again. Back upstairs we retreated, Mona grinning as she watched us go. She wanted half an hour to elapse, maybe an hour, maybe two, so she could rouse us once more from a sound sleep. Down in the smoker, she waited for the perfect moment. When I heard the fire bell, I always wanted to kill her.

Maybe if I'd gotten to know Mona better, I might have liked her. Over the years I have discovered that if I take the time and effort to learn more about the life of someone I dislike, I usually find a sympathetic tie develops. But I never did get to know Mona. Although we fifty-seven girls were bunched so tightly together, separated only by thin partitions; sharing meals; and passing each other constantly on the stairs; we were subdivided too sharply by class, by floor, even by academic majors, to form many close friendships. Most of us had a special friend or two, and probably a small group that tended to eat together or to gather in each other's rooms. Few of us could extend an intimate connection further. When I had glimpses of other lives, I wished somehow I knew more about them all. Brushed by tantalizing hints, I longed to seize and shake them until someone's full story fell out.

Because I disliked her so much, I was particularly fascinated by Mona. Private, intense, she spoke in short, enigmatic bursts, punctuated by sudden snorts of laughter that never seemed to have been evoked by any particular point in the conversation. She often staked out a corner of the living room, turning the back of her easy chair ostentatiously to the room, where she read a book and snorted aloud at unpredictable intervals. Sometimes as I passed the smoker I saw her cross-legged on the floor, almost hidden by a haze of cigarettes, deep in conversation with her roommate, Dulie. Since I adored Dulie, who had been my Big Sister, I figured that Mona must have a compelling inner self I had never been able to see.

Mona's impenetrability was increased for me by her chosen major, psychology, which was then — compared to history, government, or English — a new and rather arcane academic field. Having staked a successful claim to the advanced study of psychology in Lawrence House, Mona reveled in her solitary expertise. After Friday-night foreign films, she presided in the living room, now with her chair facing her audience, as her postulants examined myth, metaphor, and symbol. Whenever an Ingmar Bergman film was booked at Sage Hall, Mona attended both the early and late shows.

My sense of exclusion from Mona's world was complete one noon during my junior year when she caught me putting my napkin in my napkin box. Since we were issued clean linen napkins only twice a week, between changes we had to store them after each meal, with accumulated lipstick, goo, and gravy stains, in individually labeled cubbyholes in a large box on the wall. Until that noon, rolling and stuffing my napkin in my cubby had been one of my most unconscious acts in Lawrence House. But today Mona, followed by a few giggling friends, elbowed her way toward me through the crowd streaming from the dining room. Just as I reached out with my crumpled napkin, she yelled triumphantly, "THIRTY-SEVEN!" Giggles broke into snickering laughter.

"What?" I said confusedly.

"Thirty-seven phallic symbols so far today," Mona said smugly, as the girls around her nodded. "We're counting all the phallic symbols in Lawrence. We're absolutely *surrounded*. I don't suppose you've ever noticed." I shook my head, trying to smile disarmingly. Mona turned to her followers. "What was thirty-six?" she asked, as if she'd forgotten.

"The candles in the candlesticks," piped up a freshman, who was now taking Introduction to Psychology. "And before that, the newspapers in the mailboxes, and pencils in the pencil-sharpener, and the shower, and the plug in the bathtub." Mona nodded in approval. I stood awkwardly, holding my napkin. After a few moments, Mona swept on into the living room, followed by the freshman with the list. Gingerly, with a new self-awareness, I put my napkin in its box.

Sometime later that year, I saw a flash of another Mona, the hidden person I never knew. I was standing near the mailboxes, after morning mail call, idly glancing through the week's college calendar. Between classes, a handful of girls drifted past me, stopping at the mailboxes, chatting, offering cigarettes and matches. I didn't notice Mona behind me until I heard her gasp. Turning, I saw her looking intently at a letter in her hand, with open pain on her face. At that moment she crushed the letter in her hand and dashed upstairs, sobbing wildly. I was transfixed with interest. While I was still staring at her departing back, Dulie drew out of the now-quiet group at the mailboxes and moved past me to follow Mona. I put my hand on her elbow tightly. "What was that all about?" I asked timidly, but unable to disguise my curiosity. Dulie was impassive. She looked straight at me; though she had been my Big Sister, I knew her first loyalty was to Mona. "It's a letter from Lynn," she finally said, as though to grant me something, and then turned away, taking the stairs two at a time. Lynn, I knew, was Mona's fiancé, a second lieutenant in the Air Force. She hadn't seen him for months. That was all I knew, and, not daring to ask anyone except Dulie, I never found out anything more. Lynn and Mona were married the next year. When I ran into Mona in Boston twenty years later, I asked her about this incident, but she didn't remember it.

I puzzled over the mysteries surrounding the lives of other girls from whom I felt alienated, and in Lawrence House, there were many girls to puzzle about. By the time we were seniors, our entering class of ten had separated into distinct cliques. Sarah Kaiser belonged to what I thought of as the wild bunch, girls who sat up all night in the smoker, partied every weekend, and were rumored to have an illegal bottle of bourbon stashed in someone's closet. I wasn't sure where Sarah fitted in. So shy she seemed secretive, Sarah didn't seem to date, or study, or do much except follow behind the leaders of the wild bunch, falling into step without an audible murmur. And she played the piano, disappearing for hours at a time to the Music Building, where she took private lessons as well as classes.

Though in my brief, strained conversations with her, Sarah was always reticent and uncommunicative, sometimes I could see signs of another, hidden person, just as I caught an occasional glimpse of another Mona. At the dinner table, when one of her close friends whispered something in her ear, she often reacted oddly, opening her eyes wide as if shocked, sometimes gasping and choking on her food until someone slapped her on the back. Listening to general conversation, she might break unexpectedly into a discussion with a tortured, convoluted question, obviously wrung from her under great stress, her face working with feeling.

But what I remember most of Sarah is how she played the piano. An old mahogany grand jutted from a corner of the Lawrence living room, usually ignored, except at Christmastime, when we drummed out tinny carols, or when a date, idly waiting for a girl to come downstairs, plunked a few notes. On a few occasions, though, when I was studying, half-hidden in a chair, Sarah came noiselessly into the room and slid onto the piano bench. Suddenly she attacked, a ripple of runs or crashing chords shattering the silence in the room. I put my book down. Though I couldn't pretend to keep reading, Sarah's emotions ran so nakedly up and down the keyboard that it seemed intrusive to listen. When Sarah played the piano, she was wholly absorbed, bending and waving over the instrument like a reed over the water, blown by a fierce wind. I watched her face for a clue to what she was feeling, but I saw nothing I knew how to interpret. I *wanted* to know. What was she thinking of? What was bothering her? Why did she suddenly bolt from the room at the end of a piece, much as Mona had bolted up the stairs?

I now wonder how many of us, amid the bustle and noise and hurrying of fifty-seven girls, sensed themselves shut out. Few of us knew how the others felt. Aside from the difficulty of knowing fifty-six girls well, we lived in a house that put on a good show. Lawrence girls learned early to keep up a cheerful front, complaining about little things, but saving their deeper woes for the privacy of their own rooms.

There we could talk to our roommates. Although I did often feel isolated, I also found comfort in the few good friendships I formed in Lawrence. Most of all, I treasured my three-years'-roommate Sophie. She and I were a defensive league against any outside threats or terrors. Although by junior and senior years, upperclassmen could vie for the few single rooms, most chose to share a connecting suite instead, so they could have the solace and company of a roommate. College roommates forged a deep bond, one that I know has sometimes endured through years of separate lives. Twenty-five years out of college, I can still hear a special tone in a friend's voice when she mentions, "Sally, my roommate at Grinnell," as I myself speak of Sophie.

Perhaps that bond depended on our unavoidable knowledge of each other's intimate lives, the kind of knowledge most of us had only known before with our families. In the small, crowded rooms in Lawrence, one had no space to hide. A roommate could tell when you were worried about a test, even if you said nothing about it; she watched you studying late, heard you tossing in your bed, woke to your early alarm. She could see the glow on your face when you returned to the room after an important phone call, and if you came in rumpled and smeared from a date, she knew why.

Such intimacy was not always easy, and the random pairings of freshman year did not survive as long as more thoughtfully arranged marriages. A few girls remained together all four years, but most of us searched, sifted, and considered long and hard before deciding who to live with the second year and afterward. Although my own freshman roommate, Alice, and I remained friends, we realized by spring that our habits were too different, and our interests not common enough, to survive another year. After two decades, when I met her again with real affection, she reminded me, "Do you still like the door closed? Remember how we used to fight about whether or not to leave it open?" I hadn't remembered that domestic quarrel, but I did recall waking to her alarm at 6 A.M. in the winter months when she did her ski exercises, thumping and cracking on the bare wooden floor. Neither of us talked about the delicate circling around each other that preceded sophomore room choice in the spring. Sophie had a freshman roommate too, of whom she was also fond, and no one wanted to hurt anyone else's feelings. It was like asking, politely, for a divorce you weren't sure the other person wanted, and then announcing, offhandedly and as though it didn't matter, that you had in fact found a new partner whom you preferred. A few of the splits were acrimonious, with accusations reported to sympathetic bystanders: "She's so messy!" "Her friend from Northrup is always underfoot. I'm sick and tired of having someone else in our room all the time." "She comes in drunk every Saturday night, and last weekend she threw up on the floor." "She's so depressed she keeps the shades pulled all afternoon and sleeps, and I can't stand it anymore." "Have you ever tried living with someone who won't talk to you?" "Have you tried living with someone who talks all the time, yak yak yak? *Have* you?"

When Sophie, a night owl, and I, a morning person, settled down together for the rest of our college years, we knew we would have to make adjustments. Sometimes Sophie read with a flashlight under her covers, and I tried not to make conversation before breakfast. I managed to keep my half of the room fairly neat, and Sophie, though her habits were more precise, didn't scold. Perhaps this partnership was successful because, different though we were in temperament and background, each thought the other was wonderful. Sophie was tall and upright, thin and elegant. Although I tended to gathered skirts and smocks, Sophie preferred trim slacks and Chanel suits. Her dark wavy hair lay flat in lustrous coils. I ruffled my short pixie cut with my fingers, hoping I might look a little like a plump Audrey Hepburn. At my best, I thought, I was cute, but Sophie was beautiful. When she and I double-dated, she dipped and glided over the dance floor with her admiring escort, while I tried to keep time in my head and avoid my partner's feet. Social grace came easily to Sophie, as I saw her, while I had to work hard for it. I had to settle, I realized, for what my encouraging friends called "personality."

I admired Sophie's New England moral fervor, firm self-control, freedom from pettiness, and social vision. Yet I always felt I could be foolish and silly in her company, and she would still think of me as a serious person. She made me feel valued. Over the years this mutual admiration society has had its problems; remembering my visions of her dazzling future, I've heard myself admonishing her, "But what are you really *doing*?", and once, troubled by my dissatisfactions with my life, she said chidingly to me, "But Sue, you *ought* to be happy!" We have had lots of "oughts" for each other, perhaps measuring the success of our own dreams by what the other has accomplished. Roommates sized each other up quickly, and the measurements we took did not always allow for growth and change.

Roommates were doubly important for those of us who lived far from home. We needed places to go for Thanksgiving, Easter, and occasional vacation weekends. Those visits to someone else's home were high excitement, not only because I escaped from Lawrence House, but because I caught glimpses of other parts of the East. When Sophie invited me home for the first time, I could hardly wait to see the Atlantic Ocean, which, she told me, poured onto a beach a mile or so from her house in Hampton Beach, New Hampshire. Having drenched myself in the romantic fervors of Edna St. Vincent Millay, I prepared for pounding surf and roaring waves. The first night after supper her father and mother obligingly drove me to the beach. They waited while Sophie and I went for a walk. A long clean swath of sand shone along a flat coast for what looked like miles. It was late fall, with a cold wind blowing, and the gray water foamed with frothy whitecaps. Though the waves broke on the sand with a steady, monotonous crash, I couldn't really call the sound a roar. There were no rocks like the ones Millay had sat on, no bay stretching out to sea, just a long gray line of water. On the other side of the road that edged the beach were rows of shuttered cafes, hot-dog stands, motels, cottages, and souvenir shops. They looked suddenly deserted, as if everyone had fled before some invincible approaching enemy, leaving their homes and businesses at the last possible minute. I felt we were the only survivors of an unknown war. Not saying much, Sophie and I paced along the firm wet sand. I loved the smell of the salt air. I told myself I was gazing not just at any ordinary horizon but somewhere out to sea — Newfoundland, England, Europe. After a while, chilled by the cold, we agreed to scuttle back to the car. That night, tucked onto the studio couch, fussed over lovingly by Mrs. Forrest, I fell asleep trying to hear in my mind Millay's crashing surf. I almost believed I had seen it.

Before our weekend was over, Mr. Forrest offered to take us for a drive farther up the coast, past Portsmouth and into Kittery, Maine. When we crossed the magical state line, I peered eagerly out the window at Kittery. I loved to hear the way Mr. Forrest pronounced it: two syllables, "Kit-tree." Though I thought I detected a slightly rougher coastline, even quainter houses, maybe a sharper tang in the salt air, I was surprised Kittery wasn't very different from Hampton Beach. As we turned back toward New Hampshire, I looked longingly at the road behind us that wound northeast toward rocks, surf, and Millay country.

I cherished the clipped words, strange vowels, and unusual idioms Sophie and her family shared as tangible evidence that they were indeed real Yankees. Other than accent, they seemed as familiar as my neighbors at home, living with the same kind of furniture, food, and domestic habits. It was hard to romanticize their small, comfortable house, a bungalow like many I knew in Iowa, or their quiet town. Only when Mr. Forrest disappeared one late afternoon, with a promise to find some "shawts," did my fantasies pick up. "Shawts," he explained, were lobsters too small to keep legally; he knew a fisherman, though, who brought a few home with his catch and sold them surreptitiously to favored old customers. Maybe he'd be lucky enough to see that fisherman down at the wharf. An hour later he slipped in the back door, putting his finger to his lips and winking as he set a brown paper bag down on the counter. As we sat in the Forrests' kitchen that night picking away at our lobsters, Mr. Forrest warned us, with a barely noticeable twinkle, never to tell anyone about eating "shawts." We could get in trouble, he said, nodding wisely. Mrs. Forrest didn't think he was funny; looking at him with affectionate sternness, she said, "I don't like it, Herbert. Someday you're going to get caught, and pay that fifty-dollar fine." I tingled with a pleasurable sensation of adventure, half-listened for a foreboding knock at the door, and broke off another claw.

Perhaps because my visits to friends' homes were always so short, I remember them like brief, vivid snapshots, as if a flashbulb had gone off for a moment, capturing a scene, and then leaving me once more in the dark. Although it must have rained sometimes at Sophie's house, or Judy's, or Jane's, those snapshots are almost all bright and sunny. The places themselves are imbued with the warmth of the friendships that brought me there. That is how I remember Amanda's parents' music camp, a home and outbuildings set in the middle of beautiful Vermont hills.

Amanda was not a roommate, or a Lawrence House girl, or in my year's class. I'm not sure I remember when or how I met her, because now it seems that suddenly, at the beginning of my senior year, when she was a junior, we became lifelong friends. Though I was right about the importance of the friendship, I was wrong about "lifelong." Amanda had cancer, which had metastasized — it was a fancy word I had not yet heard, though in years since, as my friends and I have aged, it has been an increasing part of my vocabulary. She waited for the cancer to reappear, treated it, and always hoped it had gone forever. Perhaps her illness gave her an added zest for life, an extraordinary vitality that surfaced in her rich, deep laugh, her excitement at new ideas, and her willingness to take chances. She drew people to her, making them feel special, as though she alone knew what secret gifts they harbored or what heights they might, if encouraged, rise to. Amanda assumed each of her friends would someday do great things. She treated us all as best friends, encouraging our ideal selves. Even knowing that she was closer to my roommate, Sophie, than to me — they both sang in the same small group, shared concerns about student government, and argued ethical issues — I was not jealous, only proud that Amanda like me, too.

Although Amanda periodically disappeared to Boston or into the Northampton Hospital for treatments, she was such a spirited fighter that no one really believed she would lose her battle with cancer. We thought comfortingly about the expertise of the world's best doctors at Mass. General. We were relieved to hear she had managed to complete one history course, even though she'd had to drop another. We seized on every hopeful sign that she had not given up. It was impossible to imagine Amanda dying.

Though I remember Amanda's affection and interest in me, I do not recall much that we actually did together. Amanda had to share her time with so many of us, and she didn't have much. We had coffee on Green Street, Friday-afternoon tea in the Lawrence House living room, and occasionally a good gossip in Sophie's and my suite. The visits to our third-floor rooms stopped when

Amanda was forced to use a cane, walking painfully but with determined energy around campus.

Amanda and I said our good-byes to each other on the spring weekend of my senior year when Sophie, I, and another friend, Chris Morgan, went home with Amanda to Vermont. It was the short break between honors comprehensives and Commencement, a time when I was in a dull and depressed state. To Amanda I confided what no one but Sophie suspected, my fears that I had disgraced myself by failing to achieve a "Summa" honors degree. Though sympathetic, she encouraged me to fight my depression, go for walks, sit and read in the shadow of the mountains. When she saw I needed to be left alone, she spirited the others away. Taking a book onto the grass, I sat with it unopened in my lap and gazed at the high slopes, so freshly green they looked as if a watercolorist had just stroked the wet color on. I could hear the murmur of bees, the faraway rumble of a tractor, and the faint sound of workmen doing something somewhere with a saw. But mostly I soaked in the sunshine, the quiet, and the space. For a while the claustrophobic tensions of Lawrence House disappeared. Later, Amanda sat on my bed and told me that no matter how I graduated, everyone knew how well I had done. She assured me that I was heading into a wonderful future. "You and Sophie will both *kill* 'em at Berkeley," she said, waving her cane in the air. She had high hopes for my career as a literary critic, and for Sophie as a lawyer. To Amanda, all her friends were Summas.

When I heard a year later of Amanda's death, I went out that night with Sophie and we both got drunk. It was the only time in my life I deliberately kept drinking past satiation until finally, on a road on the way home, I was sick. Though Amanda would not have liked to see me throw up, she would have understood that I was trying to make an excessive gesture. She would not have been disappointed in me, because she never was. Perhaps that is why I still miss her.

Sometimes friends not only welcomed me into their homes, in New Hampshire, Massachusetts, or Vermont, but also introduced me into their relatives' houses. That was how, on a trip to New York City, I met Jane Greenfield's aunt. When Jane brought me home with her for Passover, I entered still another new world. Mr.

Greenfield, who owned a large manufacturing operation in Lowell, Massachusetts, sent someone from the mill to pick us up. In a way, I felt, we had a chauffeur. Jane greeted the driver, Mac, by name, asked casually about his trip, and then settled back next to me in the rear seat. It was clear we did not need to include Mac in our conversation. I had read enough English novels to know something about family retainers, but I was too shy to ask Jane if that was what Mac was. I just looked at him out of the corner of my eye and tried to decide what he was thinking. He was so silent and expressionless I couldn't tell. He drove, and Jane and I talked. When we arrived at the Greenfields' home, a house handsome and spacious enough to impress anyone from Ames, Jane introduced me to Florrie, a beaming older woman who stood behind Jane's mother at the door. Florrie, Jane told me, had lived with the Greenfields for years and had helped raise Jane and her sister Roxanne. After hugging her mother, Jane gave Florrie an equally warm squeeze, and Florrie in turn wept a little. I realized that Florrie occupied a very different place from Mac. In Dickens and Brontë I had also read about housekeepers, nursemaids, and governesses, but Florrie seemed too outspoken, too much a family member, to compare with Jane Eyre or Mrs. Rouncewell.

I had never been to a Seder before. Sitting in a carved straight-back chair at a long table set with white linen and fine crystal, sipping my Mogen David wine, I felt as if I were in some vaguely European setting, perhaps in the midst of a Henry James novel. Having grown up without a father, I always looked appraisingly at other people's, and Mr. Greenfield seemed just right: kind, handsome, expansive, and very much in charge. I was envious of the Greenfields when I saw him look proudly around the table at his family, a cherished wife and two pretty daughters. Mrs. Greenfield, petite and charming as a delicately colored bird, fluttered pleasantly on her side of the table. Still beaming, Florrie served the dinner, and then retired to the kitchen. I hoped I wouldn't use the wrong fork.

My weekend with the Greenfields had a fairy-tale quality, as if I were Cinderella transported to the ball, and it was a shock to return, Mac again driving, to drab midwinter Northampton. When, in late spring, I decided to go to New York for a weekend, and

Jane, after consulting her parents, suggested that I could stay in the maid's room at her Aunt Eleanor's, I was prepared for another storybook excursion. I wasn't disappointed. Aunt Eleanor lived in an apartment tower on Fifth Avenue, an address that sounded imposing even before I saw the granite grandeur of the building itself. A spiffily uniformed doorman looked me over, absorbed my dirty trenchcoat and spike heels, but nevertheless called upstairs to tell Aunt Eleanor I was coming. Although she was on her way out, she stayed long enough to greet me in her marble-tiled entry, show me the maid's room, and tell me to make myself at home.

I never did see all the apartment. I peeked in the living room, not wanting to intrude, and stared at the real oil paintings on the wall, some of them by people I'd studied in Introduction to Art History. Did she own a Matisse, or do I merely remember a splashy blue-and-white print that I mistook for an original? I was prepared to believe anything, and if she had collected Matisses, I wouldn't have been surprised. Though details of her furnishings escape me, I recall the cushy deep blue carpeting and a blur of pale satins and brocades. The maid's room is clearer: a large closet, windowless, with an ironing board in an adjoining utility room.

At the end of the weekend, I wanted to do something polite to thank Aunt Eleanor for her hospitality. I had not seen her since our first meeting two days before, and when I was packed and ready to go early Sunday afternoon, Aunt Eleanor was still in bed. Her maid (who, for some reason, obviously was not living in the maid's room) said she would soon be taking Mrs. Weinstein's breakfast in to her, but Mrs. Weinstein did not plan to get up for at least an hour. I thought briefly about what to do, and then I had an idea. Back at Smith, Lawrence girls often thanked each other with flowers, or, to be exact, a single flower, usually a red rose, purchased at a florist on Green Street. To celebrate a birthday or offer congratulations or gratitude, one wrote a note to go with a single (75-cent) rose. So I hurried to the elevator, rode all the way down to Fifth Avenue, and walked a few blocks until I found a florist open. He unsmilingly wrapped a single flower in green paper and gave me a small white card. I inscribed my thanks on the card and hurried back to Aunt Eleanor's apartment. Handing it to the maid and blushing a little, I went to get my suitcase.

Just as I was leaving, the maid called me. "Mrs. Weinstein would like to see you in her room," she said, pointing down a hall I hadn't explored. A few seconds later I stepped inside the bedroom door. Aunt Eleanor, in a lacy bedjacket, was propped up in a white-and-gilt double bed, a breakfast tray in front of her. On the bed was my long cone of green florist's paper with the rose poking out. "Thank you, my dear," she said graciously. "I do hope you have a pleasant trip back to Smith. Did you have a nice time in New York?" I nodded. I couldn't help noticing on her bedside table a large china vase of artistically arranged spring flowers. After thanking her again, I didn't have much else to say to Aunt Eleanor, nor she to me. Safely out on the street, I allowed myself to feel slightly embarrassed about the single rose.

From time to time I thought back to Aunt Eleanor, her airy and flower-filled bedroom, and the small white-walled maid's room at the rear of the apartment. Somehow I connected the maid's room in my mind with Mrs. Stevens, our housemother. Something about the contrast between the lives of those two, both single women in late middle age, tugged at my imagination. Aunt Eleanor and Mrs. Stevens: what did they have in common? What could they show me about my own later life? Nothing, I told myself reassuringly. But although I could push Aunt Eleanor out of my mind, Mrs. Stevens did not disappear so easily. Among the women I encountered, and tried to understand, during my four years at Smith, perhaps the one I knew least was Mrs. Stevens. Although she was our housemother, no one thought of her in a maternal way. She was the only older woman around to talk to, but we were wary about confiding in her. As head of a scholarship house — that was the title with which the college tried to endow its housemothers with dignity, Head of House — she lunched regularly with Miss Bailey, Head of Scholarships and Student Aid. According to several girls, who claimed direct evidence from their interviews with Miss Bailey, Mrs. Stevens reported on which girls were causing trouble, taking too many weekends away from campus, or even spending too much money on meals out. So to most of us she seemed more like an Establishment spy than a surrogate mother. She was always friendly to me, but I didn't trust her.

Although I had some glimmerings about the defensive isolation of many Lawrence girls, and certainly some awareness of my own bouts with loneliness, I never extended any such understanding to Mrs. Stevens. Only much later did I realize why I compared her life to wealthy Aunt Eleanor's, and then it was too late to let her know how ignorantly I had judged her.

Despite her efforts to keep up with campus life and to discuss current events at the dinner table, we all assumed that Mrs. Stevens was superficial and a little silly. Brisk and chirping, she kept up an irritating air of perpetual good cheer. We were more comfortable with, and more impressed by, moodiness and melancholy, signs, we thought, of deep feeling and sensitivity.

Although she was probably only in her late fifties, Mrs. Stevens seemed aged beyond recognition. Dressed in dark print crepes or tidy suits, with a large single strand of pearls around her wrinkled throat, she bustled around the first floor of Lawrence, plumping sofa pillows, posting menus, folding newspapers. Some days she entertained one or two other housemothers, who, elbow to elbow in her closet-sized sitting room, played cards for an hour or two or sipped tea and chatted together. Occasionally we saw her in housemothers' company at a Friday-night movie or concert; they were the only ones in the audience wearing hats and gloves.

None of us thought of Mrs. Stevens as a woman. Although I knew she had been divorced, I was still shocked one day when I borrowed her telephone directory to see written inside the front cover, with a list of other names and numbers, "David Stevens," with an address and number in Boston. It was a confirmation that she had once had a real husband. She sometimes got mail still addressed to "Mrs. David Stevens," but no one could successfully imagine her as once married, with any feelings of vulnerability, tenderness, or pain that resembled our own.

In the back hall, abutting the wall of Mrs. Stevens' bedroom, stood the one pay telephone in Lawrence. Every evening girls lined up on the back stairs, waiting their turn at the outside line that would connect them to home, boyfriends, or the local movie theatre. According to house rules, no calls were supposed to be made after 10:30 P.M., in order not to disturb Mrs. Stevens. But we mostly ignored that curfew, even giving out the pay-phone number so that our boyfriends could ring us back. Sometimes Mrs. Stevens, bristling with pin curls, emerged from the front hall, her bathrobe tightly sashed around her, eyes unusually alive, and chased the offenders back upstairs. Grumbling, we agreed she wasn't a very good sport.

After spring vacation in my senior year, I arrived so early back at Lawrence that no one else had yet returned. My train had been late, and when I walked up the porch stairs, well past 11 o'clock at night, the front door was securely locked. When I rang the bell, I had to wait a few minutes until lights went on and Mrs. Stevens came to the door. She had obviously been in bed. "I've had this dreadful cold," she explained, somewhere in the midst of her tinkling, ceaseless flow of interrogation. "I was all tucked up, just having a cup of tea. Do come in and have a cup with me." I followed her, still talking, into her suite. It consisted of three rooms, a sitting room, a bathroom, and a bedroom beyond. I had never seen more than the front sitting room, nor had any one else in Lawrence, except the house president, who cleaned the suite daily as her work assignment. Passing through the bathroom, which looked quite ordinary, though rather old and dingy, with a depressing large array of cosmetics aligned on the sink and a surprising frilly, flowered shower cap hanging on the wall, I found myself suddenly in Mrs. Stevens' bedroom. I had not realized it was so small. After she had deliberately arranged herself back in bed, I had just room to perch on a straight-backed chair next to a scuffed, nondescript dresser. Lying in her bed, all Mrs. Stevens could see were some framed family pictures she had hung on the opposite wall. An ugly standing wardrobe, in a black varnished wood, took up the remaining space.

Just as the darkness and dinginess of the room began to make an impression on me, I was startled by a loud, imperative ring from a telephone. It was clearly only inches away. Looking around instinctively, I realized that I was hearing the backstairs pay phone, ringing and ringing with an insistence that could not be ignored. Mrs. Stevens smiled deprecatingly. "Oh dear," she said with a sigh. "That phone." As she lay in bed, it must have sounded as though it were ringing in her very ear. For a few brief moments I put myself in her place, lying every night sleepless and alone in that cramped, dark room, listening helplessly to the endless, meandering conversations, the laughter, the flirtations, the arguments, the sounds of life outside her walls. I thought of her careful makeup, the powder and the rouge; her businesslike suits and determined pearls; her white gloves. For those few moments I felt sorry; I wasn't sure for what.

Then I firmly thrust aside such uncomfortable feelings, picked up the dangling end of her conversation, and began to drink my tea. I did not want to, I could not, acknowledge any connection between Mrs. Stevens and myself until I was long gone from Lawrence House.

Intellectual Butterfly 🌿

My HAND shook a little as I held the camera. "Over there," I called to James, "just in front of the sacred horns! I need a human dimension in this picture! Hurry, before the next tour group comes through!" He moved obediently a few feet to the right and, gazing into the green-gray distance of the olive-covered hills, waited patiently for me to snap the shutter. The bright white light of the Mediterranean was muffled this morning by a soft haze. I hoped my camera would adjust. Hands still shaking, my stomach flip-flopping, I talked sternly to myself. Don't panic now, you're finally here. There's plenty of time, James will let you stay as long as you want. It's real, it's real. This is it. The Palace of Minos at Knossos! Behind me I could hear the shuffle of dozens of feet and the loud bark of a German tour guide. I took the picture and skipped forward to give James a hug. "Ready?" I said eagerly. "Now, Braxton says to walk to the edge of the courtyard and turn west six steps. Next we're going to see some more storage rooms, where the oil jars caught fire when the palace was destroyed. We're supposed to watch for black marks on the charred stones." He nodded, took my hand, and we moved on.

Threading the maze that April morning, a British guidebook our matter-of-fact ball of string, James and I wandered up and down worn stone stairs, through unidentified chambers, past shattered columns. It was an eerie journey, but not just because we were trying to reimagine a vanished Minoan society, and to vault back three thousand years. While we wanted to evoke some spirits, perhaps a slim-waisted bull dancer or a regal snake-wielding priest-

ess, we were also accompanied by my own ghosts. Though James didn't see them, I was holding their hands almost as tightly as I held his. One was myself, a freshman in Art History 11 twenty-five years before, a seventeen-year-old girl sitting in a small circle of weak autumn sunshine falling from the skylights of the Smith College art library. Reverently turning the pages of an oversized, lavishly illustrated book, I shared through Sir Arthur Evans' detailed commentary some of his rapture as he discovered an unknown civilization. Though I was behind on my other homework, I stayed late in the library that afternoon so I could follow Sir Arthur through the same doorways past which James and I now measured our steps.

Until I'd seen the first slides of the palace in Art 11 I had never heard of Minoans, or Knossos, possibly even of Crete. Suddenly I had been transported into a society of lightness and gaiety, filled with dancers, magically writhing octopuses, snake goddesses, even a graceful blue monkey. The slides showed me a setting so remote and yet so stunningly fresh that I felt dazzled as if by too much light. When I stepped off our plane in Crete twenty-five years later, I felt it only right that the noonday sun bouncing off white stucco buildings and gleaming water made me stop and shade my eyes.

But young Sue Allen from Ames, Iowa, who was learning of worlds she hadn't known existed, was not the only ghost from the past who walked with me through Knossos when, many postponed dreams later, I finally got there. I also wanted to turn and talk to Mrs. Kurtz. Though retired some years ago from the Smith faculty, she surely was teaching Ancient Art somewhere. I could not believe such purposefulness could have been stilled. When she lectured in a large darkened auditorium, tapping her stick on the floor to signal a change in slides, she only had to tap once. Other, lesser, members of the art history faculty fumbled with the stick, or wielded it so feebly that the audio-visual man, probably drowsing behind his projector, paid no attention. But Mrs. Kurtz, striding across the stage to point to some detail on the screen, tapped with such authority and definiteness that the slides clicked into place almost with an audible snap of heels.

Gray-haired, square-shouldered, dressed in businesslike suits and jackets, Mrs. Kurtz appeared to me the epitome of the serious and successful scholar. Though married to another archaeologist, a short, elderly, distinguished man, she nonetheless seemed far removed from domestic life. Her husband, frail and ailing in the years I saw him, seemed only a backdrop for her formidable energies. Every summer she led an expedition to Delos, where, I was told, she was excavating an important Greek temple. A rare Smith student was sometimes allowed to accompany her; I'd heard one girl in the art history library say something about "working on Mrs. Kurtz's digs this summer." In a flash I saw myself in khaki shorts and a safari hat, bending over a hole in the ground, digging with my trowel at an edge of polished marble protruding from the upturned earth.

When I enrolled in Mrs. Kurtz's course in Greek Art, I was hoping to convince myself that I could be an art historian. For hours I pored over illustrations of Greek archaic statues, watching for their smiles to disappear and their columnar tunics to begin to twist and drape, until eventually I could date each Kouros accurately. I studied geometric patterns on vases, mentally reconstructed friezes, and compared capitals on columns. But although I did well on identification tests, I knew that I lacked a certain spark. I was never able to come up with a truly original thought for my essay exams, and I was never struck by a question profound enough to pose to Mrs. Kurtz after class. Somehow, I feared my interest in ancient art was frivolous. Burying myself in photographs of Greek temples, wanting to touch marble drapery, being entranced by ancient gods and heroes, did not seem sufficient qualifications for a career in classical archaeology. Besides, despite Mrs. Kurtz's summer camp on Delos, it seemed likely that everything important had already been dug up. I reluctantly decided to sink my spade in fresher fields.

But Mrs. Kurtz's Greek Art class left a permanent mark. Wooed by the blue skies and glowing creamy marble in her color slides, I decided that one day I too must visit the sites I could now only admire in books. The Palace of Minos at Knossos came to symbolize for me all the lost temples, palaces, and cities of the ancient world. It was the quintessential ruin, still being explored, still impenetrable. In the academic community I venerated, Knossos was also a live controversy; scholars could not even agree about its dates. I wanted to ramble at leisure in its ruins, confront its frescoes at eye level, and watch the clouds move behind its columns.

Twenty-five years later, here I was. But I was not as devoted a scholar as I once had been. Already, in an earlier stop at Athens, I had spent much less time in the Athens archaeological museum than I had intended; I was startled to find that I could scarcely recognize the various kourai in the Acropolis museum, let alone date them. Only the Acropolis had survived my dusty memories from Greek Art, to emerge more silently commanding than I had ever imagined. I put down my rather cursory inspection of the other Athens treasures to jet lag and eyestrain. Here at Knossos, though, I wasn't so sure. Although James and I were conscientiously following Braxton's guidebook, I was not quite as fascinated as I had expected. I remembered almost nothing of what I had read about Knossos twenty-five years ago. The frescoes, which I knew *best, were now stored in a section of the Iraklion museum that was indefinitely closed for repairs. Staring into the dusty spaces designated as "workshop," "queen's room," "baths," I found it hard to furnish them mentally with either things or people. Only the royal road, a paved highway rolling into the distance, seemed immediate: I could imagine throngs of people hurrying down that road, as tourists now rushed through the ticket stile at the entrance to Knossos. I had not even read anything about that road in my art class.*

So I wanted to turn to the vision of Mrs. Kurtz, sternly stalking the ruins next to me, and explain to her that I was trying. I wished I could remember more. I was sorry, I'd tell her, I couldn't do any better. James stopped for a moment to stifle a yawn. I instantly felt I had to yawn too. The sun had begun to blaze brightly again, its unaccustomed heat a blessing to bones chilled by a long Minnesota winter. Across my mind flashed a recent picture, from only yesterday: James and I basking on the beach a few yards from our hotel, as blissful as sleeping seals in the sun. It was just late morning now, and after a leisurely lunch at that little taverna, the one with fresh red snapper and stuffed eggplant, we could nap, swim, and sunbathe all afternoon. I looked surreptitiously at my watch, but James caught me. "I'm ready to go when you are, Susan," he said mildly. I knew he was thinking about the beach too.

"Well, we're almost through," I said reluctantly. "Just one more page in Braxton." I couldn't believe we had finished our tour, even moving slowly, in merely an hour and a half. Both my guidebooks to Crete had admonished me, "You will need a full day for the museum in Iraklion, and another full day for Knossos. Then you will want to return to the museum." But I wanted to return to the beach. I felt guilty. Mrs. Kurtz would have expected more than a morning, a day, or even two days, at the site of a lifelong dream. How could I possibly be ready to go? Did we need to retrace our steps? What had we missed? A tour group swept past us as we stood indecisively on the terrace. I had always scorned tours, but at the moment I did not feel very superior.

I looked at James, who was waiting. "James," I said hesitantly, "do you think Mrs. Kurtz would know if we left now, and had lunch, and went back to the beach?" He laughed, took my hand again, and turned with me to the exit. Leaving Greek Art behind, I walked on, giving in to the olive-scented breeze and the warmth of the sun on my back.

"When I saw this finger," said Mrs. Kurtz casually, "I realized at once that it belonged to *Kouros* Number 374 in the basement of the Louvre." I looked blankly at the slide, a blown-up picture of a small piece of marble. It certainly looked like a finger, but that was all. Although during these months of Greek Art I had learned to categorize varieties of the archaic smile, I was nowhere near being able to distinguish varieties of fingers. Another slide appeared, a statue of a standing young man, rather battered, with a missing finger on his left hand. "This is *Kouros* Number 374." Mrs. Kurtz continued. We looked at it dutifully. "And here is the restored hand," she added, as the image swiftly changed to one of the same statue, now with his finger reattached. The class gave a collective gasp of admiration. Mrs. Kurtz smiled slightly, nodded her head in acknowledgment, and went on to the next slide.

Leaving class that morning, I was still afloat in admiration. Imagine knowing all Greek statues in the Louvre so well that you knew immediately which ones had missing fingers! Knowing the contents of the *basement* of the Louvre, where Mrs. Kurtz made it sound like stacks of old statues were heaped like disused paint cans. Having the confidence to speak up and definitively identify a missing part! I let myself sink into fantasies of the intellectual life. Now, in my junior year, I was trying to decide about my professional future. As I considered the art historians I saw around me, I was uncertain about my ability to measure up to them. Worse, I was not even sure I wanted to. How many years of unrelenting study would it take for me to be able to recognize different kinds of marble fingers? What kind of indentured time would I have to serve? What renunciation was required?

Few of the women professors at Smith led lives I thought I wanted for myself. All the tenured women, those with rank and reputation, were well into middle age or beyond, where, as far as we students could see, most had settled with a kind of drab stolidity. Dressed in tweeds or shapeless dresses with little scarves, they blended into the dark, dusty backgrounds of office, classroom, and library. A few exceptions were the known eccentrics, usually close to retirement, who exuded a kind of embalmed enthusiasm. One, an emeritus English professor who taught me the Romantic poets, sat majestically on a raised podium before her students, her snowy white hair piled high in a careful pompadour, makeup rosy red on her pale wrinkled skin. She fervently intoned stanzas of *Childe Harold's Pilgrimage,* pausing for effect at its most dramatic moments. Interspersed with her remarks on Byron's love of freedom, or Wordsworth's spots of time, she admonished us girls about our own developing souls. Peering acutely over her glasses, she looked at the front rows. "Each of you girls is a caterpillar," she said, "just beginning to emerge from your chrysalis." Her hands described a light airy sweep. "I want you all to grow wings, to become butterflies, to fly and then to SOAR." She smiled. Though she was not looking at me, I shyly smiled back and wrote her remarks in my notebook. I found Miss Rose's little sermons more notable than her lectures. But how could she know anything about the kind of emotion Byron was describing? More a monument than a person, Miss Rose was impossible to imagine young.

Earthly passion was difficult for me to connect with most women professors. We students saw little of their private lives, though occasionally some faculty member held a seminar or a tea in her apartment or small house. Most women profs lived close to campus, many of them sharing space with each other. A few were known to be couples of many years' standing, though no one ever thought of them as anything except epitomes of devoted friendship. Single faculty women were never seen at any campus event in the company of men, and what social or emotional lives they led were so well screened from our view as to be invisible. Few had children, although privileged students at those home seminars or teas sometimes met a dog, cat, or beloved budgie.

Male professors, on the other hand, seemed to have what we thought of as normal lives. Although we could not imagine sex as ever having touched the bony angles of Miss Clemens, or having jarred the otherwordlly, dreamy Miss Holmes out of her obsession with Immanuel Kant, we had no trouble thinking of tense, leather-jacketed Mr. Aston breathing heavily in someone's ear or of melancholy, gray-headed but blue-eyed Mr. Hunter meeting a wild senior girl after hours at Rahar's Tavern. In fact, Mr. Hunter frequently *did* meet a classmate of mine from Lawrence House, a long-legged and agile girl who intrepidly climbed out a kitchen window, and those of us who'd heard of Vicki's late-night assignations wondered if she were destined to become his fourth Smith wife. Mr. Hunter seemed a bit used, but still vital. Another girl in my roommate Sophie's religion seminar was in love with their young instructor, who openly sat with her over daytime coffee at Gino's, talking of Barth and Tillich, to the envy of the other religion students.

Many male professors were married, with wives and children who didn't appear on campus but who were off-campus certification of normalcy. Some of us even baby-sat for them and verified their existence. Although in my junior year a statewide newspaper scandal accused a surprising number of male professors at Smith of bizarre homosexual practices, most of us students got over our shock at the news very quickly. We were sorry for the pain that public disclosure must have cost the professors we liked, and we speculated with appropriate chills about what it might have been like to be their wives. But my friends and I gave the men some credit for having at least committed themselves to a passionate act. I wonder now what we might have thought if they had been women. Sexual mores seemed to us as secure and as traditional as the stone campus landmark of the Grecourt Gates. The women faculty, we assumed, had simply given up sex in exchange for a life of the mind.

I did not look scornfully on a life of the mind, however. Indeed, it seemed to me that having taken a vow of abstinence and dedication, women professors had gained an intensity of feeling about their work. They lived and breathed their subjects, and in return the subjects came alive for them. "Miss Haskell *is* the eighteenth century," one of her devotees said loyally to me, after explaining how she had come to know Samuel Johnson as Miss Haskell's personal friend. When I watched Mrs. Kurtz lecture, she could animate a pediment, turn a statue, or twitch a piece of marble drapery so that it fluttered in the Attic breeze. In my class in Medieval Literature, Miss Barnes might have been hunched over on a horse just behind Chaucer, so close did she make me feel to the personalities on his ride to Canterbury. When Miss Turner, English historian, outlined the tragic lives of the Stuart monarchs, I felt she was ready at any moment to row Bonnie Prince Charlie across the sea to Skye; without anything but strict historical facts, she made me hear the whoosh of plumes, the clatter of riding Roundheads, the screams of the crowd as a king's head rolled from the block.

The intellectual life as I was introduced to it at Smith was, in fact, an exciting adventure. A few years ago, after a decade of teaching literature, I was able to audit an introductory course in North American Geography. On paper, the subjects of these lectures sounded boring: topography, crop distribution, fuel sources, railway lines, glaciers, timber, weather. But I was enthralled. Although I had of course looked at maps before, suddenly they became moving pictures. As if I were deciphering a palimpsest, I could now glimpse the actual land below: tugboats and barges, railroad yards, decaying villages, spreading cities. After years of farsightedness, I had been given a new pair of glasses. That was the feeling I had at Smith, picking up glasses to see worlds I hadn't known existed.

Worlds whirled by very quickly in Art 11. Introduction to Art History, a year-long survey, was so famous that I immediately signed up for it my freshman fall. In some ways that course determined my whole academic orientation at Smith: my sense of the intellectual life as a series of fascinating, but often terrifying, voyages to unknown lands, with boats leaving all the time for different ports and professors shouting at us hesitant tourists to get on board or forever be left behind. Our status as students was plain. We were passengers, not crew members, and only occasionally invited to dine at the captain's table. Still, we might someday be able to sail ships of our own. Meanwhile, as the Smith catalog, faculty, and my own convictions assured me, our destinations were places every liberally educated person ought to visit. This, I thought, was why I had come to Smith: to acquire a liberal education. Whatever it was, I wanted it.

Despite my eagerness, however, I often found the voyage fraught with danger. Art 11 to me was one long tack between Scylla and Charybdis, with fabulous sights along the way, but slide tests and essays always threatening to make me founder. Everyone referred to Art 11 with a certain hushed quality. "I'm behind on Art 11," "I'm looking for someone's notes for Art 11," "I need someone to quiz me on identifications for Art 11." Even now, a quarter-century later, I can say "Art 11, Art 11" silently over and over again, like a mantra, and soon find myself transported back in time to cavernous, darkened Sage Hall, surrounded by two hundred other whispering students. My pen poised and clipboard ready, I am watching for the first slide. The feeling of tension in the room is almost palpable, a thrumming wire that, when jerked, will cause two hundred pens to descend and move like lightning. For an hour all anyone will hear in Sage Hall is scratching of pens, rustling of paper, and the droning voice of a lecturer punctuated by the clicking of slides.

Taking accurate notes was crucial, since all Art 11 exams depended, finally, on how well a girl had been able to study her notes in conjunction with posted pictures. The Art History professors, who took turns teaching their specialties, hung black-and-white blow-ups illustrating each day's lecture in the Art 11 study room, a small, poorly ventilated space with movable bulletin-board partitions. To memorize slides, and, just as crucial, to have something to say about them, we had to spend many hours kneeling, sitting, or standing in front of the posted photographs. Staring intently at each picture, I tried to identify it and fix it in my mind by locating it somewhere in my frantic shorthand notes. Where, I often asked myself in frustration, was the "open perspective," or "texture"? As I searched for "repetitive curves" or "pent-up emotion," waiting girls behind me breathed heavily and elbowed their way closer to the photographs. On the day before an Art 11 exam, students stood two or three deep before the pictures, craning their necks, ruffling through notes, and sometimes muttering quietly, "Oh, God." The Art 11 Study Room was always close and hot; but on exam days, it was rank with the smell of sweat.

Not all my time in the Art 11 Study Room was panicky or unpleasant, however. At early or late hours when I found myself alone there, I could become absorbed in the delight of really *seeing* what Mr. Gamp had meant by the "lighter" architecture of Gothic compared to Romanesque, or why Mr. Stewart waxed rhapsodic about the clouds in seventeenth-century Dutch landscapes. Then, when my notes made sense, I felt as if I had literally "caught on," catching hold and hooking myself to a fast-moving boat speeding me through these foreign waters. Sometimes I saw all by myself the sharp angles of a Roman portrait bust, the dramatic shadows of a Wren facade, or the building blocks of a Cézanne still life. On those days I was pleased and triumphant when I left the study room. Unfortunately, my new confidence often led me to skip a day or two of study, and then I quickly fell far behind. Taking Art 11 tended to be a manic-depressive experience.

Art 11 exams were shock treatments. When I walked into the blackness of Sage Hall, wrote my name on my blue book, and adjusted my clipboard, my mind was always a muddle of mixed images, tag lines, and dates. When the first slide was flashed onto the screen, an audible intake of breath swept through the crowded, silent room. During three minutes we had to identify the picture, place it in historical context, and then make as many intelligent remarks as we could squeeze into the remaining seconds. Then another slide flashed on the screen. Click, flash, scribble; click, flash, scribble. It is a rhythm I can still remember, punctuated by the fast beat of my heart.

Art 11 even had its own legends. On the night before the final exam, I had just dragged wearily home from the study room and collapsed on the sofa when Mona Bragdon emerged from the smoker, puffing hard, looking bored. "Got your Art 11 tomorrow, don't you?" she asked with a pretense of sympathy, looking at my notebook flung on the floor beside me. "Well, you'd better not stay up all night studying. Did you ever hear what happened a few years ago to a girl who did that?" No, I shook my head. Encouraged, she went on with mounting enthusiasm. "Well, seems she'd stayed up several nights, actually, taking No-Doz, to study for all her exams. Art 11 was the last one. So she'd worked up to it, last afternoon of the last day of exams. And she had really crammed until she knew the stuff cold. When the lights went off, she looked up at the slide and recognized it immediately. She started to write, and she never stopped. She wrote, and wrote, and wrote, as fast as she could. She knew every slide, and she just kept writing. At the end she handed in her bluebook, went home and fell into bed. Three days later her art professor called. He wanted to see her in his office. When she sat down, he picked up the blue book that was lying on his desk and handed it to her. She recognized her name and handwriting on the front. When she opened it, she gasped. There in front of her was a single page covered with writing, a mass of scribbles, you couldn't tell what. She had written, and written, and written, all right, but she'd been too dazed to ever turn the page." Mona took a long puff on her cigarette, looked at me speculatively, and waited. I looked back. I had nothing to say.

During the same year that I rushed through three thousand years of art, I was also embarked on an only slightly less extensive tour of ancient history. Like my art course, I found this one a revelation. It not only introduced me to people, like the Assyrians and Sumerians, I'd never heard of, but it also objectively refuted my Presbyterian Sunday school certainties about the origins of the Christian religion. Confronting historical evidence, and trying to make sense of it, was confusing to someone whose previous history course had been taught by the Ames High School basketball coach. I had always thought history was what was written down in history books, but Mr. Hauptmann, our professor, wanted us to write history ourselves. He was subtle, too, I thought: assigning The Epic of Gilgamesh, comparing the story of Noah and his ark as a second-rate imitation, and then merely letting the hints seep into the sinking foundations of my religious faith. Dignified, natty, with a sharply trimmed goatee whose single strip of gray seemed artistically painted on, Mr. Hauptmann was so informed, so decisive, so nastily acute, that our class soon fell dumb in his presence. Some days he would merely raise his eyebrows and sigh expressively at our stupidity; other days he sarcastically tried to prod us beyond what he thought was our bovine endurance. I dreaded but envied his witty sallies. Of course, I thought, such a brilliant man — one whose questions no one could answer — must be right. Shocked at how quickly my securities had collapsed, I nonetheless soon agreed that civilization had stopped with the Greeks, degenerated with the Romans, and lasped into the still-continuing Dark Ages with the Christians.

Mr. Hauptmann's irony seemed so pervasive that it left little room for much else. What, I asked myself, did he care about? What did he hold sacred? Did he believe in anything? What did one find to believe in if one *didn't* believe in anything? Once I tentatively posed these questions to Olive Standish, the history honors major in Lawrence House, and she said mysteriously, "Wait till the Christmas lecture. You'll find out." Months later, I did. On the day Christmas vacation officially began, Ancient History was the last class. Since signed attendance was required, we were all there at 11 A.M., a packed house, when Mr. Hauptman walked in, and without his usual desultory remarks, took out some typed pages, placed them on the lectern, and began to speak about the life and death of Socrates. This lecture was no haphazard improvisation from notes; it was a magnificently planned performance. Suddenly the laconic, bored man who had barely endured us all semester was transformed into a dramatic orator, passionate and resonant, determined to bring Socrates alive into our classroom. As he masterfully outlined, and then filled in, a flattering portrait of Socrates as a thinker and spiritual leader, I began to realize that under his verbal decorations he was meticulously drawing a comparison to Christ from which Christ emerged decidedly second-best. But I had little time to absorb this insight, which three months before I would have found intolerable, before I realized that Socrates' life, and our class hour, were both almost done. Just as the period ended, timed to the exact moment, Socrates died. Mr. Hauptmann stopped talking. The bell rang. Although we were now free, we all sat silent for a few moments, as one does after a great pianist has played his last note. Then, spontaneously, the entire class burst into applause, clapping and clapping more and more wildly until Mr. Hauptmann, studiously oblivious, had packed his notes into his briefcase, clasped its gold lock, and strode without a backward glance into the hall.

It was no wonder I thought I might want to major in history. Like art history, history clearly brought with it self-confidence and a sense of superiority to the rest of the unenlightened world. My belief that history was an elite discipline was confirmed by my discovery that it largely consisted of uncovering other people's fallacies and biases. That illumination was due to a single candle lit by Olive Standish in one of my darker hours. On the night before my first hour exam in Ancient History, I was brushing my teeth and thinking nervously about the Peloponnesian War. In marched Olive Standish, looking purposeful as always, and plunked her glass down next to mine. "How're things?" she asked, squeezing out her toothpaste in a neat tiny ribbon. "Well," I answered as quickly as I could, spitting first, "I have my History 12 hour exam tomorrow. I'm really worried. Mr. Hauptmann said it was going to wake us up. And I get everything confused, the development of the polis, all those changes in the constitution, all those battles."

Olive turned and looked full at me, her dark eyes boring through the murkiness of my mind. I sensed she was going to help. "Listen," she said, "just remember one thing. Criticize the text."

"What?" I asked, feeling stupid.

"Don't you know about historical bias yet?" she asked impatiently. "Everybody's got a point of view. You just have to figure out what it is. So what text are you using?" I told her. "OK, just find a place where you can disagree with Muller about something and mention that in your exam. Take it from me, Hauptmann will love it."

Back in my room, I pored over Ernst Muller's *Ancient Greece and Rome*, searching for something I could disagree with. Trained to accept a textbook as the Word of God — indeed, I now figured after Mr. Hauptmann's gibes about the Bible, *more* dependable than the Word of God — I had a hard time. It was one thing to doubt Sunday school admonitions, another to doubt gold-printed Muller, embossed on a green binding. But finally I found a paragraph on the rise of monotheism, and I realized that in fact Mr. Hauptmann had said something rather different. Though somewhat skeptical about Olive's advice, I decided to try it.

During the exam next day, I managed to work into my otherwise humdrum essay a few sentences beginning, "Muller in our text perhaps erroneously claims that monotheism began . . ." I hoped Mr. Hauptmann wouldn't notice that my remarks didn't have much context, in fact didn't relate to my main point at all. The following week when he handed back the exams, Mr. Hauptmann lectured us sharply, with a tight smile, on how poorly we had all done. "Most of you barely passed," he said with a shrug, "and no grade was higher than a B—." My heart sank. But when I opened my bluebook cautiously, relief flooded through me, like the surging waters under Noah's Ark (definitely mythical): there it was, in Mr. Hauptmann's precise pen, an unremarkable but welcome B—. Leafing quickly through my pages, I found my brief criticism of Muller. Mr. Hauptmann had underlined one sentence in red, and in the margin he had written, "An interesting point." I had learned something about academic advancement.

While I was adventuring most mornings on the ancient Mediterranean, and swooping afternoons through Baroque cathedrals past Rococo on my way to Impressionism, three days a week I was also a time traveler back to the days of trilobites and dinosaurs. When I was registering for courses, no one pretended that Introductory Geology was in the same class with Art 11 and Ancient History. But everyone agreed that for someone afraid of science, who might not survive chemistry or physics or zoology, Geology 11 was probably the ideal course. As Dulie, my Big Sister, succinctly explained, "No math, lectures you can knit in, and field trips on nice days."

Low-keyed as it was, however, Introductory Geology was sometimes disturbing. It was perhaps the only course I took at Smith that made some effort to connect the world of scholarship with the everyday world around us, and I wasn't used to making that link. In art, we studied pictures of pictures; in ancient history, we pored over translated documents from civilizations long vanished; in French, we spoke a language that disappeared as soon as we left the classroom. But in geology we were forced to make immediate correlations between theoretical forms and the crowded, changing landscape that surrounded us. The Connecticut Valley, ancient, folded, glaciated, and eroded, didn't look like the diagrams in our textbook. It was covered with trees, roads, and towns, and it was too big for the eye to grasp all at once. I was baffled by the complexity and irreducibility of "the real world" — a phrase that reverberates for me with uneasiness, since my Smith training still makes me want to circle it in red, asking in the margin, "And what is *that?*"

Whatever the real world was, I only caught brief glimpses of it. When I returned to the Smith campus after almost twenty-five years, I was astonished to discover a path that led for more than a half-mile around Paradise Pond along Mill River, into shady patches of woods and past swimming holes and park lands. I had always stopped automatically after I had circled the pond, never thinking that I might be able to continue my walk, never *wanting* to continue it. Somehow my mind had closed at the boundaries of the campus, and I had never had the curiosity or temerity to explore further. Introductory Geology tried to make us push beyond those self-imposed boundaries.

Geology field trips themselves never seemed quite real. First we spent several days watching the blackboard, trying to stay awake as old Mr. Stottlemeyer, our soft-voiced, dull professor, diagrammed the relevant formations. Although when I read in our text about geological change, I often became quite excited to see millions of years unfold, I couldn't transfer this excitement to Mr. Stottlemeyer's lectures. Even when, in a wrenching moment of insight, I could see myself as the merest dot in an infinite chain of dots, I was always lulled back to complacency after an hour of Mr. Stottlemeyer's gentle drone.

Sleepiness, in fact, is what I mainly remember about the geologic field trips. On Monday afternoons in fall and spring, our class assembled after lunch outside the classroom building and separated into yellow school buses. During the ride into the country, the warm sun beat through the windows, the bumpiness of the bus kept us from reading, and the heavy feeling of lunch settling into my stomach pulled me steadily down into blankness. I began to drowse as we rattled through Holyoke or Hadley or Amherst. Soon the landscape became a blur, bouncing unsteadily outside my window, a mélange of billboards, highway signs, and patches of field or village. My eyes blinked, shut, blinked open and shut again. Despite the efforts of Miss Baumgirtle, a graduate student in her late twenties who was our guide and chaperone, many of us openly fell asleep. Lecturing in her hearty loud voice, Miss Baumgirtle even tried occasional jokes to capture our attention. But most of us didn't make the effort to look as if we were listening. Perhaps we didn't worry about being polite to Miss Baumgirtle because she seemed so — well, "out of it," as the girl sharing my seat on the bus whispered to me. A chunky, plain, earnestly enthusiastic woman, Miss Baumgirtle always dressed for field trips in heavy knickers, knee-high hiking boots, and a flannel shirt. Her B.A. degree, my seatmate added, was from Oklahoma State, "and you sure can tell." I felt sympathetic toward Miss Baumgirtle, but I wasn't sure if it was because of Oklahoma, her laborious jokes, or her flannel shirt.

Eventually the bus jerked to a stop, and Miss Baumgirtle bellowed, "ALL RIGHT, girls! Here we ARE! Everyone OUT!" After we dutifully filed off the bus, we stood in a circle around Miss Baumgirtle, who began talking eagerly the moment the last of us stepped onto the ground. Now she was in her element, firm and self-confident, and we were the ones who were unsure. "What we have here" — she pointed to a large chunk of rock protruding from a road cutting — "is some Holyoke schist. Does anyone remember how the Holyoke schist was formed?" No one did. Miss Baumgirtle furrowed her brow, sighed, and began waving and folding her hands, trying to reproduce Mr. Stottlemeyer's blackboard sketches of transverse faults. When I couldn't make the link between her gestures and the jagged, lichen-covered rock looming behind her, I gave up and concentrated instead on my left leg, which was asleep.

Geology seemed even more confusing the day Miss Baumgirtle took us to the Connecticut Oxbow. Not long before this field trip, I had seen a painting in Art 11 of that curving stretch of river, with its silt-filled backwater, an example of nineteenth-century American landscape. I had studied it afterward in the slide room. Now we stood for a few minutes at the turn of a steep road ("ALL OUT but only for FIVE MINUTES," boomed Miss Baumgirtle) and squinted down through the humid mist of a hot spring afternoon. Here in the open the oxbow, though recognizable, looked different from the painting. As Miss Baumgirtle pointed out, it had moved as the river changed course. But the difference was more than one of location; I noticed how much more complicated, messier, and distracting our view was than the painter's. Shrubs and tangled undergrowth obscured our sightlines from the road, and below us tall trees and the high hills competed for attention with the river itself. A cloud of gnats swarmed about us, and several of us slapped at them distractedly. In the slide room, I had gazed steadily at the oxbow for several minutes; now, itchy and damp from the hot plastic bus seats, and troubled by gnats, I felt that having seen the vista once, I was ready to go home. I liked the painting better.

Allowing for change and disruption was temperamentally hard for me. In geology, nothing was certain. It seemed fitting that our weekly laboratory sessions literally focused on shifting sands. Deep in a basement room in Seelye Hall, we took our places at long tables. In front of each of us was a sandpile. To the right lay a stack of colored paper markers, sticks, and a few tools, like tiny gardening implements. Following Miss Baumgirtle's often-repeated directions, we were required to reproduce in our individual sandpiles the geologic forms we were studying that week. Even if I had had

much three-dimensional imagination, which I didn't, I might have
had trouble showing how several layers of glacial deposit, each
marked with a different color, lay after a volcanic eruption had
twisted and turned them upside down. As it was, even with Miss
Baumgirtle leaning over my shoulder and whispering hints, I regularly overbuilt my sandpiles, causing disastrous collapses, or poked
my markers haphazardly in the wrong places.

Worst of all were the rock quizzes. They were a stern reminder of
my mental rigidity, since success depended on one's ability to see
through changing circumstances to quintessentials. First Miss
Baumgirtle brought out a large tray of rock specimens, each one
clearly labeled. She pointed out the rosy quartz in the Sugarloaf
conglomerate, or the black sheen that marked the Meriden shale,
or the identifying specks in the Holyoke schist. After ten or fifteen
minutes, she disappeared with that tray and returned with another. Now the rocks looked entirely different. But of course, except for a few deliberate ringers, they were not. One was the
Holyoke schist, another the Sugarloaf conglomerate, and hidden
somewhere the Meriden shale, only in new incarnations. Having
memorized a Sugarloaf conglomerate that was six-sided, with large
black chunks, I couldn't decide whether a black-studded, oval rock
or an all-black round stone was the real thing. And if this was the
conglomerate, which was the shale? Could Miss Baumgirtle be
fooling us with *two* conglomerates? Mostly I guessed wrong. Looking over my list, Miss Baumgirtle clucked loudly, though sympathetically, and marked it with firm, large, red X's.

I preferred an intellectual life that confined itself to libraries.
Just as the Smith campus became for me an outer shell, a protected greenhouse into which I had been transplanted, so the Library Browsing Room became my personal glass case. It was a
room for studying, a refuge, and a hiding place. It was where I
went when I wanted to live the life of the mind.

One was not actually supposed to study in the Browsing Room.
A neat lettered sign on its glass doors announced, "No Food. No
Studying. For Browsing Only." But since it was the only room in
the library with upholstered chairs, everyone ignored the sign.
Every morning between classes, and every night after dinner, I
trudged up the small hill from Lawrence House to the library.

From my first day at Smith, I knew I belonged there. The building itself, old-fashioned, stone, and impressive, reminded me of the Ames Public Library that had sheltered me as a child, and as soon as I pushed open the carved oak door and stepped into its spacious entry hall, I knew exactly where I was. To the left was the brightly lit Periodical Room, where I later studied whenever I needed glaring overhead lights to keep me awake. To the right was the Browsing Room.

Though when I saw the Browsing Room twenty-five years later, I was surprised to find it rather threadbare and drab, I remember it as being warm and cozy. Carpeted with faded Oriental rugs and furnished with comfortable high-backed armchairs, ottomans, and floor lamps, it was lined with shelves of Dickens, Thackeray, Balzac, and other classics, mostly in leather-bound sets. In one corner, a huge Webster's Dictionary stood on its own stand; there one day, reading Chaucer's *Canterbury Tales,* I checked for word origins to see if he had indeed known the word "fart." Anywhere else in the library I might have felt embarrassed; but one always had privacy in the Browsing Room. Girls pushed and yanked their chairs and sofas into positions where they cornered an alcove, faced a window, or monopolized a lamp. From the door, all one could see on entering were backs of furniture and backs of heads, a hostile phalanx guarding the silence.

Finding a seat in the Browsing Room took promptness, and keeping it involved aggressive determination. An unwritten code governed seating monopolies. As soon as a girl arrived in the morning and found an empty chair, she could reserve it indefinitely by leaving her jacket flung over the back, books piled on the cushions, or an open notebook on the floor. Then she could safely leave for an hour's class, or a quick snack on Green Street, and return to find her place still vacant. But honor varied among individuals. Sometimes I discovered someone occupying my chair, pretending not to notice my approach, perhaps not even lifting her head as, glaring, I ostentatiously picked up my books and clipboard she had moved to the floor. Not everyone gave up as easily as I. At exam time, low angry voices sometimes broke the peace of the Browsing Room as squatters argued over territorial rights. Every chair, including the last straight-backed wooden one, was occupied, and a few girls sat hungrily on the bare floor, like vultures, waiting for someone to rise and vacate.

Most of the time, however, the Browsing Room was heavy with peace. It blanketed the air like the rich sweet afternoons in spring when honeysuckle, lilacs, and magnolias blossomed outside the library windows. Although on those afternoons I sometimes gathered my books, decamped, and sat in the sun for an hour or two, usually I preferred to stay indoors in the Browsing Room, watching the weather from behind its tall windows. Curled in my favorite chair, my legs stretched over its padded arms, hidden from the rest of the room, I could look outward to the Smith campus, moving past me in a flow of color but with little sound. Out my window I saw a wide space of lawn, several paths, corners of a few buildings, and a little piece of sky. In the winter I stared at the intricate bony branches of bare trees and swirls of snowdrifts; in fall, changing leaves; in spring, an explosion of flowers. Periodically I pulled myself back from daydreams and turned to ancient Greece or Chaucer or the Mesozoic Age. Once I was again immersed, the world outside my window disappeared. Behind me I could hear and see nothing, except occasional murmurs, the thud of the glass door closing, and the scrape of a chair being pulled into position. I remained lost in my books until my leg cramped or my stomach rumbled, reminders that my body had been neglected too long. Stretching, I then walked home to dinner.

Different temperaments preferred different parts of the library. Dreamers, drowsers, and loners gravitated to the Browsing Room. But I sometimes felt that no-nonsense students settled instead in the Reserve Reading Room. That was where my roommate Sophie always studied. In the Reserve Room, assigned books were kept in a strictly guarded enclosure and released only for two-hour intervals. I went there as little as possible, since I found it unnerving to see long rows of tables filled with studying girls. At exam time, the Reserve Room was oppressive with the combined panic of all the procrastinators whose fate now hung imminently over them, counted down by the quiet ticking of the Reserve Room clock. Girls waited in line to put their names on lists for required readings assigned many weeks ago. As the hours shortened, some wandered the room peering over others' shoulders and asking how soon a book might be available, while even more desperate students marauded openly when someone injudiciously went to the toilet.

On the night before the first finals in January, the Reserve Room was filled to every inch of space. Anyone who whispered was angrily hushed, girls rustled ceaselessly, faces were grimly affixed to notes and texts. My friend Dulie, always a source of Smith legends, told me about an incident in the Reserve Room on a January night not long before. In the midst of the terrorized quiet, one girl, suddenly overcome and swept over the edge, had, as Dulie put it, "gone absolutely bonkers." Rising to her feet, she swept her books to the floor. As everyone looked up, astonished by the crash, she glanced around, wild-eyed, and shrieked, "There is no God! Sex rules the world!" Before anyone could move, she rushed out, leaving the Reserve Room shattered behind her. Having done time in the Reserve Room myself, I was sure Dulie was telling the truth. It was no wonder I preferred the upholstered privacy of the Browsing Room instead.

Although I had discovered a haven in the library, I knew it was not an end in itself. Soon I needed to find a lasting home in the right major. Choosing a major was a serious business, almost as important as marriage, and certainly more imminent. Although I had a few years left to find the right man, by the end of my second year at Smith I was supposed to "declare a major," a phrase that had the august sound of reading banns in church. That major would determine my career, and indeed, I thought, in the unlikely event I didn't marry, my whole future. Complicating my choice of a major was my enthusiasm for each new field I studied. Thumbing through my well-worn course catalog, I longed to advance into upper-division courses, whose titles and descriptions sounded tantalizing. Think of knowing all about "The Economics of Under-Developed Countries"! I pictured myself as an economic advisor in Africa, helping people to better lives. What about "Twentieth-Century Decorative Arts"? What fun to become an expert on all those vases, lamps, and jewelry! And how could anyone who loved literature graduate without the definitive word on "Joyce, Yeats, and Eliot"? That popular course at Smith linked them so firmly in my mind that I still tend to think of Joyce, Yeats, and Eliot together, a trio of dancers tapping across the stage of twentieth-century literature. I wanted to learn about Robespierre, Marat, and David in "The Age of Napoleon," and I wondered if I could ever read French well enough to spend a semester with "Studies in Balzac." And what about "Contemporary Religious Thought"? "Theory of Music"? "Logic"? "Comparative Government"? I wanted to do it all.

During each introductory course, I wondered if I ought to major in that field. Soon after Art 11, I had a serious affair with art history. When that ended, I briefly flirted with economics and American studies. Astonishingly, I even once considered — momentarily, on a field trip when we saw petrified dinosaur tracks — geology. But of all those possible majors, I remember my time in history with the most regret, as one might think of a long-ago broken engagement to a once-loved fiancé.

In the late 1950s, history was perhaps the most prestigious major at Smith. Or so we students thought, influenced by rumors we assumed were founded on definitive fact. Now, a faculty member myself, I marvel at how reputations of departments rise and fall, blown by the breath of student preference, ablaze with one or two star professors, borne aloft by the praise of faculty colleagues. At Smith, each department had a kind of free-floating aura. History was staid, distinguished, a demanding taskmaster. Its students, we assumed, were determinedly intellectual. As my Big Sister Dulie had warned me in my freshman fall, "Choose any history course you want, but don't look for something easy. There aren't any gut courses in the History Department."

Mulling over this daunting reputation, I signed up with some trepidation for the History Honors Program, an elite Imperial Guard of the major itself. Its director, Miss Turner, was a professor I ardently admired. Her transformation of the dull details of Enclosure Acts and Parliamentarianism into a drama of Tudor-Stuart England finally prompted me to leave art history and move into her field instead. History, Miss Turner demonstrated, was the most comprehensive of the liberal arts; one could look at paintings, read novels, absorb economics, and somehow, in a magical alchemy, turn all that information into history. What better way to study anything and everything?

For a brief while, I thought I had found my home in history. I was a member of the select few. I could carry my Harvard bookbag into the library with a sense of importance now that I was on a serious mission. "I'm in History Honors," I could say with confidence, as I used to say, "I'm Sue Allen from Ames, Iowa." Under Miss Turner's tutelage, I constructed a year's program that would incorporate a seminar in the French Revolution, a survey in government, and at least one of my beloved English courses. I was delighted to find I could work "The English Novel" into my new major.

After a month or two, however, I knew something was wrong. I was bored by the French Revolution. Instead of focusing on Marat and his friends, it dealt with taxes, acts, and assemblies. I dropped my government course because I could not digest its multisyllabic abstractions and substituted another English course in American literature. Only in English was I having fun, hurrying home from class to read Jane Austen, to pore over Emerson looking for nuggets, to wonder at Thoreau's luminous sentences. Though I hated to admit it, history wasn't fun.

Following much discussion with my friends and meditative hours staring at my ceiling, I made a fateful decision. This was my last chance, in my junior year, to shift majors. It was not an easy move. But although the English Department was not as renowned as History, although I'd have to make up a lot of courses, although I might never be truly liberally educated, I just plain wanted to study English literature. I made an appointment to see Miss Turner.

The interview was not easy, either. Not long ago I had sat across from Miss Turner's desk, planning my program, thanking her for her signature. I had only recently taken my vows. Now I needed her to sign another form so I could get out. Stumbling over explanations, I tried to get to my point, while I watched her, eyes fixed on me, tap her pencil absentmindedly on her desk. Finally I said, "I guess maybe I have trouble reading history. I seem to want to read literature instead."

Miss Turner broke in impatiently, stabbing harder at her pad of paper. "But Miss Allen," she said, with a shading of reprimand that I had not thought of this solution myself, "what is to stop you from reading novels in the summer?"

I thought for a moment. I so wanted her to tell me I was doing the right thing. Wanting to read novels did sound frivolous, and I didn't think I could tell Miss Turner what responsible work one *did* as a critic of literature. I wasn't sure I knew. "You know how you had us read Disraeli's *Sybil?*" I asked at last. She nodded. "Well, I could see it was sort of important historically, but I thought it wasn't very well written," I said apologetically. "I want to read the really good things, sort of on their own, just for their own sake. I guess I want to read stuff like *Bleak House."* I had begun Dickens in "The English Novel," and every night I looked forward to an early bedtime, so I could tuck myself under my quilt and read *Bleak House* until I fell asleep. I repressed the idea of telling Miss Turner about my quilt.

Miss Turner was silent. Her swivel chair creaked as she leaned back in it and gazed at me. I felt I had deeply disappointed her. But, like all the history faculty I idolized, I could see she was a stoic. She sighed, took a slip of paper from her drawer, and scribbled her signature on it. As she handed it to me, she frowned and spoke. "You know, Miss Allen," she said gravely. "you told me last year you were thinking about majoring in art history. Then you wondered about economics. Here you are a junior, already in the honors program, and now you want to change majors again." She paused. I held my breath. "I fear," she said firmly but with regret, as if she did not like having to pronounce someone's doom, even if it was certain and deserved, "you may turn out to be an intellectual butterfly."

I had no reply. Grasping my change-of-adviser form, my ticket to freedom, I fled. It was years before I could think of other ways I might have ended our conversation, justifications I might have made, defenses I might have constructed. Then, eventually, I gave those up, too. I began to see Miss Turner's judgment in a different light. Perhaps, instead of a condemnation, it was a release. What, after all, can one expect of an intellectual butterfly? Now when my mind wanders during long speeches; when I am unable to finish a story in *The New Yorker* or an article in *The New York Review of Books;* when I tell a friend I'll see an avant-garde Polish film she adored, but secretly know I'll never get there; I have learned to say to myself, "So what? Remember what Miss Turner said? If you were destined to be a lightweight, why fight it?"

Settling down in my English major took some time. Severed

from the rigors of history, I now found myself uncomfortably awash in "Introduction to Literary Study," required for all majors. Each section of this amorphous course depended for its shape upon the character of its instructor, and my section reflected the soft-edged, spreading image of Mr. Wedelstorm, a genial, small-eyed man who wore baggy, three-piece tweed suits and who puffed ostentatiously on a large pipe that seemed always wet. I wondered if he envied lean Mr. Abernathy, one of the most popular English professors, who smiled seldom but charmingly, who dealt in ironies, and whose fragrant, angular pipe never went out.

On my first day in Mr. Wedelstorm's class, I knew I had fallen far from the heights of history. "Let's gather in a circle, girls," he said, with a grin I thought reptilian, and motioned us close to him. I didn't like this. I had grown used to Smith formalities and the welcome sense of impersonality they gave me. Obediently we moved our chairs into a wide semicircle, while Mr. Wedelstorm seated himself in front of us, looking intently at each of our faces. He didn't talk much about literature that day. Mostly he assured us of his genuine desire to be of help in our new field of study, his easiness, his availability. "I want you girls to feel you can come to me with any problems you have," he said, sounding earnest, but somewhat mitigating his effect with a large, loose-lipped smile. "I'm the father of five, and I won't be shocked by anything you have to tell me. Even the most personal problems." He nodded reassuringly, his smile shrinking to something smaller and more intimate.

I never did learn exactly what literary study was. According to Mr. Wedelstorm, it was mainly a search for hidden sexual meanings, which evidently lay like precious ore buried beneath the most innocuous landscape. Sex, I learned, was everywhere: goats, guns, needles, purses, petticoats, trees, vases, bees, anything tall or thin, round or deep, piercing or enclosed. Now if Mona Bragdon counted phallic symbols in Lawrence House, I thought I could astonish her. Mr. Wedelstorm often spent class reading aloud to us, Elizabethan sonnets, Shakespeare, Swinburne, Auden. He didn't care much for prose. Pausing in the midst of his readings, he looked up to see if we had caught all the sexual references. "Pretty bawdy stuff, isn't it?" he'd say in a friendly way, with a twinkle and a heavy puff on his pipe. (Eventually I added "pipe" to my list.) Sometimes Mr. Wedelstorm just looked up and winked. Since I didn't always know what double-entendre he was winking at, I simply made a small red mark in my margin.

It was with relief that I signed up next semester, and the next, for classes with Mr. Abernathy. Having had to abandon the intellectual giants of the History Department, I was glad to find an English professor I could revere as well. Nor was it only reverence, as I admitted to myself. During my last year-and-a-half at Smith, I was hopelessly, but respectfully, in love with Ralph Abernathy, A.B. Harvard, M.A. Oxford, Ph.D. Harvard, Sophia Smith Professor of English. Tall, gaunt, with a tanned and seamed face, he looked to me as if he had passed through the fires of life, seasoned but unburned. From my chair in the Browsing Room I could see him bicycle to his office, his tennis racket casually slung behind him, adroitly avoiding the throngs of passing students and waving to faculty along the way. In winter, Mr. Abernathy wore tweed jackets with leather elbow patches. I was so moved by the raspiness of his leather patches that I once tried to imagine his rubbing his elbows together, like a Boy Scout starting a fire.

Sometimes when I took a study break in the library, I walked down to the dark basement to see if Mr. Abernathy was in his office. Wreathed in pipe smoke, he usually sat with his back to the open door, his floor piled high with stacks of books and papers. Even when his chair turned toward me, he never looked up. Once when I passed, I saw him stroking his thigh absentmindedly while he read. I thought I could feel the heavy khaki under my own hand.

From this cluttered den came the reviews, essays, and books that had made Mr. Abernathy one of the best-known names of the college. I had even seen his byline in *The New York Times Book Review,* which my mother had kept on her desk from the time I was a child, a cultural message as remote and valued as if it had come from the East by pony express. To sit in a classroom, listening to someone who wrote for *The New York Times,* was, I felt, the privilege of an Ivy education. I tried to jot down Mr. Abernathy's every word, especially his humorous asides. I had already begun to view irony as one of the saving graces. One day, lecturing on Thoreau, he said, "Someone once called Thoreau a 'sagacious woodchuck.' A very apt description, I think." He paused. "Come to think of it, *I* was the one who said that," he added thoughtfully.

I wondered how I could ever approach Mr. Abernathy. OK, I told myself, I'll never be one of his American Studies students, the long-legged ones with black tights and black hair, versed in socialism and Frank Norris. But maybe I might ask for one moment of intellectual communion. Perhaps I could walk into Mr. Abernathy's sanctuary, pose him a piercingly intelligent question, and watch his face break into an appreciative smile. All spring of my senior year, in his seminar in American Realism, I waited for my chance.

One late afternoon, after reading for two hours in Leslie Fiedler's *Love and Death in the American Novel,* I had an idea. In our seminar we had just finished Faulkner's *Sartoris.* Influenced by Fiedler, who seemed to me more profound than any literary critic except Mr. Abernathy, I had begun to wonder about sin, guilt, racism, and sex in American literature, all of which appeared to be joined in a complex pattern I didn't quite yet discern. Since I had studied Gothic art in art history, and had heard something about Gothic fiction in "The English Novel," I was particularly struck by Fiedler's remarks about the Gothic element in the American novel. Thinking about *Sartoris,* I had a Gothic flash of insight which now, years later, escapes me, but which then seemed to me stunning. I would take Mr. Abernathy my insight, I thought, and offer it to him.

Heart pounding, I descended to the basement. Mr. Abernathy was in his office, reading intently, his back to the door, but the door, as usual, open. I tapped timidly on the door jamb. Mr. Abernathy whirled around quickly.

"Yes?" he said, looking at me.

"Excuse me, Mr. Abernathy, I'm sorry to bother you, and I won't take a minute of your time," I said hurriedly. He hadn't asked me to come in, but I took a few steps forward and stopped. The floor was so covered with books that there was only the smallest space to stand. "It's about Faulkner, Mr. Abernathy," I began, and blurted out my idea. To my alarm, instead of sounding profound and intellectual, it sounded adolescent and confused. I wished I were back in my carrel upstairs. Mr. Abernathy listened patiently. When I was finished, he looked rather blankly at me, then uttered a few terse words that as far as I could see, closed the subject forever. Turning around in his swivel chair, he picked up his book again. With his back to me, the interview was clearly over.

Then disaster struck. Too intimidated to turn around myself, I decided I would quietly back out instead, and retreat from Mr. Abernathy's presence like a dismissed courtier. Thinking I was retracing my path in the small cleared space, I took one tentative step backward. I suddenly felt and heard a sickening loud crunch. Mr. Abernathy whirled around again. He and I both looked at my feet. Somehow I had managed to jam my right foot squarely in the middle of his typewriter, which I hadn't even seen, hidden as it was on the floor among his stacks of books. "Oh dear, I'm so sorry," I wailed, though it only came out as something between a gasp and a whisper. I tried to extricate my foot, but it was stuck. As the moments stretched into eternity, I pulled hard until I finally heard the twang of typewriter keys. My foot jerked loose. Mr. Abernathy winced. I muttered another apology and fled to my carrel. Fiedler, luck, and life had all failed me.

My worst crisis of confidence in the English Department did not come from this encounter with Mr. Abernathy, however. Afterward he continued to mark my papers with favorable comments and good grades. Although he never invited me to New York to meet Max Eastman, a trip that was a mark of special esteem for American studies majors with social principles and dangling earrings, he did encourage me, in an offhand way, to continue my life as a scholar. It was where my destiny as an English major lay, I was sure, reading and interpreting other people's work. I never thought of writing anything of my own. I always remembered the hard lesson I had learned as a freshman from Mr. Sheik.

Now that I sometimes teach creative writing myself, I have managed some sympathy for Samuel Sheik. Young, dark, aloof, and somewhat snappish, he was one of the most junior instructors in the English Department, probably sentenced to a term in Introduction to Creative Writing as part of his probation. His real field was James Joyce, which someone should have warned me was not a favorable omen. When I signed up as a second-semester fresh-man for his course, I'm not sure what I expected, but it was cer-tainly not what I got. If we were instructed in anything, I don't remember what. Every two weeks we were required to hand Mr. Sheik some writing, either a story or a group of poems, topic com-pletely open, no directions given. Mr. Sheik wrote a few comments, assigned a grade, and handed them back a few weeks later.

Such freedom should have been liberating. Perhaps for some of the writers in the class it was. They were all older than I, juniors and seniors, and I listened with depression as they conversed easily with Mr. Sheik. They were experts on love, death, and disillusion-ment; I wasn't even sure what my illusions were. Jean Stanley, a Lawrence House senior, sat in front of me and sometimes walked back to the house with me afterward. Surprising everyone, Jean had flown to Florida to see her boyfriend after Christmas and had returned married. Now she was expecting a baby. Someone said that was why she had gotten married. I felt enviously that she cer-tainly had plenty to write about. But what about me? What did I have to say? What had I possibly experienced that could make a poem or a story?

On the day before our assignments were due, I sat on the Lawrence front porch, writing pad on my lap, and stared discon-solately into the branches of the giant beech tree opposite. As the snowy, chilly spring began to thaw into the promise of summer, I watched the black scraggly twigs begin to bud, then leaf out. I had nothing to say. Nothing ever happened to me to compare with the bizarre fates of the characters in the stories we read: Seymour Glass, Kurtz, Daisy Miller. All through the bright spring afternoon I doodled, waiting for some inspiration to strike my pencil. Look-ing up into the topmost branches of the beech tree, I wished a Muse could part its leaves and whisper to me the opening line of a poem.

As the dinner hour drew near, and I knew my time was almost up, I began to write down any image that occurred to me. I tried opening lines, scratched them out, tried them again, gave up and finally stuck with them. In short bursts of desperation, my poems grew. I wrote about old men on park benches, melancholy on a spring day, hopeless love.

Not surprisingly, Mr. Sheik was never impressed. His comments were pungent but unhelpful: "I don't get it." "Not bad." "Stiff." His grades were always B− or C+. I was appalled by the C+'s, a mark I'd never gotten before, and one that I knew could spell doom to a scholarship girl. What was I to do? Toward the end of the semester, I wrote about my dilemma to my mother. Back came her advice: "Why not try writing about something you know?"

Though that sounded deceptively simple, my mother's words did start me thinking. Could I perhaps write a short story about a girl like myself? Though I could scarcely believe that I had problems and feelings worth treating in fiction, still, my mother might just be right. She usually was. So for my final assignment, I decided to tell about a freshman at college who was away from home for the first time and who was miserably homesick. Though my story didn't have much plot, it was thick with atmosphere and studded with details of life in Lawrence House. Finally, with what I thought was considerable ingenuity, I created a symbol to carry the story to its emotional climax. In a glassed frame on her bureau, my heroine kept a picture of her mother, and at a critical moment, I made the picture fall from the bureau and break, shattering shards of glass at the girl's feet.

Waiting for Mr. Sheik to return my story was interminable. Would he perhaps read a segment of my story aloud in class, as he had done for several of the more advanced writers? Would he give me an A at last? I felt my whole career as a writer was poised in the balance.

What I saw first was the grade: B−. But the worst was yet to come. I hurried to the privacy of my room to read his few scrawled, marginal remarks. One leapt out at me. Opposite my paragraph about the shattered picture, the symbol I prized, was an underlined exclamation: "Oh, God!" That was all.

Hunched on my bed, I let the implications of his comment sink in. I knew immediately what he had meant; I was a slow writer, but a quick critic. Mr. Sheik had seen my attempt at artistry as a glaring idiocy, a faux pas so gauche it had only earned his contempt. I could hear his voice, irritated but resigned, as he underlined my blunder: "Oh, God!" I began to turn red with embarrassment. How could I face him in class the next day? My only option for maintaining my self-respect, I thought, was to accept Mr. Sheik's judgment and then, resigned, move on. OK, I would never be a writer. At least I had learned something in Introduction to Creative Writing: not to waste any more time in a futile pursuit. I didn't have to give up literature, but I would have to be satisfied with the world of scholarship. I was able to do that fine. I could write reviews, analyses, essays, and maybe someday even a scholarly book. My cheeks still flushed, I folded my story carefully and put it at the bottom of some papers in my desk. I did not write another short story for eighteen years.

Living as a critic in the world of books was far from a passive fate, however. I often sank so deeply into literature that what I was reading seemed more real than what I was living. Dickens's rain ominously pattering on the Ghost Walk at Chesney Wold was much more dramatic, and longer lasting, than the humid cloudbursts soaking my raincoat as I ran to the library. Wordsworth's daffodils were imbued for me with more philosophical significance than the scattered yellow clumps on the banks of Paradise Pond, which I barely noticed, since they only bloomed at the time of final exams. Henry James's heroines faced agonizing choices with fine moral distinctions, while my own decisions appeared straightforward and comparatively banal. Isolated in Lawrence House, on a campus that seemed like a remote island, I loved to escape to the Yorkshire moors, the Castle of Chillon, or Walden Pond.

Certain at last that I was in the right field, I moved easily from the complex crescendos of Donne's sermons to the social panoramas of William Dean Howells. I never found a period of English or American literature I didn't like. Though I had worked at history because I thought it was good for me, I read my English texts because I was entranced by what writers had done with words. I began to realize how much I loved the sound of speech, the shape of sentences, and the rhythms of paragraphs.

Sometimes the richness of language was too much for me. Overcome by surfeit, I felt I had to share my feast with someone. In the midst of reading a passage, I would leap to my feet and knock at my roommate's connecting door. Sophie was at her desk, upright, concentrated, making copious notes about Barth, Tillich, or Sartre. Although she didn't like being interrupted, she knew I needed an audience. Holding her finger on the page, she looked up. "Hey, Sophie, I just have to read you this," I said apologetically. Jumping onto her bed, I began to declaim from a passage I had just marked in Carlyle's *On Heroes and Hero-Worship.* It wasn't so much what he was saying that moved me — years later, rereading it, I shuddered at the actual message — but how he said it. I waved my hands, emphasizing the italics, my inflections rising and falling, throwing pillows to the floor in my excitement. "Isn't that just great? Can you hear how it rolls?" I asked Sophie eagerly when I'd finished.

"Yes, I see what you mean," she said, smiling patiently, her finger still on the page of Tillich. "But that's enough for a while. No more breaks. Come in at ten and we'll have some tea and Triscuits." Although Sophie admitted she liked Carlyle better than Spenser, and Hopkins better than Carlyle, she also occasionally reminded me, with a touch of acerbity, that she didn't really need me to bring culture into her life. She read poetry herself, and did she bother me with Wittgenstein or Schopenhauer? Often I had to content myself with underlining luscious passages or copying them into the back of my notebook.

Life as an English major did not always lack companionship. Although I was not very friendly with the other English major in Lawrence, Lolly Turnbull, I did know several girls from our shared classes. One of my closest friends outside Lawrence was Andrea Stein, whom I had disliked so much when I first met her in Freshman English that I was determined to make friends with her. I figured she must be really interesting. In our English class she raised her hand to say things like "This reminds me of Kafka," or "Personally, I think Dostoievsky does this a lot better." From her remarks, I gathered not only that she was no longer a virgin, but that she was now actually rather bored by sex. Like me, she got all A's on her papers; we looked at each other with mutually suspicious assessment when Miss Barnes praised one of our essays to the class. Since Miss Barnes observed the usual formalities, I did not even know Andrea's first name for some time. One day, nerving myself, I asked her after class, "Miss Stein, would you like to come and have tea with me on Friday?" Andrea blinked, looked surprised, and accepted.

That teatime, when Andrea unbent to tell me about riding the New York subway alone at age twelve, graduating from Bronx Science at fifteen, dissecting fetal pigs in her biology lab, and planning a combination of pre-med and English, we began a long and still continuing friendship. We liked each other despite, or perhaps partly because of, our differences. Ames, Iowa, was as foreign to her as the Bronx was to me. We even had different literary tastes: she preferred E. M. Forster and D. H. Lawrence, I inclined to Sarah Orne Jewett and Sir Thomas Browne.

But it was to Andrea I turned when I had to share my grief about Clarissa Harlowe. During the late spring of my senior year, when lush green grass, purple and white lilacs, and red and yellow tulips brightened the campus, I was gloomily immersed in the prolonged sufferings of Samuel Richardson's *Clarissa.* Richardson could not have asked for a more avid, sympathetic reader; drawn into the novel's letters, I painstakingly followed Clarissa's adventures as if they were my own. I first hoped she might find happiness with handsome, quick-witted, dissolute Lovelace. Even realizing the odds against this union, I didn't give up until almost the end. Identifying myself with Clarissa's bravery, intelligence, and determination, I was sure she would triumph. I hadn't, however, prepared for Richardson's eighteenth-century idea of moral victory.

On the afternoon Clarissa died, I closed the book with shock and sorrow. Sophie was gone and couldn't comfort me. Knowing I had to share my feelings with someone, I hurried across the campus to Andrea's house. Tears barely in check, I took the stairs two at a time and knocked hard on her door. I hoped I was doing the right thing. Andrea and I were both reading *Clarissa,* but we hadn't discussed it yet. When Andrea opened her door, her eyes widened in surprise at my stricken face. "For God's sake, Susie, what in hell is the matter?" she asked. "Come on in, don't just stand there."

Walking over to her bed, I sat down, cross-legged, trying to look composed. "It's Clarissa," I said, audibly sniffling. "I'm sure this is going to sound dumb, but I just finished the book, and I feel terrible. I never thought she was going to die."

Andrea looked at me. "I know what you mean," she said with a wry smile. "I finished it yesterday, and I felt the same way. Like absolute shit. So calm down. I'll make us some tea."

Remembering Andrea and myself that spring afternoon, sipping tea and talking about Lovelace and Clarissa as if they were absent friends, I am filled with a sense of loss. I am seldom now on such direct, intimate terms with what I read. Perhaps I have learned to live more fully in my own life, so I do not need to find as deep a refuge in books. They still matter, but I am not sure they matter as much.

My long-ago tears at Clarissa's death are a valuable reminder to me of what I came to care about at Smith. Like Mr. Hauptmann, I too have turned out to believe in something, a learning process I am committed to continue. Although I have forgotten dates and texts, some of the intellectual habits I acquired at Smith cling to me, like fragments of a chrysalis a butterfly never left behind. When not long ago I tried to explain something to my daughter about volcanic action, I found my year's elementary geology had evaporated like the steam from a mountain's cone. I can no longer date the *Kourai* in Athens, I've long since erased Napoleon's battles, and I can scarcely translate the French phrases in Dorothy Sayers' murder mysteries. Even in my own field, I remember little about Francis Bacon, Spenser, Dryden, and other writers I never teach. But I get excited about following Peter Matthiessen into Eastern Africa, learning about basins and ranges from John McPhee, tracing the life of Woolf or Jean Rhys through their biographies. I still wish I could take all the courses in the catalog, and I am not quite ready to admit I never will.

In my office at the college where I teach, I keep an old plastic folding lawn lounge, the kind that adjusts to different positions. During a busy day, I look forward to a few moments, during my lunch hour or late afternoon, when I can close my door and take out a book. Unfolding my chair, I lean back on it, covering my legs with a small lap robe. Soon, if I am lucky and the phone doesn't ring, I find myself once again in D. H. Lawrence's mining country, or Middlemarch, or Netherfield, drawn into old quarrels, love affairs, ambitions, and sorrows. If the book is a new one and any good, I feel exhilarated, admiring the writer's sleights-of-hand and wondering what will happen next. The clock stops ticking, and I forget everything but what I am reading.

If someone were to see me, I would appear to be an ocean traveler, tucked up on deck as though for a long voyage. And indeed I am sailing away, in the direction laid out for me long ago in the Smith College Browsing Room.

In the Swim 🌿

IN DARKER moments, I sometimes think life is one long college mixer. Moving into a crowded room buzzing with activity and filled with people I do not know, I try to remember who I am. Taking a deep breath, I march up to someone and introduce myself. It is not as simple as once it was; I can no longer say, "I'm Sue Allen from Ames, Iowa," and expect that definition to make much sense. Now I vary my tag lines: "I'm Jenny's mother," "I teach English at Macalester," "I'm a friend of James," "I live at the end of the block, in the house with the crumbling chimney." Then, with luck, I start a conversation, and eventually, if my luck holds, I become absorbed into the color, sound, and movement around me. Time passes. I get tired. After a while I leave for the quiet of my own room. Sometimes, when I've enjoyed myself, I fall asleep smiling, thinking about the whirl of the dance. Sometimes I am just grateful to rest for a while before I return to the party. There are always new faces to confront, new connections to make, new attachments to form.

Sartre could hardly have devised a more frightening prospect than life as an endless mixer. Why am I sometimes haunted by this vision? Perhaps I've become sensitized by a decade as a single adult (single woman? single parent? divorcée? which tag line do I use?). So much social life in my late thirties and early forties has, after all, been reminiscent of what was happening when I was eighteen: mixers, blind dates, or dates you've barely glimpsed, possibly with eyes half shut. Mixers haven't changed much in twenty-five years. Sometimes they have fancier names, like A Really Fun Cocktail Party, or Just A

Casual Potluck Dinner For A Few Friends; sometimes they have organizational titles, offering the reassuring dignity of S.A.T. (Singles All Together), P.O.P. (Parents Without Partners), Sierra Club Singles, Westminster Adult Fellowship.

Like college mixers, most adult mixers focus on drinking to "break the ice," a phrase I've always thought implied a sudden treacherous slip into chilly waters. Over the years, white wine has replaced martinis, which once replaced beer, and, at more serious mixers, a coffee urn is a prominent emblem of the group's higher purposes. Drinking, whether chablis or Maxim, is essential to a mixer. Holding a drink, one can always sip instead of talk, or, standing alone, peer with a studied poise over the rim of a glass as if it were an invisible wall to lean on. "Oh," that pose announces, "I'm simply standing here, drinking; I don't know why I'm here, certainly not for the reasons you're here, I guess I was just thirsty." Although conversation about what is in one's cup or glass may be limited, it is often extraordinarily useful: "Can I get you another glass of wine, too?" asked ingratiatingly; or, pronounced with a severing touch of firmness, "Excuse me, I'm going back for a little more coffee. It was nice to meet you, Richard."

There are some differences. At college mixers, we didn't wear name tags. Blundering from stranger to stranger, girls struggled to remember names to attach weeks later to a voice calling for a Saturday-night date. Boys had to remember not only faces and names but some means of contact, a telephone number or dormitory or mutual friend. Now, at adult mixers, we strain not to look too obviously at a name we've been told only moments before. I try not to feel embarrassed until I've examined a tag the third or fourth time.

Adult mixers are more earnest. In college, they had only one announced purpose, for boys to meet girls, sort each other out, and set up dates. Adult mixers are often cloaked with determined cheer, health, and good sportsmanship (Bicycling Outing, Sunday at 4 P.M. at Prospect Park! Bridge Club, every Wednesday at 7 P.M., Church Social Hall!) or of psychological self-improvement. Before or after the obligatory drinking, the true adult mixer presents something called an Enrichment Program, as if it were the food, the solid main course, to which the accompanying white wine or lukewarm coffee is a mere concession to human frailty. "Pansy Perkins, M.S.W., noted family relations expert, will tell us about 'Drawing the Circle Closer Together,'" promises the program note; "Ms. Perkins is a welcome visitor to our group every year. Her peppy, heartening advice will give us all something to think about." Here in Minnesota, where we are proud of having properly labeled chemical dependency, alcoholism is a favorite topic; "Alcoholism Is a Family Disease! George W. Thomas, former director of the Kenwell Institute, will share his experiences tonight in a forthright, informal talk which will be followed by small group discussions." Fortified by whatever one had in one's Styrofoam cup first, one sits for an hour in silence among strangers to hear about "Creative Intimacy," "How to Love Yourself So Someone Can Love You," "Surviving a Family Vacation," "Budgeting Your Time," "Making Friends with Your Teenager." Afterward, before going home, everyone circulates with another cup of coffee, probably later wishing it had been decaffeinated.

Blind dates have had a few changes, too. Rather than wholly unknown ventures, they usually now involve cautious meetings between two people who have talked, briefly, at an adult mixer; or met, briefly, at someone's dinner party; or exchanged views, briefly, at a conference. Once I went out — for a long while, actually — with a man I'd met when he sat next to me at a concert. At least I knew what he looked like and that he preferred Mozart to John Cage, chamber music to symphonies, and the acoustics of Orchestra Hall to the auditorium at St. Catherine's College. It wasn't a bad introduction, one whose scope I wish I'd had more often when I was younger.

My blind dates these days take place at lunch. That's another change. In college, one usually had to risk an entire evening. At worst, one gambled a whole weekend at a man's college, where it was possible to feel sentenced to life imprisonment before Sunday afternoon. Now I briskly suggest lunch: it's short, and it takes place in daylight. I always pick restaurants with windows, so I can watch people passing if I lose interest in the conversation at my table. There's another advantage to restaurants with windows: faces come sharply into focus in bright noon sunshine flashing through plate glass. In that light one notices the comforting wrinkle of laugh lines around the eyes, discontented glances that dart restlessly around the room, a forced smile that flickers on and off too frequently.

When my lunch date and I are looking hard at each other, trying to read character in each other's faces, what are we hoping to find? Years ago, on my blind dates, I wasn't sure, either from my perspective or from his, and I'm not convinced I even know now. As if we were tapping with white canes, gingerly exploring the unknown territory before us, we wonder what is out there. While I'm venturing forth, I am aware of the other explorer making his way toward me, looking for the boundaries of my territory. Will he see my warning signs and barbed wire? Can we meet in any open space between?

What is he looking for? Who does he want? What do I want? Years ago,
when less was at stake, we asked each other questions that stayed safely on
the surface. Where are you from? What school did you go to? What are you
going to major in? Where are you going at Thanksgiving? Now we ask each
other different questions, still factual, but designed to open doors into farther
distances: What do you do? How long were you married? How long have you
been separated? How many children do you have? How old are they? Some-
times I think it would be easier if we met each other with a prepared state-
ment. Should we perhaps begin lunch, not with the usual glass of white wine,
but with a monologue? "I was born in 1940 in Ames, Iowa. My mother was
a widow. The absence of a father in my childhood probably explains . . . "

Although I much prefer a lunch date to a mixer, I often leave the table with
the same sense of relief I used to feel when I slipped behind the closing dor-
mitory door. Inquisition over, judgment either delivered on my part or waiting
to be rendered on his. Even after a pleasant encounter, I am usually tired,
what with emotional letdown, a heavy quiche, two glasses of wine and all
that plate-glass sunshine. As I take a deep breath, trying to recover energies to
carry me through the afternoon, I sometimes think of Mort Sash, a colleague of
mine. Soon after his divorce, I saw him in the halls of the history department.
Startled, I commented on his altered appearance: new beard, thinned waist-
line, a certain self-satisfied glow. "Well," said Mort modestly, "I guess you
could say I'm back in the social swim again." We're close to the same age, so
he knew I wouldn't find that phrase archaic. Later, I thought how acute it
was. "In the swim": taking a deep breath and diving into social life. It
brought back my childhood swimming pools, where I learned about chance
meetings, flirtations, overtures by dunking, and how to swallow chlorinated
water with a smile. Now it reminded me also of salmon, driven by inescapable
instinct, swimming valiantly upstream, struggling against great odds to meet
and mate, so life can start all over again. Maybe I should think instead of
paddling lazily in a summer lake, or floating down some tranquil stream,
looking at the blue sky overhead. But I inevitably return to images of heavy
currents and struggling swimmers. Being "in the swim" is hard work. That
was how I felt about social life in college.

In the beginning, there was Rahar's. For years it was such a leg-
end of Smith life that gray-haired alumnae in tweed suits could
startle us with evidence of their youth by asking, "And how is
Rahar's? Has it changed?" When I returned to the Smith campus

after twenty-two years, and found Rahar's at last closed down, I thought as I passed its abandoned site I could almost smell the overwhelming odor of cigarette smoke and stale beer that used to drift like fog out its open doors and down the street.

A tottering frame building on an out-of-the-way city street, Rahar's was not a nightclub or dance hall. Though it served pizza and a few other snacks, it certainly wasn't a restaurant. Rahar's was simply a place to drink. According to rumor, its owner was the brother, or cousin, or business partner, of either the mayor or chairman of the city council or chief of police, depending on whose rumor one believed. Whatever the reason, no one ever had to worry about being asked for an "i.d." at Rahar's; nowhere else nearby could a Smith freshman or sophomore, or indeed anyone under twenty-one, order a brandy Alexander without demur.

Probably because its free-flowing liquor was its only attraction, Rahar's was seldom frequented by anyone except college students. But it was always crammed full, small dark room after small dark room of tables crowded with boys from Amherst, U. Mass., Williams, Yale, anywhere within a few hours' driving distance, and their Smith dates. On week nights, or early on Fridays and Saturdays, Smith girls came unescorted, sitting not too self-consciously together, either talking earnestly or glancing surreptitiously to see if any unattached males at other tables might be interested in a little encouragement. Since no liquor was allowed on the Smith campus, not in the dormitory rooms, not in the student union, not even anywhere on the grounds, Rahar's was not just a place to drink: it was the *only* place to drink.

After my introductory visit to Rahar's, where my Big Sister Dulie took me one late afternoon, I could see I was going to have to learn about drinking. Dulie described a typical Northampton date: "Maybe a movie first, or something to eat at Friendly's if they've come a long way, and then everyone just goes to Rahar's." When Dulie ordered a Manhattan, with off-hand authority, I wondered what to do. Somewhere I remembered reading in one of my teen-age manuals, *Betty Bear's Teen-Age Guide to Beauty* or *Manners for Young Moderns,* or maybe it was somewhere in one of the college issues of *Mademoiselle,* how to order a nonalcoholic drink. Was it called a "Horse's Head"? Or was it "Horse's Leg"? Or "Nag's

Head"? Or no horse at all? What would happen if the bartender
didn't know what I was talking about? How could I explain, since I
wasn't sure what went into the "Horse's Head" or "Nag's Tail," or
whatever it was? Was it soda or tomato juice, with a twist of lime
or with a maraschino cherry? I decided to order a Coke.

"Plain Coke?" said Dulie, with friendly curiosity. "Don't you
drink?" I confessed that no, except for some of my mother's Tay-
lor's sherry, I didn't. "Sherry won't do," said Dulie disapprovingly.
"What you probably need to start off with is rum Coke. They don't
put much rum in it here anyway. It's mostly just Coke."

When I had my first date, I took Dulie's advice. We arrived at
Rahar's about 8 P.M., and with a Friday-night curfew of 12, I knew
I had three-and-a-half hours of drinking ahead. My date ordered a
beer and looked at me. But I never had been able to manage more
than a few sips of beer before feeling I had swallowed a whole
swimming pool. It always bubbled in embarrassing burps through
my nose. So I decided to take a chance. "Rum Coke, please," I said
firmly to the waiter, half afraid he might look at my round, pink,
seventeen-year-old face and laugh. But he didn't. My date didn't
say anything either. The rum Coke tasted strange, as if someone
had added molasses or cough medicine, making it very sweet, like
Kool-Aid. After a few swallows, I waited for something to happen.
Only the faintest warmth in my stomach, a feeling that edged on
what I identified as bus sickness, signaled the effect of my first
grown-up drink. I was a little disappointed.

Soon I realized that rum Coke wasn't going to be good enough.
Nobody else ever ordered it, and I thought I detected slight sneers
from those nonchalantly asking for old-fashioneds, Scotch and
soda, daiquiris. Listening at the Monday morning breakfast table
in Lawrence House, I heard Lolly Turnbull, our most accomplished party girl, talk about "tossing down too many Jack Dan-
iel's." She sounded matter-of-fact, businesslike, and totally in
charge. Bourbon, she indicated, when I asked her, was redolent of
Southern verandahs and wisteria, but it wasn't sissyish; in fact, it
put a woman on an even par with a man. More straightforward
than rum, it was, however, more feminine than Scotch. On my
next Rahar's date, I ordered bourbon-and-water. Rahar's didn't
give a choice of brands. This time I didn't have to wait long for an

effect. With my first sip, I had to fight my facial muscles, which wanted to wrinkle into a violent gesture of distate. On the second, I could sense not just a warmth, but a fire swirling down through my chest and spreading out in small rivers through my body. My cheeks grew flushed, and by the end of the first glass, I was a little dizzy. I felt myself beginning to relax, as if I were sleepy. I knew that was how I was supposed to feel. Bourbon-and-water was a success.

For four years, until as a senior I became confident enough to admit to myself I didn't really like the taste, I said deprecatingly to my date, "Mine is bourbon-and-water, please." Gradually I increased my tolerance, until I could manage three or four weak ones, nursed over several hours, without my dizziness turning into whirling nausea. Bourbon-and-water was perfect for Rahar's. The bartender didn't use much bourbon, and I could always ask for more ice. As time dragged on in those noisy, darkened rooms, I was grateful for bourbon's magic. It was an anesthetic that dulled my senses, making me care less what I said or what he said. After some bourbon, I didn't strain so hard to hear the conversation across the table or to follow the muttered repartee between my date and the boy next to him. Clinking my ice cubes, or chewing thoughtfully on them when I didn't want to order any more liquor, I told myself this was a fun way to spend a Saturday evening. Very collegiate. Lots of laughter, joshing around, happy people.

"Hey, George, how're things?" my date called out, reaching his foot to stop a boy hurrying past our table with a tray of beers.

"Hey, John! Well, look who's here! It's the Big John, all right!" George said heartily, pausing long enough to put his tray down on our table and hit John in a friendly way on his back.

"Having a great time, huh, George? Really living it up?" John asked. Sometimes John introduced me, stumbling over my last name or omitting it entirely, or if George had a date trailing behind him, he might motion her to our table. We girls smiled warily at each other.

"What house are you in?" I asked politely.

"Parsons. How about you?" she said.

"Parsons. That's in the Quad, isn't it? I'm in Lawrence."

"Lawrence. Is that on Green Street?" I nodded and looked wise.

If we recognized each other, we tried to figure out why, whether we had a course together or maybe were both in tennis or had often seen each other in the Browsing Room.

"So when are you heading back to New Haven, John?" George asked. They compared notes on timing, whose car each was riding in, how fast each had made the trip.

"How's about that big history test on Monday, huh?" John asked. George groaned. John laughed in commiseration.

"That calls for another drink," George said, moving off with his tray toward his own table in another room. "See ya."

There was a short silence after George had left. John's animation disappeared. I tried to think of something to say. I sucked hard on another ice cube and wondered how much more time I had to last until curfew. No one ever went home early. I wished there were something else to do besides drink. I was up to three bourbons-and-water already, and I didn't want to push my luck.

Smoking was what I decided might fill some of those silences. Besides, like drinking, smoking seemed an integral part of social life at Smith. First I needed to learn how. Again Dulie proved indispensable. For several mornings after breakfast, she coached me in the living room. We started with Kents, which Dulie told me were good starters. "When you really get into it, you'll want to change to Marlboros," she said. "Kents are mostly for smokers who aren't very serious about it, sort of ladylike types. Salems and Kools are like smoking Mentholatum. They're not actually *cigarettes*. But stay away from Camels or any of those unfiltered brands. Only guys smoke those, and they taste terrible besides." I quickly learned to puff, but it took much longer for me to gather the courage to inhale. Even with Dulie watching, guiding me breath by breath, I choked and coughed as the acrid smoke poured into my lungs. It was many weeks before I could inhale with grace.

But then I felt I had acquired a useful, and even decorative habit. Often when I was nervous, I played with my hair, ruffling my short bob or twisting a back strand under my fingers. Worse, I tore at my cuticles, removing dead skin in a perfectionistic cleaning gesture. I knew neither habit looked nice. Now that I could smoke, I fancied myself looking like a brunette model in a glossy cigarette ad, tossing back my imaginary smooth pageboy as I leaned forward, holding my Kent toward the lighter of a handsome, smiling young man. Dulie had even shown me a trick, "very sexy," she'd said, about how to light a cigarette: "You just touch his hand, the one that's holding the match or lighter, and guide it toward your cigarette while at the same time you look into his eyes. Like this." She demonstrated. Although I practiced, it made me feel phony. Only Lauren Bacall, with her long swoosh of hair, could do this properly, I decided; a girl from Ames, Iowa, had to be glad if she just managed to keep a match from going out long enough to get her cigarette lit.

Soon I became dependent on cigarettes to lighten tedious moments, relax tension, and interrupt routine. During a long morning of studying, I looked forward to a break when I read mail in the Lawrence living room and puffed companionably with other smokers, who bummed cigarettes under an unwritten code of repayment as stringent as the Honor System. One Marlboro was worth two Salems; it took three Kents to pay back a single Benson & Hedges. On the library steps I sat for a few minutes between classes, flicking my ashes on the ground with a practiced touch that said to passing students, "I'm not as uptight as you are. I have to go to class too, but I'm never in too much rush for a cigarette."

My main use for smoking was, of course, at mixers or on dates. When I wasn't sure of what to do, I could always light a cigarette. Sometimes, when I was in an uncomfortably quiet back seat of a car, returning with one or two other couples from Amherst, lighting and holding a cigarette meant I didn't have to hold hands instead. And who could lunge at a girl who held a lighted torch in one hand and was blowing thick smoke from her mouth?

Wanting a defensive weapon, even a feeble one like a cigarette, was an instinctive reaction when I walked into a mixer. Although I never went alone, I was scared when I entered a room full of strangers. Expectations hovered in the air. I not only had to meet some of these men, but if I wanted to have any social life at all, impress a few of them. Most Smith freshmen had contacts in the East already: brothers, cousins, boyfriends of older girlfriends, prepschool classmates who'd scattered into the men's colleges. But those of us who had traveled far from home, or who had attended public schools, sometimes found ourselves absolutely dependent on mixers or blind dates. Unlike my old familiar life in Ames High, I could not here meet boys in my classes, in my neighborhood, at play practice, or the swimming pool. Suddenly they had become a scarce resource, almost an endangered species, which appeared for special occasions like mixers in smooth madras plumage or shaggy Shetland sweaters. Those occasions took on the frantic air of a hunting season, during which one needed to select the best target, take careful aim, and not waste the few shells one had. Meanwhile the prey was edgy, moving quickly from shelter to shelter, and disappearing completely if frightened.

No men were allowed above the first floor of campus houses. No wonder that when a girl in Lawrence received permission to bring her father momentarily upstairs, when a janitor was needed to haul a heavy trunk, or the girl serving as receptionist ushered a maintenance man or plumber to heating duct or toilets, she was required to call out loudly down each hall, "MAN ON FLOOR!" It was a ring of triumph, the announcement of Big Game let loose for a few moments in our manless precincts. Whenever someone called "MAN ON FLOOR! MAN ON FLOOR!" I always half-expected a door to open and a girl to lean out and yell hungrily, "WHERE?"

Meeting someone at a mixer was an art of calculated passivity. Although I tried to look unconcerned, friends and I chattered nervously to each other, keeping a conversation going to give the appearance of being preoccupied.

"This skirt isn't too tight in back, is it?"

"No, no, it looks just fine. You look great, you really do. Honest. Boy, it's hot in here. I hate these things."

"I do too. I never meet anybody interesting. I don't know why I bother to come."

"Oh, come on. What about that guy from Williams you met at the Freshman Mixer last weekend? He called you up right away, didn't he?"

"Sure, but he's not going to get down here again for a month. I probably won't remember who he is by then."

"Don't look now, but I think some guy is coming across the floor. He's got his eye on you."

"What does he look like?"

"I don't know. Sort of tall, glasses, a funny nose. Pimples."

"Don't stare! Just keep talking to me!"

"OK, OK. Relax. He went over to that other group by the wall. There are a lot of girls from Hopkins over there. Everyone's laughing. They must know some of the guys here. God, this is terrible. I don't want to stay awfully long. Do you have a cigarette? If we can't smoke here, do you want to go outside?"

Moving into an open space, we tried to position ourselves so we could be seen, but not be stranded in an unprotected island. If I were talking to just one girl, and the two of us were standing too far apart from the crowd, a boy might come and ask one of us to dance. Then the other, suddenly abandoned, had to walk, trying not to hurry, across an interminable wasteland of dance floor to find the safety of other clustered girls, the crowded punch table, or the exit. If my friend was asked to dance, and I was not, I felt like a failure.

Although in Ames I had been considered bubbly and outgoing, something happened to me at mixers. Uncertain, wanting to please, I couldn't lapse into the camaraderie, flippancy, and friendly teasing with which I used to flirt. Instead I felt wooden and constrained. Rather than leading into easy conversation, my questions tended to resemble an interview. Asking questions was my only way to make contact, learn something about the boy I was talking to, and decide whether or not I wanted to see him again. I always had the sense I didn't have much time.

"Hi. My name's Tom Moore."

"Oh, hi. My name's Sue Allen. Where are you from?"

"I'm from Wesleyan."

"Wesleyan. I know someone from Wesleyan. Peter Errington. He's from my home town. He's a junior this year, but I don't know what house he's in."

"Errington. Pete Errington. Sounds familiar. Seems like I've met him, but I don't know where. What's your home town?"

"Ames, Iowa. It's a small town in the middle of the state."

"Isn't that where Iowa U. is?"

"No, that's in Iowa City. Iowa State is in Ames."

"Huh. Iowa. That's a long ways to come. Do you like it here?"

"Oh, sure, it's just kind of different, that's all. I'd never been East before. Where are you from?"

"Bridgeport."

"Oh, really? That's not too far from Wesleyan, is it? Do you get home a lot?"

"Nope. They keep us pretty busy. Besides, Bridgeport is crummy. I haven't really lived there long, but I hate it. Say, do you want some punch?"

"Hey, thanks, that'd be nice."

"Okay, be back in a minute."

While my new acquaintance was gone, I had a decision to make. How long did I want to talk to him? Given limited time at the mixer, at what point did I try to meet someone else? If I had already concluded, on the basis of admittedly superficial evidence, that I didn't want to see Tim or Keith or Clark again, how did I extricate myself? How long did I have to wait after he had gone to the trouble of getting my punch?

Sometimes Tim or Keith or Clark saved me the trouble by disappearing. Instead of getting punch, he melted into the crowd and never returned. Or he said abruptly, "Excuse me," and just turned on his heel and left. I never had the nerve for such a direct and immediate departure. Moving from foot to foot, I had to build up enough kinetic energy to burst finally into a hurried litany of farewell: "You know, I think I'm going to have to find this friend of mine I came with. I told her I wouldn't desert her, and I left her alone at the punch table a while ago. She was about ready to leave, anyway, so I guess I'd better check on her." Sometimes, if I had been at the mixer a while and was discouraged, I gave up: "Well, I suppose I'd better think about getting back to my dorm. I have a big economics test on Monday, and I had really promised myself I'd spend most of tonight studying. It was nice to meet you, though. Maybe we'll run into each other in New Haven sometime."

I never knew exactly who I hoped I might meet at one of the mixers. Just some nice guy, that's all I want, I told myself; maybe two or three, enough to keep the phone ringing. But of course I was really looking for more than one or two casual dates. Deep down, I dreamed about finding someone special, a grown-up boyfriend to replace my Iowa high-school crushes I thought I had outgrown. Here in the East I would have much more choice, dozens or even hundreds of bright young men, ambitious and upwardly mobile, ready to turn into physicists, economists, college professors, doctors, lawyers. The East seemed to me a vast reservoir of talent.

Looking hopefully around the room at a mixer, I watched for the almost-homely boys, the ones with glasses (but strong jaws), ragged haircuts (but square shoulders), shy smiles (but straight teeth). I knew I didn't have a chance with the super-handsome guys, the athletes, or the Big Men On Campus; back in Ames High, I had learned to leave those prizes to the cheerleaders and beauty queens. I quickly dismissed the obvious losers, boys with acne and bad breath, boys who squeaked or snickered or wore loud colored shirts, boys who were round or squat. Though I was fascinated by the sardonic, wisecracking young men, I was frightened by them too. They turned their glittering eyes on me as though to fix me for one paralyzing bite. I thought I'd do better with the quiet, thoughtful ones, who might be waiting for someone like me to discover their hidden depths and light their inner fires.

As I conducted my uncertain assessments, I of course knew I was being simultaneously evaluated too. I wished I knew what criteria were being used, so I could try to meet them. Perhaps if I were thinner? Prettier? Sexier? Having had plenty of dates in high school, I assumed that here in the East I would still be a reasonably valuable commodity: perhaps provincial, but on the other hand, appealing in a Middlewestern way. I was wrong. I was merely part of the large pool of available girls, two thousand four hundred, to be exact, from whom the visiting men could pick and choose. Most of us had to work hard to fill our social calendars. On weekends, many girls in Lawrence House were studying in their rooms, playing cards, taking in the foreign film at Sage Hall, or "sitting on bells" in place of a luckier girl who'd been asked out.

When mixers failed, I had two alternatives to a solitary weekend. One was to respond to the occasional calls that echoed through Lawrence on Saturday night. The phone rang in the hall, and after a few moments someone yelled, "There are some guys from Williams downstairs. Does anybody want to go to Rahar's?" Perhaps in order to nerve themselves for such a foray, the boys were usually defensively raucous and dauntingly good-humored. One had to be ready to rise quickly to the occasion, with equal laughter and an unbounded enthusiasm for an evening focused on Rahar's weak bourbon.

The other alternative, a blind date, was safer, though it too had hazards. Blind dates ranged from the spontaneous offer of a friend who knocked at your door at 7 P.M. and said, "Danny brought a friend with him who has a car. Do you want to go out with us?" to the matchmaking of a girl who knew someone you'd *really* like. "Someone" was a boy she'd known in high school, or her boyfriend's nice roommate, or her younger brother. Probably because I seemed a friendly, "down home" Iowa girl, I was usually asked to entertain roommates, brothers, and old-friends-from-highschool who were shy, haltingly conversational, or just plain silent. I ran a high statistical average of mathematicians, electrical engineers, and seminary students, well-meaning, serious, and very quiet.

Blind dates could offer excitement, however. Perhaps my most unforgettable blind date was Matthew Parker, who took me to the Deerfield–Mount Hermon football game. Early that week, Beth Thompson had approached me during the after-dinner coffee hour. Since she was a senior and well aware of her position in the Lawrence hierarchy, while I was a new freshman, we had never exchanged more than a few polite words. Now, however, Beth inquired how I was liking Smith, was it what I expected, and did I keep myself busy. "I'm asking because I wondered if you have any plans for this weekend. I thought you might like to double-date with a friend of my brother Skippy," she said solemnly. "He's driving up from Princeton on Saturday with his roommate, Matthew Parker. Of course you've heard of Matthew's father?" I had indeed. Matthew Parker, Senior, had been a renowned minister at a large, wealthy New York church, where he had made a national name for himself by combining his tousled good looks with his optimistic, patriotic, and down-to-earth sermons. He had published a best-selling volume of them; one night when I was babysitting, I had read an excerpt in *Reader's Digest* called "Jesus Was a Regular Guy." By the time he was forty, the Reverend Matt Parker had achieved the cover of *Time* and an inside spread in *Life*.

"I've asked Nancy Weiss to go with Skippy," Beth continued, methodically outlining her plans. "She seems like the right type for him." Nancy Weiss was short, tiny, and very pretty, with luminous dark eyes and curly black hair. I could see why Beth wanted her for Skippy. And why had I been chosen for Matthew, Junior? "I haven't met Matt, of course," Beth continued, "but I'm sure he's nice. Skippy says you're not to mention his father, though. He doesn't like to talk about him." As Beth went on, I gathered that she had been observing me. Now I remember seeing her at chapel last Sunday. She had probably decided I was responsible, decent, and religious. With a small-town background, and Protestant credentials, I was obviously a safe choice for the son of Matthew Parker, red-blooded saint of Fifth Avenue.

When Saturday arrived, I was ready long before noon, when Skippy and Matt were planning to drive us to Deerfield, their old prep school, for a football game. It was a sunny, cool day, perfect for escaping the campus, and I loved the idea of seeing some more of the East. I had begun imagining what I might say to Matt, and what interesting things he could tell me about his life. Though I wondered how religious he was, I figured someone at Princeton also had to be fairly sophisticated. He sounded like a wonderful combination, trustworthy, loyal, kind — how else could the son of a famous minister grow up? — and a man of the world. Princeton was a college I hadn't seen yet, but I pictured it as wealthy, beautiful, ancient, and elite. A Princeton man! The real Ivy League! An afternoon at my first prep school! Sunshine, travel, romance!

When the phone rang and I was told my date was waiting, I stopped at Nancy's room so the two of us could go down together. She looked adorable in her tight blue skirt and matching V-necked sweater, and I wished I felt less chunky in my own red plaid pleated skirt and fuzzy Orlon pullover. Matt would probably wish Nancy were his date instead. When we walked into the living room, I looked quickly at Matt. I didn't want to stare. He was good-looking, with broad shoulders and chiseled features, but he moved with a kind of lurch, glancing once at me and then turning toward the door.

Parked behind Lawrence was an enormous black square vehicle, old and battered, a kind of grandfather to the 1940s black Ford my high-school boyfriend had always driven. But Matt's car was much bigger. "My," I said with bright interest, making my first conversational effort, "what kind of car is that?"

"It's a hearse," Matt said, opening the door for me with a sudden raucous cackle, the kind I remembered hearing from the boys who darted into Lawrence on Saturday nights, yelling for girls who wanted to go to Rahar's. When I climbed into the car, I saw why. Behind the black seat the cavernous rear space had been converted into an elaborate bar, with a counter, cabinets, and a varied collection of bottles. One of the bottles was already open, and two used glasses stood on the counter.

"My," I said. "Isn't that something." I didn't want to stare at the bar too openly either.

Skippy, now settled with Nancy on the back seat, adjusted himself so he could reach the bar. "Ready for another, Matt?" he asked.

Matt shook his head. "Nah, not yet," he said. "Wait till we get on the road. Then you can fix me another Scotch. And how about you?" He turned to me. He clearly didn't remember my name.

"No, thanks," I said uncomfortably. My heart had begun to beat a little fast. I wondered how long it would take to get to Deerfield.

Conversation en route was limited. Mostly Skippy and Matt reminisced about their years together at prep school, telling each other — and Nancy and me, as a kind of aside — about past Mount Hermon–Deerfield games, a classic event which was also Deerfield's annual Homecoming. I had heard rhapsodic stories about Mount Hermon from a Lawrence girl who had attended Northfield, Mount Hermon's sister school, so I was able to chime in occasionally with comments, which the boys received in silence. Nancy, always reserved, gave a periodic low, gurgling laugh, and nursed a tall glass of gin-and-tonic.

By the time we arrived at Deerfield, Matt was already what I had learned to call "juiced." I found myself high in the stands, looking down on a formal procession in the football field below, a ceremony with the whole school marching in uniforms. I was so far away that the figures looked like miniatures, and the ceremony like some kind of Eastern ritual. I had never been to a prep school before, and of course I had never seen school uniforms.

It all looked impressively traditional. In between talking to Skippy, Matt tried to explain to me what was going on. He still didn't pronounce my name. He and Skippy kept poking each other excitedly.

"Hey, it's the old man! See him down there?"

"Son of a bitch. Hasn't changed a bit, has he?"

"And Hayward? Do you see Hayward? There, strutting along in the second row? What an ass! Where do you suppose he'll end up?"

"What if he ended up at Princeton? Suppose you'd let him into the Dekes?"

"Are you kidding? *That* asshole?"

"Who are you talking about?" I asked Matt, trying to enter into the spirit of the conversation.

"See that guy down there, in the second row, third from the left? He's a guy who lived next door to Skippy one year. A real asshole," Matt said, and turned to Skippy again.

"Oh," I said. Nancy looked at me and smiled, a kind of deprecating, pleasant, oh-why-does-it-matter-anyway kind of smile. She seemed content to sit and watch.

After the football game, Matt and Skippy wanted to hurry down from the stands before their friends got away. While they slapped backs, exchanged greetings, and acknowledged their new status as College Men, Nancy and I stood together a little apart, out of the way. Eventually we left, found someplace to eat dinner, and Skippy and Matt ordered more drinks. We got on the road again after dark. Somehow Nancy and Skippy had disappeared. Perhaps we dropped them off, though I don't know where. What I see next in my mind's eye is myself in the front seat of the hearse, watching the road anxiously as Matt, another drink in hand, pilots the huge black car unsteadily along an untraveled road. I think Matt told me he was taking a shortcut; I see woods on either side of us, and darkness closing in.

I remember asking Matt lots of questions. Partly I felt this was my only chance to get to know him, and partly I was just plain scared. I knew Matt shouldn't be driving, but I had no idea how I would get home without him. Even if I had had the courage to ask to drive, I didn't know how to handle a vehicle of this size. So I asked questions and derived some comfort from hearing Matt give more or less coherent answers. I gathered he didn't like Princeton much, didn't know what he was going to major in, was already on academic probation in his sophomore year. He didn't sound happy.

Somewhere on that dark road, with woods on either side, Matt abruptly stopped the car and turned off the lights. My questions had finally brought me to his attention. Now I was really scared. I didn't want to get into a necking session with Matt; not only did I hardly know him, but he was so drunk I had no idea what might happen. In my only experience with uneasy moments in the front seat of a car, the car had always been parked in a place where I could get out. I knew how to open the car door quickly, leap for the sidewalk, and call out a breezy good night as I headed for my own front door. But here there was no front door.

When Matt reached for me, I acted instinctively. I had no place to go, but I had to get out. Without thinking, I opened the car door, slid outside, paused for a second in the cool night air, and then opened the rear door and scrambled onto the back seat. Somehow I must have assumed I would be safe there, Matt in front, me in back. As I look back now on my panicky move, I am a little sympathetic toward poor Matt. He of course saw my action as an invitation. Given my determined chirpiness, as well as my vaunted small-town background, he must have been surprised. But, drunk or not, he rose to the occasion. Almost as quickly as I, he opened his own door and slid into the back seat next to me.

Suddenly I realized what I had done. Heavy with alcoholic fumes, Matt's breath swirled toward me. I didn't know what to do. So I gave Matt a gentle push, not hard enough for him to really notice, and began to talk. I have no idea what I said, but I know I chattered loudly and continuously, like a squawking parrot whose cover had just been lifted from its cage. Talk, talk, talk, one cheerful tidbit after another, a monologue that I pretended included him. "Don't you think?" "Isn't that true?" "Don't you agree?" I'd ask, barely waiting for him to say something, and then hurrying on. I had edged myself toward the end of the seat, with my back braced against the door and my knees hugged tight against my chest with arms clasped around them. I hoped I looked like a turtle or a snail drawn tight inside my shell. Meanwhile I talked. "Let me tell you what happened the first day I met my roommate, it's really funny." I babbled. "I've been pretty homesick, I guess. I miss Ames because I knew it so well. It's right in the middle of the state. Have you ever been to the Midwest?"

At first Matt looked puzzled. He even tried to respond, as if he was willing to play this silly game for a little while. But gradually he became aware that I had no intention of using the back seat for anything except a podium. His face darkened. He moved restlessly on the seat, making the bottles on the bar jiggle. I kept talking for what seemed like hours. Finally, he said, "Well, if you have to be back at midnight, I guess we'd better get going." He sounded disgusted. I pretended not to notice. We both opened separate doors and got back in front. For the rest of the trip home, I watched the white line in the center of the road and asked God to get me safely home to Lawrence House. Neither of us spoke until we pulled up outside the dorm. I thanked Matt and got out. He grunted and started the motor again, racing it loudly before I had closed the car door behind me. I never saw Matt Parker again. Later I heard, probably from Nancy, who went out with Skippy a few more times, that both of them had been expelled from Princeton. I wondered where Matt had gone, but mostly I wondered what had happened to the hearse with the built-in bar. I wished I had a postcard of it.

Even when I didn't have to escape into a back seat for safety, I usually kept a secure distance from my blind dates. I found it hard to feel comfortable with them. They were all such strangers. I began to realize what a luxury it had been in Ames to get to know a boy over a long period of time. If we exchanged only a few words today, we'd see each other in drama class tomorrow. If we had no classes together, we would probably pass at the bus stop or meet in the lunch line. Though during my high-school crushes I always felt as if my future hung on each agonizing moment, in fact I had all the time I ever needed to experience the natural life of any attachment — its birth, growth, and slow or sudden death. At Smith, everything seemed unnaturally speeded up.

Sometimes my longing for some warmth, the kind of acceptance I'd known back home, overcame both my scruples and my fear.

Timid and frightened of sex, I usually watched defensively for any forward moves from my dates. I was armed and ready: a sudden shift of position, a lighted cigarette, or, as with Matt Parker, a torrential flow of talk. As I told myself reassuringly, I had my standards. I was tentative about holding hands, and I certainly never kissed anyone goodnight on the first date.

Almost never, anyway. One night in my junior year, when I had endured several months of dismal weekends, scarce blind dates, and long Saturday nights in the dorm, my roommate Sophie asked me if I'd like to double with her "steady's" friend, Pat, yet another seminary student. I sighed, with gratefulness as well as resignation, and said yes. When I was introduced to Pat, I liked him right away. He was very quiet, soft-spoken, and good-looking. Before long I realized that he reminded me of my own long-time steady high-school boyfriend, Peter. He didn't talk much, he smiled slowly but with real pleasure, and he seemed to like me. True, I couldn't find out much about him, and we chimed in with Sophie and Don's conversation rather than hazarding much of our own, but the evening passed pleasantly. I had a feeling that Pat wasn't very intellectual, but I didn't have to strain to talk to him either. He was OK.

After dinner and a movie, Sophie and Don separated themselves from Pat and me. They were a serious couple and needed time alone together. I knew Sophie's morals were as strict as mine, though since she and Don were practically engaged, I assumed they had advanced farther in courtship rituals than I ever had. Except in general terms, Sophie and I didn't discuss sex. Perhaps knowing that Sophie was parked somewhere with Don made me feel easier about my own behavior. Perhaps my thinking about Peter, whose arms had always felt so strong and loving, jarred loose some of my emotional locks. Perhaps I was simply, overwhelmingly lonely. For whatever reason, I found myself encouraging Pat in wordless ways I hadn't known I knew.

It was a misty spring night, cool and moonless, and we walked slowly along the deserted path by Paradise Pond. After a while we stopped. Pat knew what to do. He put his arms around me. He felt just like Peter: solid, reassuring, very much there. From then until curfew, less than an hour away, we kissed and hugged, walked a little, stopped and kissed again. Neither of us said much. I was breathing hard, experiencing a sharp physical hunger. I was shocked to feel such warmth for someone I barely knew. Pat was breathing hard too. We still didn't say much. I knew things would not progress much further, since we had no car and we had no other place to go. With the grass so cold and wet, we couldn't even sit down. So we continued to walk and stop, walk and stop.

When we parted on the Lawrence porch, I was still in tumult, dazed and puzzled. Pat seemed uncertain too. We didn't look at each other too closely as we muttered thank-yous, and a few phrases about seeing each other again. Upstairs, when Sophie came in, I said something about Pat's physical attractiveness, his niceness, and his intellectual dullness. She agreed. I went to bed, something still burning inside that I didn't know how to put out.

Later the next week Sophie came into my room with a broad smile on her face. "You sneaky sexpot, you," she said to me affectionately.

"What are you talking about?" I asked her.

"I'm talking about Pat. Don just called and we talked about last Saturday. He says Pat had to leave his white shirt in the trunk of the car because it was covered with lipstick stains. He's too embarrassed to take it to the cleaners. It's got red all over it like blood. My heavens, what were the two of you doing? Don says he didn't know you were such a hot number." She grinned again. I blushed, not knowing what to say. "Do you think you'll hear from Pat again?" Sophie asked curiously.

"I don't know," I said. I really didn't. We hadn't gotten acquainted in the usual ways, and I wasn't sure we were actually friends yet.

"Bet you will," Sophie said. "Do you want to?"

"I don't know," I said. I thought for a moment. I guessed I expected I *would* hear from him, though I didn't want to appear to Sophie to be overconfident. But did I want to? He had been nice, not the kind of guy who got drunk and grabbed you, like Matt Parker, but he hadn't been all that interesting. Aside from his resemblance to my old boyfriend Peter, maybe he didn't have much to offer. "I guess I'll wait and see," I finally said hesitantly. "But let me know if Don says anything more about him, will you?"

As the next week passed, and the week after, I realized that I was not in fact going to hear from Pat. I didn't feel too bad — it was like having a large sunfish slip off the hook, when you were really fishing for walleye — but I couldn't help thinking I'd been rejected. What had happened? Had I scared him? For weeks afterward I thought of Pat's ruined white shirt, crumpled in Don's trunk, its lipstick stains a visible testimony to my uncharacteristic abandon. I wished Pat hadn't shown the shirt to Don. I hoped maybe by this time he had thrown it away. Eventually I decided I never wanted to see Pat again.

If trying to get to know someone on a blind date was difficult, my other alternative — a "college weekend" — wasn't any easier. "Going on a weekend" was a ritual that varied in detail but consisted, at least for me, of the same uncomfortable elements. Although I never took a chance on a blind date for a whole weekend, I seldom knew my escort well in advance. We had usually met at a mixer, or perhaps briefly in the Lawrence living room when someone was dropping off a sister, or visiting a high-school friend, or maybe concluding an unsatisfactory evening. One of my discoveries was a young man who had had a blind date with Claudia, a friend of mine; they didn't get along, and since he was at Smith for the whole weekend, she ran out of ideas to entertain him. Helping out, I volunteered to talk to Blake for an hour while Claudia showered and changed upstairs. When Blake called me the next week to invite me to Yale for a weekend dance, I hesitated, made some excuse, and asked him to call me back for an answer. I felt obligated to consult Claudia. Lawrence rules said Blake belonged to her. Claudia, however, was relieved. "He's all yours, and welcome," she said. "But do you really want to go? He's awfully boring. I think you're nuts." I nodded defensively. I had never been to Yale, I hadn't had a date for weeks, and I thought maybe Blake just needed some drawing out. Still waters run deep, I said to myself, and decided on the spot to accept. "I think he seems sort of sweet," I said to Claudia. She snorted.

First I had to decide how to get to New Haven. The train was expensive, the bus ride long and inconvenient. According to weekend protocol, the girl paid for transportation, the boy for lodging and meals. Mrs. Sullivan, secretary in the Office of Scholarships and Student Aid, had already told me, encouragingly, about a "discretionary fund" that might, under special circumstances, pay train fare to a man's college. "Just last year, Margie Mack, the student body president, came in here in tears because her fiancé, whom of course Miss Bailey had met, had asked her to the Princeton Senior Prom, and she couldn't afford to go. We were able to give her *twenty-five dollars* toward the train and the first new dress she'd had in two years." Mrs. Sullivan smiled. "Of course, Margie had done so much for Smith." I decided I could manage the ticket. I didn't think an ordinary fraternity dance, with a boy I'd only met once, and whom I'd in fact sneaked from under another scholarship girl's nose, qualified for Miss Bailey's grant.

Blake met me on the platform in New Haven, looking not quite as handsome or as full of potential as I remembered. I thought sinkingly of the forty-eight hours ahead of me. First, Blake told me, we would drop my suitcase at my rooming house and then go right to the fraternity. On a residential street near the campus, we stopped at a worn-looking, faded house. A large woman with a spotted apron greeted us noncommittally at the door and showed us up the stairs and down to a dark hall to a small room with a double bed, a wicker rocking chair, and a painted nightstand. "I lock the doors at two," she said to Blake, and left us standing next to the bed.

Blake looked away. "I hope you don't mind, but because of all the house dances this weekend, everything is real crowded. Two of you will be doubling up. Maybe you'll meet her at the house tonight. I think her name is Chrissie. She's the date of a brother of mine I don't know very well," he said.

"That's fine," I said quickly. I wasn't surprised. On my last college weekend, three of us had been packed into a largish bed that wasn't nearly large enough. I had gotten used to sharing a bed with one or two girls I didn't know. I did hope Chrissie didn't toss and turn too much. I wanted to be the first back to the room at night, so I could pick the side near the wall. Lying alone in the bed, I liked to listen for a while to nearby sounds — cars outside, a chiming clock, a slamming front door — until I had made tentative peace with my surroundings. When the new girl came in, I would keep my eyes tight closed and pretend to be asleep.

Careful to position my suitcase on the wall side of the bed, I smiled at Blake and followed him outside. At his fraternity house we walked through a large living room and down the basement stairs to the party headquarters. It was only late Friday afternoon, and not many dates had arrived yet. Two couples sat on a bedraggled sofa at one end of the windowless, pine-paneled room, a few boys leaned on the bar at the other end, and one couple was dispiritedly dancing to the scratchy sounds of a portable phonograph in the corner. The smell of old beer, mixed with cigarette smoke and basement damp, hung in the air. I could see a tapped keg at one end of the bar, and a stack of tall glasses piled on the counter.

"Want a beer?" Blake asked.

"Yes, thank you," I said. I hated beer.

During the two days that followed, in my memory we seldom left that basement. Sipping beer, talking desultorily, occasionally trying to draw in another couple, dancing jerkily, sitting down again and sipping some more beer, we worked hard to make the hours pass. By midnight Friday I pleaded travel fatigue, with an additional excuse about having stayed up late studying for an exam, and escaped to my safely reserved portion of bed. Alone in the dark, savoring my privacy, I was happier than I'd been all evening.

Saturday morning Blake didn't pick me up until eleven. Having woken early from force of habit, I dozed for a while. I didn't want to disturb the girl sleeping so soundly next to me. She hadn't come in until two. After three hours, my stomach was growling crossly. I got out of bed carefully, sat in the wicker chair, and read, but all I could think about was breakfast. So I was glad to see Blake when he finally arrived. Instead of finding a restaurant, however, we went back to the fraternity, where the basement bar was now heaped with coffee cups and Danish pastries. We ate and drank, chatting with the other couples who were yawning and complaining about hangovers. I felt self-conscious about not having one.

In the afternoon I pressed Blake to take me on a tour of the campus, past the looming, ivy-covered Gothic cathedrals that turned out to be classroom buildings, dining halls, or libraries. Neither one of us could think of much else to do. By Saturday evening, we had nothing more to talk about. As Claudia had warned me, Blake wasn't a sparkling conversationalist; and my own jaw ached from talk and tension. After a while, we went back to the basement.

Now, a fraternity brother behind the bar was serving mixed drinks, wiping his hands on a loud colored towel and cracking jokes with the couples loitering nearby. As the evening wore on Blake began to drink more seriously. He held my hand a lot and pressed me close when we danced, rubbing his hand up and down the small of my back. Filled with people and spilled drinks, the basement was hot and humid. I could feel my clothes sticking to me in the places Blake pressed, and under my own hesitant touch, Blake was clammy. He grew more and more silent. Finally he asked me if I'd like to see his room. I couldn't figure out how to say no. Up the stairs we climbed, still in silence. On the way we passed one of his roommates. "Going up?" he asked Blake. Blake nodded. The boy grinned at me. I smiled back, knowing what he was thinking but not knowing what to say.

Once in Blake's room, he sat down on one of the beds. I stayed on my feet, admiring the posters on the wall, asking which was his desk, examining the books on it. I had had some practice now in maneuvering. "Want to come over and sit down?" he said, patting a place next to him on the bed.

"I don't think so," I said in the friendliest way possible. "Girls from Iowa get nervous upstairs in men's rooms. It takes us a long time to get to know people, if you see what I mean." I had found that a useful line before. "Girls from Iowa . . . " had several variations. "Girls from Iowa go to bed early." "Girls from Iowa don't drink much." "Girls from Iowa are shy about that."

Though he was a little blurry from drink, Blake was still a nice guy. After a half hour during which nothing happened, he sighed and got up. "So what do you want to do?" he asked, with something close to desperation in his voice. Just then someone knocked on the door.

"Hey, Blake, you in there? Can we come in?" I recognized Blake's third roommate, whom I had liked.

"Sure," said Blake flatly. "Just a sec." He turned to me. "Well?"

"Let's go back downstairs and dance some more," I said, thinking with resignation of Blake's slow-moving, heavy feet. I glanced surreptitiously at my watch as we passed Blake's roommate and date in the hall. Only two more hours till one o'clock. I thought that was a reasonable time to ask to go back to the rooming house.

Sunday morning wasn't bad at all. They served milk punch at the fraternity house, a rich concoction that reminded me of eggnog. I knew I was going home soon, and Blake and I were much more relaxed as we sat with our drinks and said very little. I felt almost as if we were old friends. I asked Blake to walk me around the campus once more, so I could fix the cathedrals in my mind. I might not get to Yale again, and I wanted to remember it.

In the train going home, I looked out the window. I was sad, not depressed, really, but wistful. Someday I wanted to go on a weekend with someone I cared about. Then everything would be different. I would have a wonderful time. I would get silly and tight, stay up till three or four, sleep all morning. I would *want* to go to someone's room and I would know what to do when I got there. I could see myself laughing, dancing, drinking, sitting happily with someone in the dark. Someday maybe I would have a weekend like that. Meanwhile, though, the train was noisy, the air was stale, and I was tired. Without caring, I knew that I would probably not see Blake again. If he asked, I would be busy, and he probably wouldn't ask. The weekend was over, and that was that. Of course I would write him a nice thank-you note. Girls from Iowa had good manners.

Not all relationships resolved themselves so easily. From time to time I became ambiguously entangled, not in tortuous love affairs, but with nice young men. That was how my mother would have described them, in an approving tone, quite different from that she used to label the ones I usually preferred, who were difficult, skittish, stubborn, unstable. The bad ones were "interesting"; the others were "nice young men." If she had met Matt Parker, she might have pronounced him "interesting," hesitantly drawing the word out to underline her doubts. When she met Bob Boylston, as she eventually did, and I told her how unexciting he was, she sighed and said, "Well, perhaps, but he *certainly* is a very nice young man." The sigh was partly intended for Bob, who had insisted on drying the dishes after dinner, and partly for me, who had already shown signs of extremely fallible judgment in the men I chose to love.

I felt sorry for Bob, too. That made things worse, because I couldn't feel attracted to someone I felt sorry for. When I first saw Bob, I had been at Smith for only a few weeks. One of the Midwestern girls I'd met on the train called me to say a prep-school friend from Amherst had arrived at her dorm with his Iowa roommate. Would I like to go out with them? Happy to see someone from home, I quickly agreed. At first I felt hopeful about Bob. Although he was rather short and light, he had a pleasant face and a suitably tweedy look. His friendly but uncertain air made me feel he too was a stranger to the sophisticated world of the East. Since he was already a sophomore, he was eager to show off a bit. Grasping my elbow, he piloted me to what he said was his "favorite corner" in Rahar's. "There are better places to drink, of course," he said, proudly informative, "but you really ought to get used to Rahar's first. Everyone does." Bob laughed at my small ironies, even when they weren't very funny, and eventually kept an almost perpetual smile on his face so he would be ready when I *did* say something. He was almost visibly relieved that I was untried and impressionable. "Rum Coke?" he repeated after me, and patted me gently on the shoulder. "Hey, of course, that's OK. There's nothing wrong with a rum Coke. Hey? Hey?" He tried unsuccessfully to get the waiter's attention. "Sir? SIR?" Turning a little red, he raised his voice and snapped his fingers. The waiter ignored him and moved on to another table. "Well, I'll try to get him on his next round," he said apologetically. I smiled reassuringly. He leaned back and loosened his necktie. Now he only looked as if he had unaccountably forgotten to knot it.

When Bob escorted me to the Lawrence House porch, I knew he wasn't going to try to kiss me goodnight. I thanked him effusively, bouncing up and down a little on my toes, exuding encouragement. After all, he was from Amherst, a definite social possibility. He beamed and promised me he'd call soon. I *did* like him enough to go out with him again, I told myself, I *did*.

Two days later, Bob called. Soon we were dancing around each other at arm's length, both frustrated. Neither Bob nor I knew how to adjust our different needs: he wanted me as a girlfriend, I just wanted him as a respectable escort. Too much a gentleman, and perhaps too unselfconfident to press hard for real affection, he seemed glad to settle for whatever I would provide. Since no other prospects hove into view, I continued to accept his invitations, but without enthusiasm. Not intending to be unkind, I nonetheless pushed Bob's tolerance to its limits: holding hands but not kissing him goodnight, asking to be returned to Lawrence an hour before curfew, sometimes turning him down for dates with flimsy excuses. He became querulous, hurt, and even a little huffy, but he always called back. I felt ashamed of myself, but I rationalized that I was, after all, playing by the rules of the game.

At Christmas, Bob called from his home in Davenport to ask if he could drive to Ames to see me. His parents turned out to be old friends of a dean at Iowa State, a man who was technically my mother's boss, and he would of course stay with them. Again I didn't know how to say no. But I didn't want to spend too much of my precious vacation time with him. I consulted with my mother. "He sounds like a nice young man," she said judiciously. "Of course I'd be glad to meet him. The Hunts just called me this morning to tell me how glad they were you had become a friend of Bob's."

I have blanked out most of Bob's visit, probably because I behaved so badly. He came to our house for at least one meal, because I remember his drying the dishes. None of my other dates had ever done that. I also remember an uncomfortable lunch at the Hunts', who weren't quite sure what to say or what inferences to draw from Bob's visit. I didn't spend much time with Bob. I disappeared for several hours to the library, claiming I wanted to do homework for upcoming exams, and I think I told him the first evening not to come over until lunchtime the next day, just before he had to leave. In those days, without an interstate highway, Davenport was a long drive.

After Christmas, I didn't see Bob again. But I hadn't really learned much from my connection with him. Before long I began to date another nice young man, who was more compelling than Bob — he tended to sulk angrily, throw temper tantrums, and in general show more signs of life — but who still did not, as a friend of mine succinctly once put it, "race my motor." Again I did not know how to find a middle ground where we could meet. As with Bob, I simply let Steve's frustration level build up, along with his temper tantrums, until he finally disappeared in fury, somewhat to my relief. That relief was tempered by the fact that I then had no one else to take me out of the dark halls of Lawrence House on Saturday night.

As I looked around Lawrence House, I was not the only girl who had trouble with her social life. Few of us had friendly, continuing relationships with men. Most, it seemed to me, had disasters. Sophie went steady for a while with a man who treated her so meanly that her friends nicknamed him, much to her chagrin, "Lou the Louse." Judy, another friend, had a year-long affair of the heart, chaste but tender, with a Harvard man so intelligent, funny, and altogether desirable, that we called him "Bill the Snowman," from the then-popular verb, "to snow," meaning "to deluge with overwhelming attractiveness." But at the end of the year, Bill inexplicably stopped calling, Judy developed chronic red eyes, and no one ever mentioned the Snowman again. Even Molly O'Brien, whose dignity and self-control I much admired, was not immune. Once when we had taken a weekend trip to Boston together, she told me she wanted to call someone she had known when they were both counselors at a summer camp. I could tell Thad was special. Although Molly went out now and then, in the three years I had known her she had never had a steady boyfriend. "He's someone I've always dreamed about," she said, with uncharacteristic openness, but she couldn't say more. Late that afternoon Thad appeared at the Y, where we were staying. All I could see in the few moments before they disappeared from the lobby was his hooded dark eyes, impassive face, and old leather jacket. He had brought his motorbike. Hurrying to the entrance, I was just in time to see Molly, looking a little flustered, perched on the back of the bike, head erect, her arms around Thad's waist. She had told me not to wait up, but she was back in little more than an hour. "It was OK," she said. "He has lots of work to do on his honors paper. He's real busy right now." She looked sad.

Most of us probably did not know what we wanted, or how to look for it if we did. I think I knew less than most. For years I thought I had missed my big chance by not recognizing the merits of Duncan Douglas McDougall, III, though now I am beginning to wonder. When I first met Duncan, I was enjoying an unusual social rush that temporarily occupied a few weeks of my freshman year. Just having dropped Bob Boylston, now dating sulky Steve, I had, briefly, the heady sensation that boys were going to be plentiful in my life once again. So when I met Duncan on a double date, I was in a picky mood. Tall, lanky, Duncan had his hair cut far too short in an army crew cut that exposed his oblong head. He was loud, making frequent bad jokes and then laughing at them himself. He wore an ill-fitting sportcoat in a plaid that was too large and too bright. When he called to ask me out, I fixed him up instead with Sharon down the hall, who spent most of her time dissecting frogs.

I didn't see Duncan again for two years. Then one day he reappeared in Lawrence House, part of the offbeat entourage of Penny Davis, leader of Lawrence's wild bunch. Penny's boyfriends, some of whom she dated and others who just attached themselves to her vicinity, were mainly from Amherst, so they came to Lawrence often, sometimes even on weekday afternoons. Determined entertainers and deliberately noisy, they scandalized Mrs. Stevens. Sometimes one limber boy hung by his heels from the giant beech tree next to the porch, while another sang risqué verses to the tune of "America" accompanied by a tinny banjo. Into our quiet living room they swirled in white-water eddies of excitement.

When I caught a glimpse of Duncan in that tight knot of laughing, gesturing boys who surrounded Penny and her friends, I almost didn't recognize him. His hair had grown out, so long it was almost bohemian, and he sported a slightly rakish mustache, which made his eyes seem to twinkle and added, I decided immediately, at least five years to his age. He was wearing an old sweater and scuffed loafers, which, although they did not look fashionable or even especially "Ivy," suited him. Someone in the group must have said something funny, because everyone roared for a few minutes. I could hear Duncan's laugh, still loud, above the others, but now it sounded bold and confident. As I walked toward the stairs on the way to my room, Duncan glanced in my direction. His expression did not change.

Later that fall I was complaining at the lunch table that I had
no one to invite to our Christmas house dance. Penny, who ordinarily ignored me, broke into my conversation. "Do you really
want a date?" she asked. "I could get Dugal for you." She pronounced it to rhyme with "bugle." It was a nifty name, snappy and
vaguely foreign. I had heard her call Duncan "Dugal" before, so I
knew who she meant. Quickly I reviewed when I had last seen
Dugal alone with her; not for a long time, I realized, because
Penny seemed to be going steady with someone else.

"Well," I said doubtfully. I did want to go to the dance, and
since Dugal lived in Amherst, I wouldn't have to worry about having him on my hands all weekend.

That was how I began going out with Dugal. I no longer called
him "Duncan," a name which fitted a clumsy sophomore, but certainly not the intriguing young man who now called me just often
enough to make me feel he was interested, but not often enough to
give me any security. From a chance remark of a fraternity
brother, I learned that Dugal was also dating a girl from Mt.
Holyoke. "Hey, Dugal, are you driving back to Holyoke tonight?"
he asked, looking at me. Dugal never blinked. "Nope," he said.
"Tonight's Northampton."

When he did call, Dugal always had something fun in mind.
One Saturday afternoon he arranged for us to borrow two bicycles,
and we pedaled around the Amherst countryside, looking for old
cemeteries. When we found one, Dugal brushed aside the weeds
and long grasses so he could read the oldest epitaphs aloud. On the
way home, enveloped in the warm humid haze of spring, we
puffed, perspiring, along the edge of the highway; shouting out
new epitaphs we had just invented. Dugal liked words. Once he
showed me a poem he had written for his grandfather, Duncan
Douglas McDougall, I. He had done it, he said, in a verse form
imitated from his Greek Literature course. Someday he was going
to take Greek as a language so he could read all the Greek tragedies
in the original. I was sure he would.

Dugal's fraternity, known sardonically on campus as "The Zoo,"
was filled with eccentrics, foreign students, and rejects from the
staider, more conservative houses. I liked them and felt at home
there. In one corner of the living room stood a television set turned

to the wall. "I got so mad at one commercial I just got up and kicked the screen in one night," Dugal said smugly. I couldn't tell if he was joking. Though I had never seen him lose his temper, he often spoke with a kind of violence that puzzled me. I sometimes wondered how happy he was, living on the outskirts of campus life. We certainly never went to any dances, proms, or fraternity parties. Mostly we talked. On the nights we hung around "The Zoo," Dugal never asked me to come up to his room. I never had to make excuses, parry, or fend him off.

As winter melted and spring began to blossom, I wished Dugal *would* do something. Although I could tell he liked me, he didn't seem to want to be physically close. Was he shy? Wasn't I encouraging enough? Although I only gradually found him attractive, I then began to feel rejected. I wished Dugal would put his arm around me when we sat on the sofa, or give me a long hug when we said goodnight, or at least kiss me with more than a quick, moist swipe that made me feel as if he were applying a rubber stamp.

I had trouble planning even a small advance. One night in early spring, when a sudden storm had buried the Connecticut Valley in wet heavy snow, Dugal and I were riding back from Amherst in the back seat of someone's car. Dugal was holding my hand but talking to the driver, so I was able to sit and think. I had had one of my nicest evenings with Dugal, entertaining and funny, and he looked especially appealing tonight, in a huge fur hat and Salvation Army topcoat. Letting my thoughts wander, I pictured myself on the Lawrence front porch, snuggling close to Dugal for a goodnight kiss. But suddenly my efficient mind came to a horrified stop. There on the floorboard of the car were my winter boots, scrunched next to my feet. Since I hadn't needed them on the sidewalk from the fraternity house to the car, I had carried them in my hand. But what would I do with them on the porch? If I had my large, bulky boots in my hands, how could I kiss him goodnight? But if I paused, set the boots on the floor, and waited, what then? Wouldn't Dugal feel as if he *had* to kiss me? After all, sometimes he just patted me and then bounded from the porch in several ungainly leaps. How could I survive that moment when I didn't know whether to put the boots down or not?

As Dugal continued to talk, still holding my hand, I looked out the window. We were already on the outskirts of Northampton. I had to act quickly. Reaching toward my feet, I began to put my boots on. Since we were sharing the back seat with another couple, and we were jammed together tightly, it was not easy. As I struggled, wiggling, tugging, and zipping, Dugal finally noticed something was going on. "What *are* you doing, Sue?" he asked curiously, and indeed the other couple were looking sideways at me too.

"I'm putting on my boots," I said.

"Putting on your *boots*?" Dugal echoed incredulously.

"My feet are cold," I said. The heater was going full blast, and together with the body warmth of so many people, the car was uncomfortably hot. But I already had one boot on and was working on the other.

"Huh," said Dugal, not unkindly. "You really *are* crazy."

"Guess so," I said, settling back again and reaching for his hand. Both boots were firmly zipped. When we reached the front porch, I had a desperate confidence born from this maneuver. Without waiting for Dugal to make a sign, I flung my arms around him and kissed him. He opened his mouth a little, and I did my best. But after a few moments, he pulled away and headed for the steps.

"Goodnight. Have a good week," he called, as he ran back to the car waiting at the curb.

Toward the beginning of May, with Dugal's Amherst graduation only a few weeks away, I realized our relationship was not going anywhere. Dugal, of course, *was* going somewhere: he had been accepted at a good medical school in Utah, far enough so he could not come back to Smith for weekend visits. It was a school that specialized in family-centered medicine, he told me. Family was important to Dugal; I remembered the poem he had written about his grandfather. That was the kind of man I wanted; why, I asked myself, had I taken so long to recognize him?

Wanting was not getting, however. Dugal graduated and said good-bye with a careless wave of the hand. The next year he wrote a few letters, none long or personal. He was almost through the Greek tragedies, though not yet in the original, he said. Salt Lake City was wonderful. Med school was a grind, but he had his first family case load to work on. Once, just before my own graduation, Dugal came back on a quick tour of the East. He stopped overnight in Amherst and we went out together for dinner and a long walk. Dugal was friendly but aloof as always; I was unaccountably sad when he left.

For the next two years I thought about Dugal. If I had been bolder, would he have responded? Why did he still bother to send an occasional card or note? What had not clicked, or had it just clicked too softly for me to hear it, or too late for it to matter? Even after I met the man I was eventually to marry, I still dreamed about Dugal. Although the sexual attraction between my fiancé and myself was powerful, I knew Dugal's interests and mine were closer and more compatible.

During the summer after my first year in graduate school, I was back in Ames, writing daily letters to Larry at Berkeley, and feeling disconnected from both my life in California and my old life at home. Smith seemed even more remote. One suppertime I had a long-distance phone call from Des Moines. "Hi, Sue," a familiar voice said. "It's Dugal. A friend and I are driving cross-country and we've stopped for the night here in Des Moines. How's about if I drive up tonight to see you?" After I hung up, my mind was buzzing. Had he deliberately planned to stop in Iowa? If he didn't care about me, why was he taking an hour's drive from Des Moines on a hot August night? But why hadn't he let me know he was coming?

Although my mother said there was no reason we couldn't spend the evening at home with her, my stepfather, and sister — they would like to get to know him, and besides, we could take our iced tea onto the screened porch and be perfectly private — I knew I had to get Dugal alone. With a transparent excuse about showing him downtown Ames, I managed to spirit him away for a beer in the Sportsman's Tavern. Afterward, we parked at a deserted spot on the Iowa State Campus. Windows rolled down to let in the night air, radio on, Dugal leaned back against the door. I sat as close to Dugal as I dared. Nothing happened. We talked, the radio played, and finally Dugal said it was time for him to drive back to Des Moines. When he walked me to my front door, he gave me a hug. "Great to see you. Keep in touch," he said, and drove away, giving a final beep on the horn as he pulled out of sight. When I went back to my room, I shut the door and cried, quietly, so my mother wouldn't hear me. The next morning at breakfast she asked how our evening had been. "He seems like a nice young man," she said. I wanted to scream. "Yes," I said. "Dugal is nice. It was fun to see him again."

Perhaps if I had been able to talk openly with some of my friends at college about sex — how I felt, how *they* felt, what I knew, what *they* knew — I might have better understood what was going on with Dugal, or Bob Boylston, or Pat. Certainly I would have been less frightened. But most girls I knew weren't much help. They shied away from specifics. Instead they issued general bulletins: "I wanted to do it, but I knew I couldn't." "It was easy. It didn't hurt at all." No one exchanged much actual information. I was too embarrassed to quiz even my roommate, who knew more than I did, and I couldn't think of anyone else to ask. Finally, as a senior, I thought I saw an opportunity to learn something safely.

As chairman of the Student Curriculum Committee, I decided the committee should arrange and sponsor some sex-education classes as an addition to our curriculum. Although the dean was initially uneasy, she finally agreed to a strictly regulated lecture, unadvertised, open only to Smith students, and presented by a family physician from Columbia. In Lawrence House, Penny Davis was unimpressed; "There's nothing he can tell me," she said at the lunch table. But even Penny had decided to go.

Most of Dr. Brugger's presentation was decidedly unexciting. It reminded me, in fact, of an advanced version of the Ames standard eighth-grade gym talk, in which all the boys left the room, the physical education teacher mentioned a few facts about menstruation, and then all the girls watched a filmstrip about eggs, pollen, and large mammals. If *I* already knew most of what Dr. Brugger was saying, everyone else must have found it even more tedious. But things picked up during the question period. Dr. Brugger had agreed to let white-dressed student ushers collect anonymous questions, from which he would choose a few to answer. As he opened the slips of paper and read them to himself, I could see that he rejected several. Finally he smiled and reached toward the microphone. "Here's one problem I think I can solve," he said genially.

"The question is, does intercourse hurt?" The room was silent. I strained to hear his answer. I wasn't so sure I believed Penny Davis when she said it didn't. "Let's put it this way," said Dr. Brugger, leaning a bit on the podium. "It's rather like helping your boyfriend change the tires on a car. I'll bet some of you have done that, haven't you? Well, it takes some effort, and teamwork, and it isn't always easy. Sore muscles, and all that. But you do it together, don't you? And it's worth it?"

I winced. I knew Penny Davis would never let me forget I had sponsored this man.

"And here's another," Dr. Brugger went on, warming up. "This one reads, 'Doesn't the missionary position get boring after a while?' " A few girls in the audience gasped at the daring of this question. I was envious of the experience that obviously lay behind it. I had a vague idea of the missionary position, but I was unsure of details. I certainly didn't know about any others. "Well," Dr. Brugger said, grinning in a conspiratorial way at his audience, "in answer to that question, ladies, I guess I could say that I've been married twenty-five years, and no, it hasn't become boring yet." Everyone laughed, and a few of the housemothers clapped. It was twenty years later that it occurred to me perhaps we should have also heard from Dr. Brugger's wife.

Without much information from my friends, and a blank from such sources as Dr. Brugger, I struggled on, sometimes drifting with the current of my feelings, sometimes fighting upstream. Then I thought I was unusual in my lack of confidence, ignorance, and confusion. Now I know better. Although my women friends and I are still reticent about discussing our current sex lives, we talk more freely about the past. Mostly we exchange horror stories, anecdotes that may sound amusing but at which we shake our heads in sympathy. We recognize that, for many of us, our lives literally changed direction because of what we didn't know or learn in those college years about men, sex, and our own needs and feelings. Swimming blindly along, some of us found ourselves lost in unmarked channels, marooned in hopeless backwaters, or simply run aground.

Twenty years after leaving Smith, I spent an evening in the bar of a large Minneapolis hotel with a Lawrence House acquaintance who was attending the same conference as I was. At Smith I had scarcely known Marcia. She had been a year ahead of me, quiet, hardworking, and very self-contained. She had also been very pretty, tall and dark-haired, with long lashes everyone envied. None of us had been surprised when she began to go steady her sophomore year with a handsome, if somewhat stolid, senior from Dartmouth. Both of them attended the Episcopal church, canoed, and liked music. But we *were* surprised when, in the fall of her junior year, Marcia suddenly announced her engagement, planned a Christmas wedding, and decided to transfer to the university of her new husband's law school back home in Colorado. Some cynics wondered if Marcia had *had* to get married, but her postcards the next year never mentioned a baby. We decided it had just been a case of overwhelming love.

Now, leaning urgently toward me in the gloom of mahogany and Tiffany lamps, Marcia told me about her life. We were both divorced, college teachers, raising single children alone. "I know you all assumed I had to get married," Marcia said. "And in a sense I did, but not in the way you thought. You know, I liked Foster all right, but I was never in love with him. He was kind of dull. He really pursued me, though, and I didn't know how to turn him down. Still, we never would have gotten married, if it hadn't been for my mother."

"Why?" I asked. "Did she just think it was time for you to get married, or did she think Foster was wonderful?"

"Neither one, really," Marcia said sadly. "But you know, Mother and I never talked about sex. I don't suppose many of us did." I shook my head in agreement. "I didn't know anything about it, and I didn't really have anyone I could ask. At Thanksgiving my junior year, I went home to Denver for the vacation. While I was there, I went to see our family doctor because I'd been having all kinds of urinary tract infections. Anyway, during the exam, he said that I seemed to be really tight and he might as well make an incision to save me a lot of trouble later. Of course I let him do it. It only hurt a little." Marcia sighed. "When I got home and told my mother, she wept. Now, she said, I was ruined. No decent man would want to marry me. She said I ought to take Foster if he would still have me. Three weeks later I announced our engagement. Do you believe that?" We looked at each other. I had lived in Lawrence in the 1950s, and I remembered. I knew something about the fear of not being wanted. Yes, I believed that.

Late that night, as I was getting ready for bed, I noticed a smear of lipstick on my good white sweater. I realized I must have made a smudge in my hurry to get dressed. That bright orange would never come out. I thought for a moment of Pat, the seminary student on whom I had taken a chance, as he on me, for one fumbling, uncertain evening. I remembered his white shirt, covered with my lipstick stains. Perhaps some of my memories of social life at Smith were, like that lipstick, ineradicable.

Summa 🌿

I STILL sometimes hear the Summa Voice. That's what I call it, having finally recognized where it comes from. In the distance someone waves a winner's banner, while simultaneously a voice whispers softly of possible failure. A job, a short story, a loaf of homemade bread: someone trained to compete can hear that voice almost anywhere, anytime. Will the interview go well, or will I talk too fast, sound too eager, and forget everyone's name? Will the editor like my story, or decide I'm hopelessly banal, as the Black Hole Review hinted? Will the loaf rise, or will it sag in the middle, proving to the Bunsens, fabled gourmets, that I only pretend to bake bread?

I know that voice now. For years, when it offered me a challenge, I felt I had to take it up. Strip the wallpaper? Write an article? Shepherd twenty-six students through a semester abroad? Learn the breast-stroke? Yes, yes, of course I could do it. But gradually I have learned that it is possible to say no. No, I don't think I want to. No, not this time. No, I'd rather stay home. No, let someone else win the prize.

I wish I had learned to say no when I was in college, when I thought I had no choice but to run — and win — the race. Not everyone at Smith heard the Summa Voice. When I was trying to recall our Commencement, I called a close friend who graduated with me, though then I didn't know her except by face and name. "Say, Tukie, do you remember how many Summas graduated in our class?" I asked, pencil poised. "How many what?" she asked. I explained. She laughed. "Are you kidding? I have absolutely no idea," she said. "I never paid any attention to anything like that."

As we compared notes, I could see the distance between her college world and mine open into a chasm. Hearing the pain in my questions, she said ruefully, "No wonder we never knew each other. While you were hiding in the library, I was probably at a party. Or huddled in the basement of Hopkins House talking about sex. I was determined not to play the academic game. I'd had enough of that in high school." She paused, and then said thoughtfully, "How we all needed to prove something."

Rueful in my turn, I agreed. As if shadows of the past had parted like curtains, I saw us then, struggling with ourselves, Tukie in the Hopkins basement, me in my library carrel. While Tukie was acquiring something I didn't learn for years, I was embarked on a long session in success and failure. The spring of my senior year I did not think much about sex. Mainly I thought about Summas.

Everybody knew who would probably be a Summa. That was how people talked about it: not who would "graduate Summa," or "get a Summa," or even "make Summa," as one might make an Olympic team, or, at Smith, make the Rally Day Show, or the College Choir, or Phi Beta Kappa. No, as I heard it, and I began hearing it already in my junior year, a few extraordinary seniors on campus were already assumed to "be Summas," — maybe Nancy Boulding in English, that tall, rangy girl who leaped like a wounded stag across campus, her bulging Harvard bookbag tossed over a squarish shoulder — maybe tiny Ruth Morris, political science, who looked tidy and severe as she marched through the library on her way to her messy carrel, crowded with typing paper, notebooks, and books flung open face-down with their bindings splitting — maybe Carol Greenberg, pale and dark-haired, so colorless and insignificant that I was astonished when someone taking a history course with her told me that Carol, too, was rumored to possibly "be a Summa."

That was how I always heard it: to "be a Summa," the ultimate somebody. Anointed, and then blessed, at graduation. As the seniors formed for the march into the Commencement ceremonies, the girls who had completed the Honors Program moved to the front of the line. The order of march was laid down in the heavy, cream-colored, engraved program. First came the Summas, that handful of six or seven names from a class of five hundred, separated by its exclusive size from the much larger group of "Magnas," thirty or forty girls who had not achieved the highest pinnacle, but who could at least write "B.A., Magna Cum Laude," after their names for the rest of their lives. Behind the Magnas marched the Honors graduates who had not tried very hard, or who had flubbed their exams, or who should not (as some of us whispered) probably have been in Honors at all. They were mere "Cums." Then the rest of the seniors trooped together, a large and undistinguished crowd. They were picking up plain B.A.'s.

Countdown for Summa began early. Each fall, in a special assembly, girls whose grades the previous year had included more A's than B's were designated First Group Scholars. This honor was more elite than Dean's List, which merely demanded a straight-B average. Next step was Junior Phi Bete, incoming seniors elected on the basis of their past high grade-point average. In Lawrence House, everyone paid a great deal of attention to what grades everyone else was getting. Making Dean's List was the essential minimum; more than one semester off this list almost certainly meant losing one's scholarship. To be a First Group Scholar ensured one's money for the following year, perhaps even with a slight increase. And to make Junior Phi Bete — well, Miss Bailey herself, Head of Scholarships and Student Aid, invited the winners into her office for a congratulatory chat.

Lawrence jealously guarded its reputation of academic excellence. We might not have as much money as girls in other houses, but we were sure we had more brains. Gathering around the house bulletin board, we read the week's calendar aloud: "Hey, Wednesday's the Honors Assembly. Is Olive going to make Junior Phi Bete? I'll bet she is. And what about Melanie?" One senior told me, with solemn pride, that two years ago Lawrence had had *three* of the eleven Junior Phi Betes, more than any other house on campus. Good grades were a kind of exhaustible natural resource, needing to be replenished with each new class, and demonstrating like a heap of diamonds hacked out with heavy labor the glitter and gleam of the scholarship girls in Lawrence House. None of us actually talked about our grades, of course. We preferred to look as if our grades had effortlessly burst forth from the dark mines of the library stacks.

Not only did the girls who lived with me notice and care who made what grades, so did my professors. When I made Junior Phi Bete, I was invited with the other new members to a celebratory dinner at the home of the Dean of the Faculty, Mr. Strachan. Aside from a brief job ironing clothes for a member of the Education Department, I had never been asked into a professor's house. Though raised in a faculty home myself, I thought Mr. and Mrs. Strachan's vine-covered, shaded, colonial brick house was far removed from the unpretentious ramblers I knew in Ames. Nervous, grateful, and wanting to please, I tried to make polite conversation with Mrs. Strachan, our hostess, by complimenting her on our dinner, a mixture of ground beef and sour cream served over small heaps of white rice. Mrs. Strachan, gratified, leaned over to me and said in a low voice, "We always feel we have to do something extra for our Junior Phi Betes. You are, you know, a very special group of people. It's different from being chosen for Phi Beta Kappa later, with all the others. You Junior Phi Betes will always remember who you are." I looked around me, feeling I needed to memorize the names of the other girls who were balancing their plates on their laps with much more poise than I. To be a Junior Phi Bete, I thought, was an honor but also something of a burden. Next day, Mrs. Strachan sent me her hot-dish recipe, gracefully written by hand on a personalized recipe card. I saved it for twenty years; although I never made Mock Beef Stroganoff, I somehow didn't feel I could throw the card away.

Those girls chosen for Junior Phi Bete were publicly in the running for high academic honors. All my senior year the possibility of a "Summa" hovered in the air like a wispy, insubstantial, but ever-present cloud. I could no longer pretend to be just one of the crowd, working hard for B's. When I complained about a paper I was having trouble with, or worried out loud about an exam coming up, some of the girls around me would hoot. "What do you have to gripe about?" they'd ask scornfully. "You're going to graduate Summa, we all know that." "Oh, come on, come off it," Mona Bragdon once snapped. Mona's scholarship had been trimmed last year because of her C in chemistry. "You're bound to get an A, you always do."

Even my professors seemed to know I was supposed to perform.

The spring of my senior year, I enrolled in what I thought would be a "fun" course in Restoration Drama. The plays, I knew, were bawdy and entertaining, and compared to the soberly tweeded other members of the English department, Mr. De Winkelmann, the professor, was reputed to be witty and theatrically flamboyant. He paced the floor, acting all the parts out loud, curling his tongue around the convoluted dialogue. I planned to sit in the back of the room, say little, and breeze easily through the semester.

So when I received my midterm back, with the grade C+ and the notation, "Rather dull," I was stunned. What had happened? Had I suddenly lost my ability to write? Could my other teachers have been wrong? How could I get a Summa if I didn't get an A in every English class? Heart pounding, I hurried to Mr. De Winkelmann's office. Our interview was short but to the point. "There is still a paper, you know," he said, fingertips pressed in an arc over his nose, as he looked off into a corner of the room, his eyes darting back and forth from me to the flickering shadows. His face was permanently contorted, I thought, from the expressions he had to assume reading Congreve or Wycherley. "If you do well on the paper, you may be able to balance this grade. In fact, we might be able to forget about it." He gave me a sudden sly smile. "This exam is not what I expected," he said. "I've heard about you, you know."

Mr. De Winkelmann had heard about me. That was what echoed in my mind as I walked slowly across campus, back to my room. He knew I was supposed to be an A student, one of the English Department's stars, a Summa candidate. We were not the only ones who watched the Commencement programs, I thought. Right after each name was the notation of that Summa's major department: Government sometimes had two Summas, History and English almost always one each, Education never. From Mr. De Winkelmann's remark, I concluded that the English Department wanted its name in lights, too, and they were depending on me.

As the New England spring slowly unfolded, the pressure I felt began to rise, as gradually but inevitably as the temperature. All fall and winter of my senior year I had been able to live under that faint but threatening cloud, because graduation — and the final honors awards — had seemed so far away. Summa depended on three faculty assessments: grade-point average, a senior Honors paper, and a three-day set of comprehensive examinations. Grades I had always worried about; they were nothing new. "Comps," the exams, were in the distant spring. That left my Honors paper, which in the first semester became a mountain standing in the way of my other courses. As I buried myself in the library on the dark rainy days of fall, or lay on my bed reading on snowy December afternoons, I tried not to think of the end of January, when my paper would be due — all forty pages of it! an unbelievable length. Instead I plunged into my work.

In a hurried, last-minute choice, I had decided to write my paper on the seventeenth-century essayist Sir Thomas Browne, and there seemed to be so much to learn about him I despaired. Thumbing through periodicals, looking up dissertation titles and obscure references, pulling down books on history, philosophy, and literature and wondering what I was supposed to do with them, I stumbled from topic to topic. As I found books that looked important, I carefully lined them up on the single shelf in my library carrel. Sometimes I was reassured to see these titles so impressively arranged in front of me — look what I had accumulated! what industry! what thorough scouring of the library! — and sometimes I was appalled. How could I ever read all of this stuff? Why did I keep forgetting things? Could I ever take enough notes? Then the books glowered at me, filling my cramped carrel with their threatening bulk, and I fled back to my room and the comfort of reading on my bed.

As I blindly pursued Browne, I was not entirely alone. As an adviser, I had fortunately been assigned a young instructor, new to the English Department. Since he didn't know much about me, I felt free of my usual burden of expectations, and though he also didn't know much about Browne, he gently corrected my essays and listened attentively to my reports. Mr. Billings was eager, kind, and disarmingly stiff, wanting to keep his precarious position as professor but also wanting to be friendly and encouraging. I was his first Honors student, he was my first Honors adviser. We hoped to do right by each other, though we didn't always know how. When I turned in my last chapter, I was anxious for his opinion; it was my best effort so far, I thought, in which my wanderings had finally taken a definite direction. Mr. Billings and I met in an echoing, empty office he was borrowing from someone on leave. Even the building, a ramshackle annex at the edge of campus, seemed temporary, as insecure as Mr. Billings, with his blond cowlick that kept falling over his forehead and his graying tennis sweater. As I entered his office, Mr. Billings rose from behind his desk. He held his hand out to me in a determined formal gesture. "Congratulations, Miss Allen," he said, a shy pleased smile lighting his face and lessening the distance of his words. "You have just written a fine chapter." I shook his hand vigorously and we beamed at each other. Then he picked up his bookbag, looked briefly uncomfortable, and blurted, "I don't really have any criticism today. Do you want to join Mr. Robertson and me in Alumnae Gym for a game of badminton?" I nodded, speechless. Playing badminton with my thesis adviser and with another English professor was an unimagined honor. Although I do not remember the game itself, probably because I undoubtedly missed all the easy returns, I know I sat down in Lawrence House for dinner that night in a rare glow of contentment.

When Mr. Billings, with real pleasure in his voice, called me in the middle of spring semester to tell me that my thesis had been judged a Summa, I was both delighted and frightened. I knew there were not many Summa theses. Now there was no escape. With fewer of us in the running, I was in the competition for good. All that remained were the Honors comps.

Almost as soon as I hung up from talking to Mr. Billings, the phone rang again. This time it was Chris Morgan. "Hey, kiddo, didja hear yet? Well? Didja get it?" I knew Chris would not have sounded so boisterous if she had not gotten a Summa on her own thesis as well. All that senior year it seemed as if Chris were mentally at my side, whispering into my ear, jogging my fears, buzzing at me about Magnas and Summas. She was a new friend; in the spring of our junior year, we had both run for different collegewide student government offices. Though I had lost, I was later appointed to another office that meant I sat with Chris on the Student Executive Board. During our campaigns we had taken each other's measure, as equally determined and ambitious.

I wasn't sure what Chris thought of me, but I certainly admired her. She was thin, wiry, and electric, emanating a kid of continuous energy. I envied her cutting intelligence, decisiveness, and absolute aplomb. During heated debate, Chris never lost control of herself, while I tended to redden and to feel my knees shake. She knew how to call the shots and how to keep score. She predicted who would cast what votes, and why, and she was always right. Once she told me of a persistent boyfriend she had just conclusively dumped. "Frankly," she said with a flick of her wrist, as though she were brushing away a bothersome fly, "I told him I liked him fine, but" — and here she raised her eyebrows suggestively — "he just didn't race my motor." Since at the time I didn't have any boyfriend at all, I was awed not only at her cavalier disposal of a scarce resource, but by her awareness of her precise physical responses. My own sexual instincts were often confused. Chris never seemed confused at all. As a final touch to my admiring picture, I knew Chris was honoring in government, known to be a theoretical and extremely difficult major. Talking with her, I sometimes felt by contrast English had to be a bit soft.

So when Chris began to seek me out, asking me to join her for coffee between classes, or to share a chocolate malt on Friday night, I was flattered. To be singled out by Chris, to walk across campus matching her stride for stride, was like being seen walking out of Alumnae Gym with Mr. Billings, each carrying a badminton racket. As we sat in the dingy, smoke-filled room in Gino's Coffee Shop, sipping lukewarm and bitter coffee from pale-brown plastic cups rimmed with faint smears of lipstick, girls in twos and threes passed us. Chris knew many of them. "Hi, kiddo, how're you doing?" she'd ask with a brief smile as they greeted her deferentially and passed by. Sometimes someone would rise from a nearby table, her knitting flung over one arm, and stop in front of Chris to ask some question about a government course, or a term paper, or a current campus issue. Chris's answers were snappy and self-contained. After a few exchanges, the questioner would readjust her knitting with dignity, and retreat to her own table with her half-done sweater under her arm. I sat and listened and sipped my milky coffee. Chris, definitive even in that, drank hers black.

What did Chris and I find to talk about? I now wonder. Although we probably spoke occasionally about student government, I don't remember those conversations. Since I was by my senior year conscientiously reading *The New York Times* every morning, we must have sometimes also aired our political opinions. Chris, to my astonishment, was a Republican; until I'd met her, I'd assumed that all intelligent human beings were Democrats. But I don't remember significant political discussions with Chris either. I'm sure I listened more than I argued. Mostly what I recall from our meandering walks across campus or our smoky visits in Gino's are Chris's precise, calculating assessments of our mutual current and future achievements. What did my adviser think of my Honors paper so far? Was I starting to prepare for comps yet? Had I been nominated for a Woodrow Wilson? Was I going to apply for a Fulbright? Where did I think I'd go to grad school?

Perhaps one reason these conversations made me uncomfortable was the distance I sensed between Chris's self-deprecating remarks and her innate awareness of her own superiority. "I'll never make Summa, kid, but I *know* you will," Chris said over and over. I protested, but Chris swept away my disclaimers with the same brisk efficiency that sent the knitters back to their tables trailing wisps of yarn. "Of *course* you're going to get a Wilson, if you don't who possibly would, and I'll be so *pleased,* I can't imagine who would make me more pleased, you're a snap, an absolute snap, and let's not hear anymore about it."

As the winter of our senior year deepened, she moaned about our Honors papers. "I'll never get mind done on time, never," she complained, but whenever I asked her how many pages she had finished, I was always demoralized when, pressed, she finally told me. "Do you mean you've already written eighty pages?" I bleated once. Government majors did not have the forty-page limit set in English, another sign, I knew, of how easy we undoubtedly had it. "God, I still haven't typed my first chapter." Even though we both eventually completed those Honors papers on time and with the same grade, I was still somehow convinced that I had finished behind Chris Morgan.

Although Chris was my Mephistopheles that year, tempting me with dreams of academic glory, others joined her insistent voice. Not only a chorus in Lawrence House but even students I marginally knew would bring up from time to time the notion that I had already been set apart as an A student and that I would doubtless be rewarded once again at graduation. "*You* don't need to sweat about the final paper," one girl in my English Novel seminar said to me. "You always write such wonderful essays. I don't know how you do it. I heard you got a Summa on your thesis." She smiled. I could see that she was friendly. "I'm sure you'll graduate Summa," she went on, "and anyway, I hope you will, more than that snooty Delores Rathbone. She was in Joyce, Yeats, and Eliot with me last fall and she was an awful show-off."

More and more I worried that I might let everyone down. If I didn't graduate Summa, how could I face my professors? Mona Bragdon, who sneered at me every morning in the Lawrence dining room? All the Lawrence freshmen, some of whom looked up to me? My roommate and best friend, Sophie, whose moral dedication to social causes I could never match? That girl in my English Novel seminar? The ones in Gino's who had seen me all spring having coffee with Chris Morgan? How, in fact, could I ever face Chris Morgan?

Most of all, though, I worried about facing my mother. Even as I write that sentence, I feel it sounds unfair. My mother probably didn't ever wonder if I was going to graduate with a Latin word tacked after my name. I do not think she ever asked about my grades or even urged me to do well. She didn't need to. All my life I had wanted to make her happy, to make up to her somehow for her pain and trouble, to reassure her that no matter what, I was doing OK. More, I wanted to show her I was doing wonderfully. I was pleased when I could bring an honor home, whether it was a "100" on my spelling paper, a prize for an essay on the United Nations, or a report card full of A's. From some deep inner place that had no connection with how often she told me she was proud of me, I felt that nothing I could do was ever enough. A Summa might be, though, I thought. To march with the other Summas past my mother, who would have driven all the way from Ames, Iowa, to let her see the culmination of her years of care and effort, to be crowned with the highest academic honor Smith could offer: surely that would be enough.

Spring in Northampton was warm and languorous. As February

melted into March, and March drifted into April, I hoped the inviting spring weather would mask the tumult I felt inside. May would bring the Honors comps, and then graduation. By early spring I knew that I would be continuing in school, entering a graduate program at Berkeley in the fall. Now, at the end of my college career, Smith had become a small, secure world which I was uneasy about having to leave. I remembered how hard it had been to part from Ames and how strange and frightening the East had seemed. I knew no one in Berkeley. I'd never been there. Unlike my arrival at Smith, no Big Sister would be waiting for me. Sophie talked of going to law school at Berkeley, but she wasn't sure. Perhaps even more than at Smith, competition would be fierce: women from all the other schools I'd been taught to admire — Radcliffe, Wellesley, Vassar — and men from Harvard, Yale, Dartmouth. How would I survive? In the back of my mind was the secret thought, one which I scarcely admitted, that at least I would probably enter Berkeley with the security of a Summa Cum Laude. Armed with that assurance, I could make my way.

Back and forth my moods swung that spring, as uncertain as the succession of sunny, gloriously green days and the sudden squalls of cold and damp. Much of being a senior was fun. Since Honors students were excused from the regular final exams in their senior spring courses in order to prepare for the three days of comps, we did not have to work very hard in our classes after midterms. Early in March, at an all-college assembly, seniors were given their graduating caps and gowns. For a modest rental fee, we could keep them until Commencement, and seniors traditionally wore their gowns whenever possible, as trenchcoats, jackets, coveralls, and bathrobes. Even in conservative Lawrence House, a senior could come down to breakfast in her pajamas, otherwise forbidden, if she was wearing her academic robe. I reveled in my black gown. Loose, insouciant, it billowed behind me as I swung across campus, signaling everyone that I was a graduating senior. Soon I would sail into life with a whoosh. From a distance I could spot other seniors flapping their way between classrooms and houses. Though I barely knew most seniors who were not in my house or major, I felt friendly toward them now.

Some mornings I joined my roommate Sophie, or Chris Morgan,

or a few other friends, for coffee in the Alumnae House. An elegant white Colonial building, it was just past the campus proper and ordinarily off-limits to students, until the spring of senior year. Then, in an attempt to woo us into the active Alumnae Association, the Alumnae House administration threw open its doors each morning, providing free coffee and doughnuts to seniors. Inside the cool, spacious rooms we balanced our china cups, chatted in low tones, and smiled at other seniors whom we didn't know. Occasionally I would hear one of them put her cup down firmly, announce that she had to get back to the library to study for comps, and leave. Then I felt an unpleasant sensation in my stomach and quickly left too. Outside, the glowing sun added to the deceptive air of morning leisure. Spring, sunshine, coffee, doughnuts: but I knew the library was waiting.

Although I saw little of the off-campus world, in spring the sloping lawns, ancient spreading trees, and gracefully scattered shrubs made the Smith grounds seem like a flowering private park. Camped with my notes beneath a clump of white lilacs, I breathed in the rich fruity fragrance while I tried to review my blue-penned synopses of the major Shakespearean tragedies. Everything seemed unreal, both the balmy spring and the compulsively neat notes, the wildly luxuriant lilacs and the cold fear that kept me turning pages. As April swept on, I felt I was part of that urgent, relentless rush toward summer. I wanted to ride the flood into May, and yet I wanted to hold it back.

As the weeks dwindled toward the Honors exams, I became numbly philosophical. Either I would do well, or I wouldn't. Chances were I would. I had looked at past tests on file in the library, and I could answer most of those questions. After all, we would have choices. I would be able to study on the two in-between days that separated the three exams. I would certainly be able to write something on Restoration drama or seventeenth-century prose, and I could stumble through the rest with a bit of luck. I could define terms, and reorient the questions to what I knew. Four hours weren't really so long, if I took a break in the middle to get a drink of water. I could do it, of course I could do it.

Suddenly, unimaginably, the week of comps arrived. I was almost glad. I had stopped retaining my crammed notes, I was sick of thumbing through books, I wanted the whole damned thing to be over with. I was not sure I could have held out much longer. The first day was not too bad. Gathered into the rare-book room of the library, we English Honors students eyed each other, then took our arranged seats at the long shiny library tables. High leaded windows above us reminded me that outside the sun was shining, crab apples were dropping their white blossoms, and other students were walking, laughing, and talking together. Inside this ominously quiet room the air was heavy with unspoken pressures, and all I could hear was the quick flap of a turning page, the scratch of a pen, the muffled thud of a chair being pushed back. The questions were not as obscure as I had feared, and, with a heartfelt prayer of thanksgiving, I saw that one passage for identification was actually taken from Sir Thomas Browne. Although my hand trembled, and I sometimes had trouble organizing my essays, I wrote steadily for four hours, standing once or twice to stretch, and handed in my booklets with the feeling that probably I had done all right.

All I had to do was last four more days. "One down, two to go," one of my friends, a junior, caroled at me when I sank into my chair at lunch. I wished I were more hungry. Next day, both worn out and let down, I began to feel funny. I did not know then that I sometimes had migraine headaches; I was aware that I seemed to get "flu" more often than most of my friends, especially a kind of feverish sickness that carried with it a pounding headache and violent nausea. It lasted a day or two and then disappeared. By the morning of the following day, when I had to leave for my second exam, my head was throbbing badly. I don't remember much about the exam, except that I plodded through it, doggedly and without inspiration. That night, in an effort to shake the miasma that had now settled over my brain, I went with two younger friends to a movie. I didn't want to talk to any other seniors. Despite the movie, I slept badly, head pulsating, vague nightmares washing across a luridly lit screen just behind my eyes.

The morning of the third and last exam, I wondered about going to the infirmary, reporting sick, and postponing the test. But that seemed cowardly. All I had was a bad case of nerves, I told myself, nerves and fatigue. Besides, if I didn't have a fever, which I probably didn't, the doctors would just assume that I was trying to get out of my comps. I decided to take two more aspirin, grit my teeth, and march out the door.

It was a long morning. As I sat, rubbing my head, waiting for the notebooks and test to be distributed, I carefully lined up in front of me a small collection of emergency aids: aspirin, Alka-Seltzer, chewing gum, Kleenex. They looked reassuring. But nothing distracted me from the increasing pressure in my temple. As my head hurt more heavily, my stomach began to heave. Several times I left the room, hoping I'd manage to throw up. I didn't. One of the few clear memories I have of that morning is standing inside a toilet stall, telling myself I only had another hour and a half to go and thinking it was forever.

When the exam was over, seniors were tossing notebooks in the air, hugging each other, and exchanging eager comparisons about test questions. I didn't want to talk to anyone. Back in my dorm, I lay on my bed, drained and deadened, waiting for my headache to subside. I knew I had not done well. I could only hope that the professors who read my paper might grade generously; sometimes when I thought I'd badly erred, I had in fact done just fine.

The remaining days between comps and graduation ticked by. I had looked forward to this hiatus as my first real vacation, a time to be freed from the fears and pressures that had assailed me for four years. But my mood of drained depression lingered. Some sunny afternoons I took long, aimless walks, passing through the flower beds of the botanical gardens or watching the sun glinting on Paradise Pond. I had seldom taken time during my years at Smith to savor its landscape. Now I sat on the banks of the pond and stared at the boathouse, its glossy varnished canoes on the same racks I had seen that first September. Two years ago I'd taken a canoeing class there; yet it still seemed private, a clubhouse to which I didn't belong. Smith held secrets, I thought as I admired from across some remote gulf the orchids in the conservatory, the flamboyant rows of creamy roses in the gardens, the rich carpet of grass edging the pond. I would never know what they were.

Most afternoons I returned to my room to pack. All my clothes, books, and papers had to be shipped home to Iowa, there to be sorted and repacked for my trip to Berkeley. Part of my depression lifted as I methodically stacked and fitted piles of books into cartons small enough for the post office to handle. As I wrapped each package with brown paper, tying it tenderly as if it were a gift, I felt relieved. But at night I would be daunted by how little I seemed to have done. Would I ever clear this room out? Books, folders, jumbled sweaters, a dresser full of socks and underpants and pajamas, a favorite coffee mug, a portable radio: now my nightmares were of heaped possessions, overflowing their boxes and drawers, burying me. Would I have to stay after graduation, desperately packing on a deserted campus, while my mother and stepfather waited in their car? Nothing any longer seemed within my control.

Listening as I was to these inner voices, I at least did not hear Chris Morgan and others talking about Magnas and Summas. Seniors now had other things to think about, some of them taking regular exams and others just basking in the sun and smoking cigarettes on the lawns. A kind of hush had descended even over Chris, who was busy trying to wind up her affairs and arrange accommodations for her relatives. No one knew when the news about Honors would be announced. I waited, with some dread, but not without hope.

One morning I saw a small white envelope, unstamped, lying alone in my mailbox. I knew what it was. Glancing quickly around to make sure no one saw me, I ripped it open. Did it say "Congratulations," or "We are pleased to tell you," or "You have been awarded . . . "? Perhaps. All I saw was the phrase, "Magna Cum Laude."

I stood for a few moments with the envelope in my hand. Almost immediately, as if she had known instantly what had happened, my roommate, Sophie, appeared. She too had been given a Magna, but although she was pleased, she tactfully turned aside my congratulations. Upstairs, a few minutes later, in the privacy of our two connecting rooms, I let her put her arm around me. That noon, feeling I could not face what I was sure would be the pitying glances of the other girls, I went out with another friend to get a hamburger. She tried to comfort me, and I tried not to show her how much it mattered. Late that night as I lay in bed sobs welled up, but they did not make me feel better. I did not think anything could make me feel better.

"For God's sake, it was only a meaningless Latin phrase," another voice, scolding and sensible, has often since said to me. "You act as though it were the end of the world. People dying of starvation and torture and disease, and you still carry on about a stupid Honors degree." The voice is, of course, right, but also, like most sensible voices, partly wrong. For me, it *was* the end of my world, one that had enclosed me ever since I had grown up, nurtured and cosseted, in a small Iowa town. Rightly or wrongly, I knew I was no longer a golden girl. Something had happened to Sue Allen from Ames, Iowa, of whom much had been expected and to whom much, I felt, had been promised.

A few days still remained until my mother and stepfather would arrive from Ames for Commencement. Dazed and tired, I listened to Sophie when she urged me to get away, leave campus, forget things for a while. She and I had been invited, with Chris Morgan, to our friend Amanda's remote Vermont country home. "Come on, Sue, it'll do you good. Amanda really wants you. And I'll be there so you won't have to talk all that much to Chris," Sophie said encouragingly. Vermont in May was New England at its most endearing, green mountains rising into newly washed blue skies. Amanda's parents were welcoming, her house homey and comfortable. Yet those few days seemed interminable. Still dragging the dull weight of my failure, I did not want to follow Sophie or Amanda on their long walks, but even less did I want to stay behind reading a book in the same room with Chris. Not that Chris wanted to talk about comps, or honors. Within an hour after I had opened my white envelope, she had called. "Well? Did you hear yet?" she'd asked eagerly. When I had told her, she had fallen silent, not knowing what to say, It was the first time I had heard Chris at a loss for words. She, of course, had gotten a Summa.

The last night before we left to return for Commencement festivities, Sophie sat at the foot of my bed. I had lain there all afternoon, trying to nap, and Sophie wanted to know what was wrong. "I don't know what happened, Sophie," I said haltingly. "Even if I didn't do as well on that last exam, wouldn't everything else have balanced it out? Why didn't I get a Summa anyway?"

"Maybe they made a mistake," Sophie said. "You know, it's possible. Why don't you find out? You could call Mr. Slater —isn't he the head of the English Honors program? He wrote you a recommendation, and I'm sure he likes you. He might tell you what happened."

Back on campus, I took her advice. Although all I said was that I wanted the chance to talk with him, Mr. Slater sounded a little strained over the phone. He asked me to stop by his home that afternoon. Seated in his formal living room, I thought perhaps I should not have come. Our interview was short. "I'm sorry, Susan," Mr. Slater said. He was reserved, gray-haired, close to retirement. Though not unkind, he had a hard time eschewing his usual studied rhetoric. "Your first exam was a Summa, and the second a Magna. But alas," and here he imperceptibly paused, "the third day you only achieved a Pass." I gasped. That was a grade below "Cum" and almost equivalent to a D. If you got a Pass on your Honors thesis, you didn't graduate with Honors at all. You were considered fortunate just to get a degree. "I am terribly sorry," Mr. Slater said again. "I don't know what happened. We were all quite surprised. Quite surprised." He looked puzzled, as if waiting for an explanation. I had none to give. I tried to smile, made some polite noises, and headed for the door as quickly as I could.

When my parents arrived, they were happy to be in Northampton and proud of my approaching graduation. Mrs. Stevens, the Lawrence housemother, told them what a credit I had been to the house. Miss Bailey, Head of Scholarships and Student Aid, squeezed my mother's hand and said how much she would miss me. For a few moments at a parents' reception I managed to corner President Mendenhall, who clapped me on the shoulder and said to my parents, "Well done. Well done." My mother tsk-tsked sympathetically when I told her about the comprehensives, but she clearly had no sense of the magnitude of my disappointment. I did not know how to tell her, and besides, I did not really want her to know. And as the whirl of Commencement activities caught me up, sometimes I forgot for hours at a time. I chatted as a sudden near-equal with Mrs. Stevens about my future plans. I ate lobster and Indian pudding with my parents, Sophie, and her parents, at

Wiggins Tavern, crowded with other visiting parents. Dressed in my Smith ceremonial uniform, a white dress, I marched in the Ivy Day Parade with the other white-clad seniors, each of us carrying a long-stemmed red rose. My steamer trunk shipped and all my packages miraculously mailed, I jammed everything else into my one remaining suitcase. The room was bare, stripped to its institutional dark wooden furniture, its scuffed floor clear of boxes, lamp, spare bookcase. As I looked around it, I felt both alienation and relief. I was at last ready to go.

The night before Commencement, the college strung colored Japanese lanterns among the cascading trees on the central campus. Dressed in white, alumnae of all ages floated by in the dark, serenading each other, as well as the president, who sat enthroned on the steps of the library. Even the president wore a white suit. Wandering with my parents under the colored lights, listening to the songs rising and falling in the warm May night, I almost didn't know where I was. This enchanted enclosure was part of the same precincts as the varnished, secret boathouse, the velvety banks of Paradise Pond, or the luxuriant orchids in the college conservatory. Tonight I had at last been briefly admitted to it, perhaps only because I was about to leave.

Next day, at Commencement, I lined up with the other Magnas and marched down the outdoor aisle in the open Quadrangle. The ceremonies were what I had expected, impressive but a bit dull. I tried not to feel bitter as I looked at the groupings in the heavy parchment program. There it was, in black and white, for everyone to see: "Summa Cum Laude." A few names, including Chris Morgan's. "Magna Cum Laude." My name. "Cum Laude." After a few names, I saw the word, "Pass." It made me shiver. Then the long list of the other seniors, graduating without special honors. Suddenly I was holding my diploma in my hand. After hurriedly packing my final things and exchanging hasty farewells, late that afternoon I climbed in the back seat of my parents' car for the long trip across country. Slowly but steadily, stopping here and there, we would return to the Midwest, carrying my confusion, regret, some satisfactions I tried to list over and over, and my apprehensions about the future.

As our car moved past the familiar outskirts of Northampton, and beyond the few landmarks I recognized near Springfield, I settled back, content to watch the changing landscape, listen to my parents' desultory conversation, and doze. As though I were a child again, knowing I would be taken care of, I relaxed into the rhythms of the journey. After a few hours had passed, Smith seemed as far as if it were across an ocean, a land where I had learned to speak a foreign language but which I had now left behind forever.

Late in the evening we stopped for dinner at a Howard Johnson's somewhere on the New York Thruway. All Howard Johnsons I had ever seen looked alike; I was still in a peaceful limbo as we walked past a row of booths toward some tables in the rear. Suddenly I heard a voice calling my name. "Sue! Hey, Sue Allen!" Shocked, I turned around. There a few feet away was another Smith girl, Judy Halvorson, who had also just graduated that day. She was a good friend of Chris Morgan's, and a girl who often sat at our table when I ate at Chris's dorm. But we were not close, and I did not care whether I ever saw her again. Now here she had appeared with her parents in a booth at Howard Johnson's, an unwelcome reminder of what I thought I had left behind me.

My parents paused, waiting for me to follow. I motioned them over, we exchanged introductions, and then my parents and I continued to our table. My tenuous sense of security had been shaken. Even here, I thought, was someone who knew me, someone who remembered my life at Smith, someone who might well be saying right now to her parents, "Too bad. We all expected her to graduate Summa today. But she didn't."

Hers was the last voice I remember hearing from my Commencement, and even that was probably imaginary. Judy Halvorson most likely turned back to her menu and ordered a hamburger with fries. Though old Smith friends have stayed in touch, my roommate Sophie calls occasionally, and college acquaintances pop up in bookstores and airports, none pulls me back to that small obsessive space into which I had withdrawn the spring of my senior year.

Even Chris Morgan's voice is silent. Twelve years after graduation, following a long break in communication, she appeared on short notice in my Minneapolis home. Once thin and wiry, she was now plump and pasty-faced; too much beer, she admitted wryly, and asked for one, then a second. Beer was all she drank now, she said. She had recently been hospitalized for something she wasn't specific about, and she had had to give up mixed drinks. But beer was fine, and she soon went to the store for another six-pack. All evening we talked. Behind Chris's rapid, enthusiastic catalog of her flourishing career and extensive travels, her law practice, congressional contacts, friends and parties, I could hear something else. I did not know what it was then, and I am still not sure. It evaded my gentle probing until late that night, and many beers later, when Chris turned to me suddenly, with no smile and a quiet fervor, and said, "You know, Sue, my problem is that I had everything I ever wanted by the time I was twenty-eight. And now I'm thirty-five." That was all. Two years later, I read in the obituary column of our alumnae magazine that Chris Morgan had died of a liver ailment.

So no one from Smith, or indeed from anywhere I have lived or traveled, has ever shown the slightest interest in what degree of Honors she, or I, or anyone else received long ago. After that Commencement afternoon, I have not heard another voice mention "Summa."

Except, of course, my own.

Up, Up and Away 🌿

I HAD HOPED it wouldn't still be so beautiful. Standing on the corner of Fillmore and Broadway, I looked past the creamy whites and soft pastels of the Victorian houses, with their gaily colored flower boxes and front gardens, down the steep hill to the blazing blue of San Francisco Bay. Once I had thought Smith was far behind me; then, after graduate school, I thought I had also left the Bay, never to return. Now, twenty years later, I was back in San Francisco, remembering the young college graduate who had brought her dreams here from the East. On this June morning, the sun had burned away yesterday's fog, and the air was cool and clear. Below us dozens of sailboats dotted the bay like white birds, fluttering and skimming across the waves. Beyond the boats Alcatraz and Angel Island hovered in the water, looking remote and mysterious. Behind us someone opened her front door, and for a moment I could hear the sounds of Chopin on a piano, before the door closed again, a woman in silk shirt and jeans slid into her Porsche, and the car disappeared around the corner.

"You see?" I said, turning to Jennifer. "This is what I meant. This is how I've always pictured it. This is what it was like. Imagine me arriving here from Northampton, where I'd been so closed in, and finding myself one day at the top of a hill just like this."

"Do you wish you had stayed here, Mom?" Jennifer asked, posing as she often does a perceptive but painful question.

"I don't know," I said to my daughter. "Of course, I couldn't stay, because

I married your father and he got a job in Minnesota. But I'm not sure what I'd be doing now if I had stayed. Or who I'd be. Or whether you'd be here at all. That would have been awful." We looked at each other and smiled. But as we walked on, admiring houses and glancing in windows, I kept trying to answer her question for myself. It was one that had haunted me for years, not only with San Francisco as a background, but with some of the other places I'd lived or paused or even just passed through. Who would I have been if I'd returned to that quiet Maine fishing village where a friend and I once spent twenty-four hours? Could I have lived there in a faded clapboard house, raising my own vegetables and taking in lodgers? Would I have become more tranquil, more contented? And who would I have been if I had settled into an Iowa college town like the one I'd known as a child? Or if I'd gone to graduate school in Boston, found an apartment in Cambridge, pursued a career in publishing there?

Now, standing on that sunny San Francisco street corner with my daughter, I remembered how I had once seen the whole Bay area in a golden haze of possibilities. Arriving in Berkeley for graduate school, I was ready for a new life and a new identity. For my first sixteen years, I had been "Sue Allen from Ames, Iowa." That was how I introduced myself when I got off the Boston & Maine commuter train in Northampton, Massachusetts. When I was at Smith, I had become for four years a "Smithie," a word I regarded ambivalently, disliking its intimations of glossy superficiality and secretly cherishing its undeniable elitism. I had been born into Ames, Iowa; but I felt I had been chosen for Smith. So although I still thought of myself as an Ames girl, I had added Smith as one might don, carefully, a heavy velvet traveling cloak: substantial, luxurious, and distinctive. Once I had left Ames, people asked me, "Where are you from?" and then, for some years after college graduation, "Where did you go to school?" My answers seemed like logical coordinates on which to locate my position: I was from Ames, and now I was from Smith.

At first, Berkeley seemed like a logical continuation of Smith. A high-powered university naturally succeeded an elitist college. Only gradually did I begin to realize that Berkeley was both an end and a different beginning. For four years at Smith, I had anticipated what might happen when I emerged into what commencement speakers called "the real world." I wasn't sure what "the real world" was. I thought it was a place where one worked, developed a career, loved, married, had children. Smith hadn't taught me much about those choices. I decided to try to postpone all of it by entering a Ph.D. program in English. "Where should I go?" I asked my revered professor

Ralph Abernathy. "Yale," he said. "Best program in American literature."
"No," I said timidly. "I want someplace different, not in the East, with a
city, and men."
"Oh, then Berkeley, of course," he nodded. "Henry Nash Smith is out there
now. It's a good department. You won't go wrong at Berkeley." I went back to
my room and sent for an application.

But Berkeley turned out to be only a temporary answer. One spring morning
in my first year there, I sat in the International House coffee shop with my
college roommate Sophie, who had become a law student at Boalt, and her
current boyfriend, Josh. Two years younger than Sophie, Josh was a one-year
transfer student from Chapel Hill, but his far-ranging intelligence and articu-
late conversation had won him an equal place among older grad students. Although I was already in love with Larry, the man I was to marry, I adored
Josh. He and I sometimes linked arms and skipped along the sidewalk, singing nonsense songs, or trying to remember all the words to "Jabberwocky."
Josh also knew how to ask hard questions, and this morning he was probing
Sophie and me about our futures.

As we sipped our coffee, I could look through the front windows all the way
down the hill, past the university buildings, and beyond to the Bay. In the
distance the early sun lit up the white and pastel stucco of San Francisco so
that the whole city seemed to shine, sparkling above the blue water, a fairy-
tale island surrounded by a crystalline moat. I was going to cut my classes
today and take the bus into the city. On such a glorious morning, who could
study? But Josh kept insisting on answers to his questions. Did I really think
it was worth while to do advanced work in English literature? What connection did it have to anything? After the M.A. exam next year, was I going to
continue at Berkeley? I hedged, not wanting to think about my answers too
deeply, and drank my coffee. The sun was warm, the city blinked and glit-
tered, and I was happy.

"And then what?" Josh asked.

"What do you mean?" I asked in return, realizing I hadn't been listening
very closely.

"I mean, after you get your Ph.D.? In four years, or whatever? What will
you do then? Where will you go?"

"I suppose to some college to teach, maybe back East," I said uneasily. I
couldn't imagine myself all alone, heading to a strange city. Coming to Berkeley, I'd had Sophie.

"Yes, but then what?" Josh persisted. I looked dumbly at him. His question terrified me. All I could see in response was a blank white space. Or was

it a long dark tunnel? I hated not knowing what was ahead. I looked again out the window at San Francisco. Did it hold my answers? What did it promise, as it winked and beckoned? What did I see in those shining lights that I wanted?

"And then what?" Josh said again. I shook my head.

"And then what?" was a question I had already vainly asked myself during my four years at Smith. I knew that during college I was supposed to decide what I was going to do with the rest of my life. I thought it was a decision I would make only once, a definitive gesture embracing the next fifty years. Yet I could hardly imagine even becoming twenty-one. "And what will you do after graduation?" old family friends asked politely. I murmured something about graduate school, which seemed to satisfy them. "And then I suppose you'll be getting married," they usually added, smiling, the women fondly, the men derisively. I protested, vigorously denied any such intention, and thought of course I would. When I was a senior in high school, Miss McNally, a farseeing English teacher, asked us to write a paragraph describing what we wanted from life. "I will graduate from college, become a foreign correspondent, get married at twenty-eight, have two children before I'm thirty, and then relax and enjoy life, probably working part-time on a big-city paper," I wrote. In college those did not appear, in outline, to be unreasonable goals.

When I came to Smith, my ambitions had new scope. Around me, female professors offered the challenge of their own dedicated lives. Names of illustrious alumnae were invoked in classrooms, all-college assemblies, and commencement ceremonies; every year some were awarded college medals or honorary degrees. Smith women were everywhere, it seemed, doing all kinds of things. We students presumed we were heading into promising futures. Perhaps that is why one Lawrence friend said to me at our house reunion twenty-two years later, "I was afraid to come back, because I really haven't done much." She had raised two children alone, returned to school for an advanced degreee, taught in an inner-city school, and now held a new and challenging job in a lab. But, comparing herself to what she thought Smith had expected of her, she felt that wasn't much.

What made us talk briefly that reunion night about noted Smith alumnae? Was it years of reading the college magazine, which flagged its public figures in every issue? Was it fearful self-comparison? Did we keep an eye out for Smith alumnae in the news so we could share vicariously in their success? We knew, it turned out, who most of the famous Smith graduates were. What, someone asked, did Julia Child, Sylvia Plath, Madeleine L'Engle, Meg Greenfield, and Gloria Steinem have in common? Someone else mentioned Nancy Reagan and Julie Eisenhower, and the rest of the dinner table groaned. "They're only famous," another woman said firmly. "They haven't really *done* anything." There was a moment's silence at the table, as if each of us was instantaneously assessing what *she* had done. I suddenly remembered the life plan I had drawn for Miss McNally. Whatever I had done had certainly been different from my plan. A broken marriage; only one child; nothing to do with newspapers or foreign correspondents at all. As for "relaxing" at thirty, as if life were over then — I smiled to myself. Then I thought about Miss McNally, only recently retired. What had she thought, year after year, as she examined her students' dreams, knowing how seldom lives fit into preconceived plans? In the margin of my paragraph she had written, heateningly, "I think you'll do it, Susan!" Did she ever wonder?

At least my vision of becoming a foreign correspondent, though quickly abandoned at Smith, fitted into the pattern there. Smith women were literally, as well as figuratively, supposed to go places. Many took Smith's Junior Year Abroad, usually to Geneva or Paris. Although foreign travel was still rare in my home town of Ames in the 1950s, girls at Smith planned to get abroad sooner or later. It was a question of when, not if. Should one spend a junior year in Florence, or apply for a Fulbright, or join the Experiment in International Living?

While waiting to get to Europe, Smith girls explored Boston and New York. Although I seldom left the campus, I heard enough tales about bohemian parties in the Village, roast beef and Indian pudding at Durgin Park, the Upper East Side and the Square, the Met and the Brattle, the New York New Haven & Hartford and the Mass Pike, so that I felt both cities beckoned just beyond my doorstep. After graduation, many girls "went to New York"; it was a vocation in itself. There they found apartments, jobs, parties, and men. I assumed they lived happy young lives ever after; I couldn't imagine anyone aging in New York.

Like a constant current of wind, sometimes blowing in small puffs, and sometimes gusting in dizzying spirals, I sensed at Smith that we were all upward bound, wafted by our training, the hopes others had for us, and the hopes we had for ourselves. In the air was a feeling I later heard expressed in a song of the sixties: "Up, Up and Away," sang the Fifth Dimension, soaring in their beautiful balloon, their voices part of the new sounds I was hearing by the end of my stay at Smith. "We can fly! We can fly!"

We could indeed fly. Although I began college by taking long-distance trains, two days out and two days back, by the time I was a junior, planes flew regularly into Des Moines from the Springfield/Hartford airport, with fares not much higher than trains'. For spring vacation my junior year, my mother sent me a plane ticket home. I had never been on an airplane before. Tremulous, I was glad to find myself sitting next to Lolly Turnbull, who was an old hand at flying. As we taxied down the runway, I held my breath. But as the plane suddenly revved its motors and roared into a burst of speed that lofted it into the air, Lolly grinned widely and pressed her foot hard against the floor. "I love this part!" she said excitedly, above the noise of the engines. "It's just like stepping on the gas! Wow!" For a moment I felt that Lolly, her delicate foot forceful on the pedal, was driving the plane and urging it upward. Her face was lit with exhilaration. The ground fell away, and I saw the tilted wings carrying us into the sky. I could fly! I could fly! Looking into the fluffy white clouds, I too was soaring free. When the plane touched down in Iowa just a few hours later, I could hardly believe I was already there. I thought of long nights of sitting up on the train, trying to cradle myself against the raspy wool seat, and long days reading and napping. Now I knew how to surmount time and boredom. I had flown away from Smith once; I could do it again. The world was out there, just waiting for me to get on a plane. Up, up, and away!

But when I finally got to Boston, I arrived on a bus. From the time I came to Smith, I was headed for Boston. When I read in high school about America's literary heritage, I focused on New

England: Hawthorne, not Willa Cather; Thoreau, not Sinclair Lewis; Millay, not Edgar Lee Masters. In high-school history, I learned that Boston was where America had started; I had once waded across the springs of the Mississippi at Lake Itasca, and now I wanted to see the beginning of the Revolution at Boston Harbor.

As I debated my selection of a college, my mother urged Radcliffe and I leaned toward Smith. Although I wanted to be close to Boston — and on the map, Northampton seemed close — I was afraid of leaping right into it. I did not want to live in a big city. I was not even comfortable in Des Moines. So I settled on Smith, thinking that I could of course get to know Boston on weekends, day trips, vacations.

Once rooted in Northampton, however, I found Boston impossibly far away. I seldom had a weekend free from the pressures of tests and papers, or the subtler pressures of social life. When did I first see Boston? Was it my freshman year when I went to visit a friend at Radcliffe, stayed in her dorm, and ventured down a few of the streets around Harvard Square? Was it my sophomore year when Sophie and I took a two-hour, bumpy bus ride, spent a night in the Y.W.C.A., and window-shopped among the expensive shoe stores and dress shops on Boylston Street? On one of my two or three trips in those freshman and sophomore years, I rode the M.T.A., sampled German sausages in a dark beer-washed cellar, and walked in awe through the Museum of Fine Arts. I loved it all.

Most of all, I reveled in Filene's basement. My freshman roommate, Alice, from Framingham, had told me about Filene's, a landmark as notable as the Old North Church. Already an obsessive bargain-hunter from my early days of allowance-stretching, I had practiced my skills only in the relatively small confines of Des Moines' Younkers. Once I walked down the steep basement stairs into Filene's acres of bargains, my horizons suddenly expanded. As I wandered from bin to bin, tantalized by torn-out labels I couldn't quite decipher, I felt as if the inexhaustible wealth and resources of a glamorous city had been culled here for my personal advantage. If I didn't feel at home on the streets of Boston, here I was an experienced hand. I snatched a crumpled blouse from another shopper's reach, and jostled my way to the mirror. Identifying it with Boston, I took Filene's to my heart.

These brief excursions into the Big City whetted my appetite for more. During my sophomore year, I began to think about the possibility of spending a summer there. Shouldn't I get some job experience besides my internship at the *Ames Daily Tribune*? Could I justify the expense of a shared apartment in Boston by some kind of work in publishing? Miss Bailey, Head of Scholarships and Student Aid, agreed that I could; she would waive the requirement that I earn at least $300 during the summer toward my college expenses. Soon my friend Molly O'Brien and I began talking about living together in Boston. When Molly's best friend, Katie Hill, heard about it, she immediately decided she wanted to join us. With uncertain expectations, we all began sending out job applications, I in publishing, Molly in art-related fields, Katie in summer teaching. To our surprise, we all succeeded. Smith, Katie said, sometimes paid off. Although *The Atlantic,* Houghton Mifflin, Little, Brown, and the Boston *Globe* decided they didn't want me, the *Harvard Business Review* invited me for an interview. Would I like to serve as a vacation replacement, partly in subscriptions and circulation, partly in editorial, wherever they were shorthanded? I would indeed. Did I like Smith? I did. Did I know Art Simpkins, the college business manager, who had been the editor's best man? Sort of. Had I ever met the editor's son, Jack, who was a freshman at Amherst? I hadn't. But I was eager and anxious to please. I mentioned the thrill of learning about publishing by working on a Harvard magazine. I was hired.

On the weekend of the interview, Molly and I looked for a place to live. Following ads, and our strict budget, we fled from several tiny, dirty cells and finally decided, with exhausted relief, to sublease a largish one-bedroom, first-floor apartment on a dead-end street, just barely walking distance from Harvard Square. I ignored the musty smells from the alley. Molly said we could manage with the stove, whose oven didn't work, and the refrigerator that had to be defrosted every week. The tenants, three young men, said we could use their furniture, two beds and a sleeper sofa, but we would have to bring our own towels. We thought Katie's mother could send some from Marblehead. Everything looked perfect. I could walk to the Business School and its *Review.* Molly and Katie would both take the M.T.A. to downtown Boston.

Cambridge, we thought, offered more opportunities than Boston to meet people. People meant Harvard men.

Although I was apologetic about abandoning my mother in Ames, she promised to try to come to Boston to visit. As June approached, I longed for the freedom and promise ahead: my own apartment, a job, Life In The City. Even now the anticipation seems more real in my memory than the summer itself. The weeks passed so quickly, and everything took more time than we expected. First we had to get settled, locating grocery stores and wine shops, bank, bakery, laundromat. Then we cleaned, airing the dampish mattresses and scrubbing the greasy stove and kitchen cupboards. Meanwhile we also worked, leaving before eight — Katie, who had farthest to travel, had to be out the door by seven — and not returning till past five. Once home, someone had to make dinner, someone else did the dishes, and the evening was almost gone. The summer nights were hot and humid. The smell of garbage settled through the back windows, as I tossed and turned on my bed, waiting for a bit of breeze. I fell asleep to shouts in the street behind, a clattering and clinking of bottles, cans, and garbage-can lids.

Never having shared housekeeping with anyone, I wasn't prepared to find it so tricky. We all had different standards of neatness, competing preferences for where we wanted to sleep, even disagreements about whether we should eat in the kitchen or the living room. Afraid of confrontation, we hinted our distrust. Did Molly spend too much of the food budget on ice cream? Did I deliberately forget Katie's favorite brand of catsup? Should Katie turn off her alarm before it woke the rest of us? Why did Katie and Molly sometimes whisper in the front room?

I never saw much of Boston. I intended to visit the Isabella Stewart Gardner Museum, where Molly worked. I kept planning to tour "Old Ironsides," see the Statehouse, feed the ducks in the Public Garden. But I never did. I think I only got to Filene's three times. Once Tony, an inarticulate but good-natured young man who lived above us and worked nights at the Gillette factory, offered all three of us a ride in his sports car on his night off. We took turns straddling the gearshift and crouching sideways in the back seat. Whizzing out of town, Tony shouted a commentary as we passed various stadiums, factories, and turnoffs to other towns. At my request, we headed to Concord, where I wanted to see Walden Pond. When we got there, everyone waited while I walked along the shore for a short distance, kicking at the gum wrappers and empty Coke bottles that littered the swimming beach. It was impossible to imagine Thoreau even as a ghost here. Soon Tony revved his motor. It was late, and we had to be up early for work the next day.

During my days at the *Business Review,* I told myself I was learning about publishing. First I sat at a desk in Circulation, where I opened envelopes, sorted checks, tallied new subscriptions, and once in a while laboriously typed a form letter to dissatisfied customers. The circulation manager, Marty Donalds, jumpy and short-tempered, spent a lot of time on the phone talking in low tones. Sometimes I could hear the words "New York," and I gathered Marty felt he was in exile here. Every day he came to work with what I thought was a Madison Avenue look, a gray well-tailored suit and pale colored shirts, but with a rumpled tie that never quite lay flat and spoiled the effect. From time to time Marty would come and stand behind my desk, drumming his fingers on the chair back, while he watched me slit envelopes and stack checks. "Fine, fine," he'd say. "Any problems this morning?" I shook my head. He sighed and went out to lunch.

Although I looked forward to moving upstairs to Editorial, my post there wasn't much more interesting than Circulation. To my surprise, "editing" did not consist of talking to authors or rewriting parts of manuscripts. Since I scarcely understood most *Review* articles anyway, it was probably just as well that my main "editorial" work was proofreading galleys. Now, however, I had a desk between the two editorial assistants, both attractive single women in their early twenties, whose easygoing talk and confidences to each other were more intriguing than Marty Donalds' telephone calls. When the editor, Sheridan Stanhope, strode through their office, Annie and Dot bent over their desks. But often they leaned back in their swivel chairs and exchanged stories about dates, friends, and arguments with their parents. I joined in with a few questions. Once Annie looked at me and said to Dot, "God, she's so young. Were we ever that young?" Annie was twenty-four; I was nineteen.

I blushed, but I felt accepted. For a while I studied Annie and Dot as possible models for "career women," but they didn't quite fit my ideals. Both of them saw the *Review* as what Annie, who was almost engaged to an airline pilot, called a "holding pattern." "Listen, if you're bored now, imagine what it's like reading this stuff all year," said Dot to me comfortingly one afternoon, when my desk was piled with statistical galleys. "Remember, sweetie, this magazine isn't *supposed* to be literature."

Walking home from the *Review* office in late afternoon, I could hear the sounds of rush-hour traffic in the distance, the city coming alive and hurrying home. When it was my turn to market, I detoured through Harvard Square, where I never tired of watching people swirling past me, aristocratic men with umbrellas and briefcases, bearded wanderers, women loaded with parcels, or long-haired girls my own age carrying green Harvard bookbags. I paused at bookstores, studied prints and posters in shop windows, admired the thonged sandals at a shoemaker's where someone was always visible behind the dingy plate glass, seated at a small table with a companion, playing a never-ending game of chess.

As the summer advanced Molly, Katie, and I admitted that although our jobs were all right, and our apartment was satisfactory, we had not done well at meeting men. Making our plans that spring, we had anticipated many possibilities: "I can look up Peter Schwartz, an old friend from high school," or "Sally says she'll give our number to Doug," or "Clark may be at Harvard summer school for six weeks." But none of these contacts ever materialized. We couldn't find anyone willing to become escorts, basic transportation, or safe conduct into the Boston nights, let alone dates. Tony didn't have many evenings off. Most of the time we were stuck at home. Once I had a drink after work with an older foreign student at M.I.T., a friend of a friend; he was small, dark, and voluble, and although I struggled with his broken English, I liked him. Next night he showed up at our apartment, this time with three other foreign students, whose English was even worse. Katie took one look and disappeared into the kitchen, where a buddy of hers in town from Marblehead, Doug-O, was having a cup of coffee. To Katie, all men had "O" attached: Bobbo, Hanko, Wayne-O. In the front room I tried to carry on a conversation. My guests were willing but understandably inarticulate. We all laughed a lot. After a while Doug-O appeared in the doorway. "Can I see you a minute, Susan?" he asked abruptly, ignoring the men crowded on our one sofa and floor. Excusing myself, I walked into the kitchen, where Doug-O shut the door. Katie looked down at the table. "Katie told me that these guys might be making a nuisance of themselves," he said in what he meant to be a brotherly tone. "Do you want me to get rid of them?" I looked at him in disbelief. Katie didn't say anything. With a loud "no," shaking my head, I went back to the living room. I wondered if my visitors had heard us. Conversation continued, but it was harder, and my laughter was strained. Eventually everyone left, Doug-O last of all. Although Katie and I didn't discuss her or my guests, the foreign students never came again.

So we agreed we needed to meet suitable men. There they were, all around us, walking down the Cambridge streets, in their olive drab summer suits, chino pants, button-down shirts. But we had no idea how to do it. Once Katie found out about a summer-school mixer, a late-afternoon ice-cream social, and left work a little early so she could slip into Harvard Yard, where it was being held. When she came home late for dinner, I was furious that she hadn't told Molly and me so we could go too. At least she hadn't met anyone. "Practically all girls," she said apologetically. At dinner that night I said we needed to brainstorm. Did Tony have any friends? Was there anyone we hadn't called yet? Who did we know at work? But none of my ideas were fruitful. Finally, taking matters into my own hands, I decided to haunt the source of supply itself. For many nights, before it got too dark, I left our apartment and walked to Widener Library. I liked being part of the Harvard crowd strolling through the twilight. The Yard was leafy and sheltered, a private enclave far removed from the bustling streets just outside. Walking up the long flight of stairs to the library, I felt as if I were entering an exclusive club.

Once inside the library, I tried to look both for interesting books and for interesting men. Mostly I focused on the men. One night, browsing in the stacks, I saw a vision. Seated at a dimly lit carrel was a young man, probably in his late twenties, fair-haired and broad-shouldered, with an aquiline nose and a strong chin. He was almost handsome without being pretty. He clearly went to Harvard. His horn-rimmed glasses added just the right note of studiousness, and his collar was unbuttoned, his sleeves rolled up, with casual self-confidence. Profoundly absorbed in his reading, he did not glance up as I wandered past him, even though I paused ostentatiously nearby and pretended to read part of a book on Thoreau. He looked mature, sensitive, full of character. Once I saw him smile at what he was reading.

For many nights I scrutinized the stacks in that corner of Widener, wishing I knew how to intrude into that blond young man's world. I decided he might be unattached. He never left his carrel for coffee with anyone, and when we both departed at closing time one night, I saw him walk briskly toward one of the dormitories. Once he was smoking a cigarette on the library steps as I walked up. With a desperate courage, I stopped. "Pardon me, do you know how late the library is open tonight?" I asked.

He looked up at me, friendly but reserved. "Ten o'clock," he said.

"Thanks," I said in return, and walked past. Later that night, passing his carrel, I whispered, "Hello." Startled, he looked up, smiled after a moment, and then turned back to his book. Eventually, after riffling through more nearby scholarly dissertations on the New England Transcendentalists than I ever thought existed, I gave up. He was never going to notice me. Furious with fate, I started reading lurid novels in the periodical room. Although I had grown up with the ingrained refrain, "Some DAY Your PRINCE Will Come," I had never stopped to consider what would happen if he came, and I couldn't get him to talk to me. Now, of course, I am almost glad I never found out who he was, because I was never disappointed. If he was married, gay, dull, or narrow-minded, I will never need to know. Like the sandal shop with chess players, the ducks in the Public Garden, and the sausages in the Wursthaus, the picture of his bent blond head under the library lights remains part of my mythology of My Summer in Boston.

Suddenly it was time to go home. In fact, my life had taken an unexpected turn, so I left even sooner than I'd planned. While I had been dreaming of Harvard romances, my mother, twelve years a widow, had had one of her own. Having asked for a ride East with a shy bachelor colleague, she had fallen in love with Buell, and he with her. Although during her few days in Cambridge with me, she gave no signs of her attraction, I could tell she had had a lively trip. "On the first night at a motel, Buell marched up to the proprietor and announced, 'This woman is not my wife!' " she recounted, amused. "He wanted to explain why we needed separate rooms. He was worrying about my reputation!" A month later, she called from home. What would I think if she and Buell got married? I was stunned but pleased. I had worried about what would happen to Mother now that I was well on my way to being launched. I offered to quit my job three weeks early and fly home for the wedding. Sheridan Stanhope was at first somewhat disconcerted, but then he became quite paternal, wishing my mother good luck and walking me to the door and patting me on the shoulder as I left his office. Now there was no time to see any more of Boston, no time for anything, no time even to make a last trip to Widener. Molly would have to return my books. I did my laundry, mailed my cartons, and packed my suitcases. On the day before I left, I paid a farewell visit to Filene's. I wanted to buy my mother something special. With odd feelings — I had never quite imagined my mother marrying again — I picked out a lacy, long nightgown, in a quiet blue, the kind I imagined a mature bride ought to have. "It's for my mother," I said to the bored clerk who stood behind the register, looking just over the customers' heads. "She's getting married." A powerful current of regret swept over me. I thought of my summer ending, of my leaving Boston, perhaps forever.

Of course I didn't really think it would be forever. Surely I would come back to Cambridge, perhaps for graduate school, maybe for a real job. Boston would be waiting for me, the men playing chess in the sandal shop, perhaps the Harvard student still working nights in his Widener carrel. But in fact I did not see Boston again for almost eight years. When I did, I found I did not belong there anymore. That return trip was perhaps the real conclusion to my summer in Boston.

Five years married the summer of my return, I knew that my marriage was not going well. I was also mired in the midst of a dissertation that spread around me like a never-ending marsh. Although I told my husband that I needed to do some research in a manuscript collection at Harvard, I really wanted to return to Boston and Cambridge for less communicable reasons. I wanted to affirm the existence of my earlier self, a frightened adventurer who nonetheless wanted to explore new lands, a girl whose world was just opening in front of her. For a few days, perhaps, I could become once more a Smithie at loose in the big city.

After we had spent a week with his family in Connecticut, Larry reluctantly agreed that I could go to Boston for three days. Aside from my visits to my mother, it was my first independent trip since our marriage. All by myself, I reserved a room at the Holiday Inn in Cambridge, where I thought I'd be on familiar ground near Harvard Square. When my commuter plane left Hartford, I looked happily down at the disappearing ground as I sipped my Manhattan. Three days of peace! I shivered with pleasure. For some reason, which I decided not to examine too closely, I had developed just that morning a painful small boil on my ring finger. I had never had one there before. On the plane, I carefully removed my engagement ring and placed it on my little finger, where it was too big but still fitted fairly securely. When we became engaged, Larry and I had shopped together for a ring. "I am going to spend a thousand dollars," Larry had said proudly. "I want my wife to have a ring she's not ashamed of." In 1963, a thousand dollars was half my year's graduate fellowship. I was impressed. Larry had to empty his bank account to afford the ring. For the first few years, we insured it, but just that spring, Larry had calculated the odds on my ever losing it, and we had dropped the coverage.

After leaving my suitcase at the Holiday Inn, I went with clipboard and paper to Houghton Library. There in a stuffy, hushed room, rare and old manuscripts were doled out to properly screened applicants. I felt quite professional as I sifted through letters, copying extracts in soft pencil, sometimes gazing around me at other preoccupied scholars. The room had none of the bustle of Widener. After an hour, I found I was having a hard time concentrating on my manuscripts. I wondered if, outside the library, beyond Cambridge, Boston had changed much. Hadn't I only just arrived? Wasn't I going to be here for another two full days? Couldn't I maybe sneak out for a while?

An hour later I was on the M.T.A., heading for Park Square. I hadn't forgotten how to take the subway. Once I'd emerged in downtown Boston, I soon found my way to Filene's basement. For half an hour I rummaged happily among purses, shoes, blouses, slips. Nothing had changed, except I had more money to spend. Bargains still abounded. As I dug deeper into one bin of handbags, I suddenly looked at my left hand. My diamond engagement ring was missing.

I stood in shock for a few moments, looking blankly at my empty hand. My ring had fallen off. Where? In what bin? Looking around me, I tried to retrace my steps. Had I lost it here, in the bin of purses? Over there, among shoes? My eyes began to glaze. The hordes of shoppers, milling around me, blurred together. I tried to imagine calling Larry and telling him I had lost my thousand-dollar ring in Filene's basement. He would ask what I thought I was doing in Filene's. It wasn't as if I'd lost it in the stacks at Widener. Could I say it had been stolen? Could I pretend I'd been somewhere else? I didn't think I could lie. The only alternative was not to go home at all. Maybe I would have to remain in the East, find friends to stay with, hope everything would blow over. I thought of my meager store of travelers' checks, barely enough to cover three nights in the Holiday Inn.

But I had to do what I could. Beckoning the clerk who was nearest, I said to her in a near-whisper, "Pardon me. I think I've lost my diamond ring somewhere in this bin, or maybe over in shoes." She looked disbelieving. Next to me, a woman began to rummage furiously in the bin.

"I wouldn't say that so loudly, if I were you," the clerk said. "Don't spread it around or we'll have a mob here. Just a minute, I'll get a stock boy."

A young man who looked about fourteen, but was probably twenty, appeared at my side. He didn't seem very smart: his eyes were dull, and he kept pushing back his greasy hair with one hand. Although I didn't think he could be much help, I told him my story once more. Nodding, he turned and vigorously began to empty the bin of purses, tossing them out like a terrier scrabbling down a gopher hole, scattering clods of dirt. Soon bags were heaped on the floor. I stood helplessly, still transfixed by my doom, and asked myself where I could go when I left Filene's. "Huh!" he said abruptly. "Is this it?" He held up my engagement ring.

My relief was so strong that I felt a little faint. I took the ring and jammed it over the boil on my third finger. Then I hugged the stock boy, kissed him on the cheek, and fled. Out on the street, I realized I should have given him some money, but I was too shaken to return to the basement. Making blindly for the subway, I went back to the Holiday Inn, where I lay down on the bed until dinner. That night I became ill, feeling panicky and as if I couldn't breathe, and then I developed a migraine headache. Next morning, too sick to go to the library, I called Larry on the phone. We agreed I should give up and fly home to Minneapolis. In the airport, between throbs, I wondered briefly if the same elegant shoe store was still on Boylston Street, if our old apartment had been renovated, and if Humphrey Bogart was still playing the Brattle. I'd never know. I was too late. Life had swept me along in a different direction, almost as if I'd driven by the freeway signs for Boston without ever noticing that I'd passed the last exit.

After my college summer in Boston, I wanted to extend my boundaries farther. During my junior year, I began thinking of Europe. I had been to the city; now it was time to go abroad. During the fall, I heard a charismatic black New York minister lecture on an African program that combined Christian renewal, charitable work, and living with natives in their villages. I glowed with altruism thinking of this unusual travel experience. It wouldn't be like one of those European tours where one only saw the surface of things. To earn our way, the minister explained, we would spend Christmas vacation talking to service organizations, churches, high schools, or any group in our home town that might contribute money for the program. That weekend I called home, anxious to share this exciting opportunity with my mother. "And I'll just ask the Chamber of Commerce what groups I can talk to," I explained, "like Lions, or Kiwanis, and various groups at our church."

Mother didn't seem as excited as I was. She asked some questions about living conditions and food in the villages. "And I'm really uneasy about your going around asking everybody in Ames for money," she said. A few days later she called back. My new stepfather had offered to provide money for a summer school in

England. Would I trade a summer in the African bush for a summer in London? My altruism vanished immediately. I would!

Perhaps I fell in love with London because I had few preconceived ideas about what to expect. Perhaps my rides on the M.T.A. and my modest explorations of the winding streets around Harvard Square had convinced me that I could find my way around London. Perhaps almost every college student who goes to Europe has a wonderful time. Whatever the reasons, I began that summer an affair with London that, despite our frequent separations, still continues. What I remember with most pleasure about my London summer was how self-confident I felt. Armed with a folding street map, suitably dressed in a wool tweed walking suit I had borrowed from Mother, I tapped my way along the drizzled gray sidewalks with a steel-tipped umbrella I'd bought in Oxford Street. I thought I probably looked Canadian, a part of the Empire. Click, click, click, I tapped, thinking when I walked home from the Underground late at night that I could stab my assailant with that steel tip. Who would assault anyone armed with such a weapon, anyway? Click, click, click. But London didn't seem to be a city where bad things could happen. It was a city with cheery colored maps of the Underground, helpful bobbies at street corners, and large-bosomed, gray-haired women in amorphous felt hats who gave crisp answers to my inquiries. Here I felt, I was free in a way I had never been before.

When my summer school was over, I had a few weeks to travel with a friend from Smith, Joyce, another English major. Tours or train fare looked prohibitively expensive. We also had both spent more money already than our budgets allowed. What now? Trying not to picture my mother's horrified face, I suggested hitchhiking. Together, I told Joyce, we'd be quite safe. Everyone said hitchhiking was perfectly OK in Europe. And we could use hostels, travel with light backpacks, and save lots of money. "I don't think I'll tell my mother until after it's over, though," I confided to Joyce. "She'd only worry. I'll write from our hostel stops, but I just won't say how we got there."

On the morning when I stepped onto a country road and stuck out my hand, I felt naked. As I stood there, my thumb stretched like Pinocchio's nose, until it was a mile long. The first few cars whizzed by. My face turned red. Joyce, giggling, was sitting by her pack a few yards away. I had agreed to try first, but I wasn't sure how long I could keep my nerve. What would happen, I began to wonder, if we couldn't get any rides? How far could I walk in a day in my canvas sneakers? A car suddenly screeched to a stop. Joyce and I looked at each other. "Let's go," I said, and she nodded. Climbing into the back seat, I took a deep breath. Up, up, and away!

A year later, back in Ames, I remembered the damp green mists on a road in Wales, a chill wind sweeping through the ruins of Tintagel, the rosy red glow of the brick at Kenilworth Castle. Last August, and England, seemed impossibly far away. Now, bound for graduate school, I was marking time in Ames all summer, making what money I could, and walking restlessly around the town. Had my time in England been real? Would I ever leave home for good?

I always came back to Ames. Although in my imaginary scrapbook I proudly labeled my summers in Boston and England as "The City" and "Going to Europe," I had many large, empty pages of summers in Ames that filled up without my noticing much what went into them. Even during my two years of graduate school at Berkeley, I spent all my vacations at home. I thought I needed to return to my roots, and I felt I owed my mother something to balance the time I was taking away from her.

Whatever did I do during those long summers? I was often alone. Few of my friends lived in Ames anymore. During the days I worked, mainly at the *Ames Daily Tribune,* where the job was now too familiar. My last summer home, when I was supposed to be recuperating from mononucleosis acquired at Berkeley, I only worked part-time, shelving books in the airless tunnels of the Iowa State Library. I carried sandwiches for lunch and sat on the clipped green lawn outside the library, wondering if I should try to meet some of the summer students who were passing back and forth to classes. But the glare of the July sun, combined with the drowsiness I felt after two hours of sorting books, turned my lassitude into paralysis.

When the day was over, I went home. After dinner, I curled in the coolest corner of the living room and read. Every summer I had ambitions: I'd finish next year's Elizabethan reading list, or maybe even just *The Faerie Queene*; I'd prepare for the honors exam; I'd read the rest of Dickens. But instead I checked out best-sellers from the Ames library, the ones with a five-day limit and shiny plastic covers, or other novels that caught my fancy and just might fit somewhere in my studies eventually. One summer, after my trip to England, I read nothing but British mysteries, Dorothy Sayers, Ngaio March, Josephine Tey, Margery Allingham. Once safe in an English village, I could escape boredom. I happily let Peter Wimsey swoop down in his Daimler and carry me off to Oxford.

Without Charlie, my evenings would have been even longer. Until my last summer at home, Charlie, an old friend from high school, worked at an Ames bank during vacations. All his cronies had disappeared too, so we sought each other's company for movies, walks, and Sunday drives around the countryside. Since Charlie and I had never been romantically involved, our friendship was easy. My mother and stepfather liked him too, and some evenings we just stayed at my house, where Charlie drank beer and read books about Franklin Delano Roosevelt, and I wrote letters or tried to do my daily number of pages in *Piers Plowman.* In the new music room my stepfather played the piano, a black concert grand that was another addition to our family. When cascades of Bach no longer poured into the living room, Charlie and I put down our books and waited for my stepfather to join us. My mother came in from gardening or sewing or reading *The New Yorker,* and we all talked for a while. Sometimes, if I was very tired, I even went to bed before Charlie went home, leaving him sitting comfortably in the living room with my parents, smoking a last cigarette.

Occasionally, after my frustration with Dugal at Smith, and during my tempestuous courtship by Larry at Berkeley, I allowed myself to wonder why my romances always seemed so unhappy and my friendship with Charlie so pleasant. I decided that probably love with sex in it was different, harder, and more troubled. Once at the dinner table my parents asked me if I had ever thought of marrying Charlie. I was startled. No, I hadn't, I told them, though I could see it was hard to explain why. "We are *very* fond of each other," I said, "but we just aren't *attracted* in that kind of way." My stepfather grunted, an explosive sound that indicated a disbelief in the general good sense of whoever had caused it. My mother said, "Well, that's too bad, dear." No one mentioned the subject again.

Before I went to sleep each night, I made sure my pillow was only inches away from the open window in the study where I now slept. The heavy warmth of the summer night lay over me like a wet towel. The same crickets I had heard all my life chirped in the backyard, the same tires squealed around our sharp corner, the same dogs barked far down the block. Lying on the bunk bed, I let my mind wander back to Smith. Scenes and people floated behind my eyes, like snippets of movies rerun, distant and insubstantial. I felt not eighteen, or twenty-one, but the child I had always been in this house, yet with a load of years piled on top of me. The summer after I had graduated from Smith, still depressed by my failure to achieve a Summa, I wondered if everything since high school had been a mistake. I had thought I had a sure path to follow, but somehow it always ended here, in this narrow bed, in the unmoving summer heat.

When I stepped off the train in Oakland the fall after my Smith graduation, the cool air from the Bay blew across my face like a promise. Driving up University Avenue, I noticed Spanish-style stucco buildings, dusty palm trees, liquor supermarkets, Mexican restaurants, and the large modern blocks of university buildings. Everything looked almost new. I could tell that people here lived in the open: I saw their outdoor tables at a restaurant, sports cars with tops down, tanned faces and sandaled feet. Things were certainly going to be different from Smith, I thought to myself. Inside my new home, the graduate dorm called International House, I liked its Moorish flavor, iron scrollwork, and ceramic tile. Peeking into the central courtyard, I saw a few students seated at glass-topped tables set among trees and flowering shrubs. After Smith, Berkeley seemed as exotic as Casablanca.

But the Ivy League had extended its tendrils farther than I'd thought. In a registration line of English graduate students a few days later, when we introduced ourselves we sounded like a roll call of Eastern colleges. The young man behind me was from Princeton, the girl in front of me from Radcliffe. She already knew several of the professors, she told me, because her Radcliffe tutor had studied with them. She and the Princeton man exchanged recommendations: "I hear Traugott is absolutely terrific, and so is Orgel. Renaissance or eighteenth century is the only way to go." "They really stress the eighteenth century on the M.A. exam, I guess. You have to know *everything* about Boswell and Johnson, and Dryden absolutely by heart. Did you know only a third of the people who take it pass with a recommendation to proceed to the Ph.D.?" As I listened, a familiar depression settled over me.

Walking across crowded Sproul Plaza, I felt as comfortingly anonymous as one of the I.B.M. cards I constantly filled out and filed. But once I entered the classroom of "Studies in Middle-English Literature," I might have been back in a Smith seminar: students taking notes, studying each other impassively, and, though seated, plainly tensed as if ready at any moment to jump the starting line. After class, drinking coffee on the sunny terrace of the Student Union, I felt the pressures of the classroom recede. I often joined a gossiping table of grad students, though I was careful to pick ones who might grumble about a lengthy assignment, but who would never inquire whether I had done the extra reading. In 1961 and 1962, no one yet talked politics or student revolutions. All around us undergraduates laughed and called to each other, exchanging news about sororities and dances and meetings. A few professors I didn't know sat by themselves at a corner table. Surrounded by lives which didn't impinge on mine, I relaxed. But once I left the terrace, and reclaimed my spot at the library study table in front of the English shelves, scowling graduate students, deep in concentration, looked up, noted my arrival, and stared down at their notes again. A few, lost to the everyday world, never looked up at all.

During my second year at Berkeley, competition heated up, as we M.A. students began to prepare for our oral exam, whose toughness was legendary and whose subjects were as unpredictable as the faculty who took turns administering it. "Frankly, we use it to weed people out," one professor said to me in an advising session. I felt my scholarly roots were so shallow all they would need was one firm tug. Even at my favorite terrace table, otherwise easygoing students began to compare notes. "Have you read all of Chaucer? How well do you know the *Troilus*?" "Do you really think we have to read *The Romance of the Rose?*" "Is it true they think that the minor Spenser poems are as important as *The Faerie Queene?*" There was no reading list for the M.A. exam. It presumed, its description read, "a knowledge of the main periods and important authors in English literature from medieval times through the nineteenth century." That covered a lot of territory.

As I approached the M.A. exam, I could hear the "Summa" voice in the distance, coming closer. I wanted to silence it. But it appeared in a new form, the nasal accents of Antonia Quincy, an English graduate student from Wellesley who was also living in International House. Very tall, with bright red hair and copious freckles, she carried her large frame with defiant self-deprecation. When we were in one class together, Antonia always checked on my progress. Had I finished all the Cowper? Could she borrow my notes for the lecture she'd missed last Friday? How had I done on the last paper? For the next one, she thought of doing a detailed scansion of the opening of "The Hind and the Panther," because it had so many subtle cross-rhythms. Did I think my Woodrow Wilson Fellowship would be renewed next year? Hers might be; Mr. Smith had been very encouraging. After a while, I learned to avoid Antonia, letting her advance in the lunch line, brushing my teeth noisily if she stood at a nearby sink, waving but walking away quickly when we passed on the campus.

But during the fall when we were both studying for the M.A. exam, it was hard to miss Antonia. She seemed to pop up everywhere, asking me questions about dates, chronologies, and sequences. It was well known that many favorite exam questions focused on lists: the reigns of the English kings and queens, the dates of Shakespeare's plays, the sequence of pre-Renaissance drama. Many of us bought large rolls of paper and covered our walls with lists, trying to squeeze all the important dates into their proper places. I always had a hard time memorizing numbers, and my lists grew increasingly befuddling as the weeks before the exam shortened. When did Chaucer write "The Parliament of Fowls"? Which came first, *The Winter's Tale* or *Cymbeline?* When was Queen Anne, and where did she fit with all the Georges? Sometimes Antonia caught me at the breakfast table, where I always ate with a group of chemists, and asked me questions I had never thought of.

"What was Shelley's most important work?" "Have you read much Scott?" "Do you have anything I could borrow on the late tragedies? I'm going over them the second time now." Her voice began to haunt me, carrying echoes of my old competitor at Smith, Chris Morgan. I wondered if Chris — indeed, the fierce academic rivalry of Lawrence House itself — had somehow spanned the miles and unfairly metamorphosed into the person of Antonia Quincy. One night, after a late night with Larry, I was taking a shower in the communal bathroom. The warm water beat on my back like a friendly masseuse. I was half asleep, thinking of nothing but the sensation of pounding water. The room had been empty when I entered, but before I finished, someone else came in and took the stall next to mine. As I was drowsily toweling myself dry a few minutes later, Antonia's high, nasal voice came over the partition. "Sue, is that you?"

"Yes," I said.

Antonia's shower stopped. "Oh, good. I looked for you tonight and couldn't find you. I've been working all night on chronologies. Tell me, can you date Pope's canon?" There was a silence for a moment as I stopped toweling. "No," I said abruptly. "I can't."

"Oh," said Antonia, complacently. "Someone told me that got asked on an exam last week. I just wondered." Walking down the hall toward my room, I was filled with murderous rage. But now I think I was angry at something more complex than Antonia. I didn't know how to escape, not just from her, but from the competition itself. I hated the fact that Antonia could tap so easily into my own fears, making my mind race and my stomach churn ("Pope's canon? Is that really important? When was 'Essay on Man,' anyway? What will happen if they ask me that?") Driven as she was, Antonia made me realize how I was driven too.

Fortunately, sometimes I forgot Antonia. Berkeley was wonderfully distracting. Politically unaware as I was, it also seemed serene. When I climbed its labyrinthine streets, and sat looking out over the East Bay, I sensed my anxieties dissipating somewhere behind me in the sun-browned hills. I was also distracted by men. Living in a graduate dorm in which men outnumbered women two to one, and taking classes with men, I found myself recovering some of my social confidence that had drained away at Smith. I flirted, dated, went to parties. Although almost immediately I met my future husband, for a while I dated other men too. I often felt as if I were whirling on a crowded floor where willing partners were waiting for the next dance. California, I thought to myself, was indeed a land of plenty. It had siphoned off the cream of the Ivy League, mixed in the best of students from everywhere else — Beloit, Chapel Hill, Toronto, Pomona — and set them all down in the few square miles surrounding the Berkeley campus. If I couldn't find the right man here, I would probably not find him anywhere.

Who might sit next to me at the breakfast table? The tall lanky chemist from M.I.T.? The Indian economist? The Canadian philosopher? Hurrying to my first class, I caught up with two men who were taking it too. One was short, blond, quiet; he smiled shyly when I asked him a question about the assignment. Did he date anyone? I wondered, smiling back. I mentally filed him away for possible future investigation. After class, I surveyed the terrace of the student union until I saw a table of three men from my afternoon seminar. In the library, between concentrated bouts of translating Middle English lyrics, I let my attention wander to the men who came and went at the tables near me. Which of them was married? Which was smart? Which looked as if he had a sense of humor? Late in the afternoon, I took time to sit with my friend Josh on the steps of International House. What would happen, I idly asked myself, if Josh, so bright and lovable, were two years older and not already involved with my best friend, Sophie? After an evening with Larry, I passed the young man on duty at the I House Information Desk. He sat there night after night, intriguing and remote, casually brushing back his thinning reddish hair. Sophie told me he was a law student. He answered the hardest questions, she said, and was undoubtedly bound for the Law Review. What could I think of to catch his attention? Was he the man I'd been waiting for?

Waiting for a man was something I took for granted. It required patience. Although I could perch on a coffee-shop stool next to someone I wanted to meet, or invite someone already in lunch line to join me on the student union terrace, I had to wait after those overtures to see if he might call. Even Sophie, with her wider experience of men, had to wait. One night she went out with an older teaching assistant, divorced, a promising physicist and a witty raconteur. They danced, dined, drove through San Francisco, and walked on the beach until dawn. She never saw him again, and since she couldn't call him, she never knew why.

In International House, such waiting was symbolized by a bobby pin attached to a string. On the wall of each room was a buzzer with a black button no bigger than a fingernail. When a phone call came to the house, the downstairs operator buzzed the recipient's room. After hearing a loud "BRRRRRR," you had a few moments to hit the button. That signaled the operator that you were racing down the hall to pick up the phone at the head of the stairs. If you were not in your room, you of course missed the call. Few of us spent much time in our rooms. So in some primeval period of I House history, an ingenious girl had discovered that the loud "BRRRR" of the buzzer caused the button to vibrate slightly. If one balanced something on top of the button — it was just deep enough, perhaps a quarter-inch, to support a bobby pin — the vibration would make the bobby pin fall off. To save one's hunting for the bobby pin on the floor afterward, it could be attached to a piece of string, which was then Scotch-taped to the wall. Upon returning to the room, one could instantly tell whether anyone had called. I focused on that pin so sharply I can still see its precise shape, wavy bumps on one side and straight metal on the other, a dark brown line silent against the creamy plaster wall. Who had called? Was it the guy I had coffee with yesterday, or the one in my seminar who said we should have a drink sometime? Was it Larry, wanting to make up after our fight last night? Will whoever it was call again? Almost every woman's room had its bobby pin. When we were allowed to visit the men's rooms in I House, I was interested — though not surprised — to see that none of the men had anything on *their* buzzers.

What hung upon the buzzer was a serious business. Although my social life now had some of the same variety and spontaneity I remembered from high school — lots of friends, lots of dates — I felt uneasily that any day I might find myself involved in something with lifetime consequences. Already, in my second year of graduate studies, I was one of the few girls from either my high school or Lawrence House class who had not married. Sophie had been engaged twice. After graduate school, what next?

I wondered about consequences the night of Roger Solomon's phone call. It was a blistering hot summer July in Iowa when the ringing phone woke my stepfather from a sound sleep at midnight. After he tapped at my bedroom door, half-irritated, half-incredulous, I had a hard time clearing my own sleep-encrusted mind to take the call. Then I could scarcely hear what Roger was saying. I even had a hard time for a few minutes remembering who Roger was.

As a fellow student in my Victorian Lit seminar that spring, Roger had caught my attention as a possible date. Reasonably attractive, a Harvard graduate, he had a beguiling eccentricity that was either quirky intelligence or lack of discipline. His reports were always on strange, unknown writers he had dug from a dusty bin in a used-book store on Telegraph Avenue, or traced through an obscure footnote in a minor history of the period. His remarks wandered, occasionally focusing to a point either so fascinating or so off-the-mark that our dozing professor, looking out the window, jumped a little and cleared his throat. The other students just stared at him, puzzled. When I spoke with him after class, or at a table of coffee-drinking students, Roger was vivacious and energetic, but somehow not always quite there.

When Roger invited me to dinner, followed by a Handel oratorio, I was already close to "going steady" with Larry, but I accepted, partly from a wish to state my independence, and partly from curiosity. Roger had also invited Monty Beacham and his wife, a professor so eminent that no mere M.A. candidate usually met him. As far as I could gather, Roger had simply called up Mr. Beacham, introduced himself on the phone, and somehow managed to snag the superstar into an acceptance. It was an odd dinner. The only kitchen facilities Roger had were a hot plate and a toaster. Seated on the floor in Roger's basement room, we ate creamed tuna and peas on toast. Pop! went the toast, and Roger ladled tuna onto a paper plate and handed it to Mr. Beacham. Pop! went the toast again, this time for Mrs. Beacham. Since it was all we had, Roger had made a great deal of creamed tuna. Attempting polite conversation while balancing the wobbly plate on my knee, I admired Roger's cheerful aplomb. The Beachams looked as if they didn't know quite what they were doing there. When Roger urged them to come back to his apartment after the oratorio, they politely declined. He didn't appear at all taken aback. He obviously considered the dinner party a success.

Everyone had a lot to drink. Roger, who had borrowed crystal wine glasses from his landlady upstairs, poured from a large jug of Gallo mountain red. When we finally rose from the floor, I felt unsteady. The oratorio passed in a haze. Afterward, Roger insisted that we stop at his place for another drink before going home. Leaving his apartment, I belatedly realized that Roger was very drunk. The car wove back and forth across the road, which fortunately was residential and untraveled. Once, when he aimed unerringly for a tree that grew in the middle of the street, I grabbed the wheel and steadied the car. When we stopped in front of I House, I leaned over and gave him a friendly kiss. "This was fun, Roger, but you're in no shape for driving," I said. "Would you please go very slowly on the way home? And would you also call me as soon as you get there, so I'll know you made it safely?" I was thinking of the tall, spreading tree. Roger promised. When my buzzer rang some ten minutes later, I was relieved to be done with the evening.

In the few weeks that remained before summer vacation, I didn't go out with Roger again. Once he called me and asked me to dinner with his father, who was visiting from the Virgin Islands. Knowing how angry Larry would be, I declined. That was my last contact with Roger until the July night in Ames a month or so later, when my stepfather woke me and told me I had a phone call.

"Susan?" A faraway voice asked. It was Roger. After some desultory conversation, he suddenly changed the subject. "I've been thinking, Susan. My brother married a Smith girl, and they get along fine. I think maybe that's what I should do myself. How about it? What do you say?"

As I stumbled through a response to my first proposal, I was distracted by the sight of my stepfather silently laughing and gesticulating wildly to my mother, now also roused from sleep. They could tell from my answers what was happening. I said something to Roger about not knowing each other very well, about how being a Smith girl wasn't enough to base such an important decision on, and finally about how I would write him a letter. The next day I did, telling him I was in fact involved with someone else. I hadn't been able to say that on the phone, probably because I was reluctant to relinquish the proposal until the clear light of day forced me to. When I saw Roger on campus the next fall, he avoided me. We exchanged a few words when we met by chance, but neither of us mentioned the phone call or letter. When I told Larry about it, he said Roger had probably been drunk. I supposed he was right.

So marriage was in the air. As I patiently explained to my friend Josh, who as a mere junior felt any idea of marrying was absurd, "At my age, it's something I *could* do." I didn't think I was ready, but I was old enough. And how long could I continue going to mixers? When I left International House, how many men would I meet? The unknown looked even more dismal when I thought of Larry, an eligible and compelling young man who wanted to marry me. How could I give him up? By the end of my second week in Berkeley Larry had entered my life and, like an erratic magnetic field, instantly disturbed my emotional compass. Hungarian and quick-tempered; highly intelligent and ambitious; boyish and curly-haired; he was irresistible. Had I always thought I needed someone smarter than I was? Larry was planning to complete his Ph.D. in two years. Was I leery of supersophisticated men? Larry, claiming a European heritage, had old-fashioned ideas about women that I found comforting. Was I trying to loosen my Ivy League values, without letting them go completely? Larry let me know that he *could* have gone to Yale but pronounced it inferior to Cal Tech. And finally, I argued to myself, if I was so strongly attracted to a man, didn't it have to be love?

While moving, though with some fear and reluctance, toward a binding relationship with Larry, I still felt the pull of other possibilities. Larry promised tight security; but Berkeley and San Francisco tempted me with the beginnings of different paths leading to unknown destinations. "If you don't stop now," the Director of Graduate Studies told me after I had successfully passed my M.A. exam, "you could finish your Ph.D. in four more years. Then we could place you anywhere — Swarthmore, or perhaps even Smith, for example. To come out of Berkeley at twenty-eight with our

Ph.D. is a ticket to virtually anyplace you want to go. That's if you don't stop now."

But I wanted to stop. Something out there was stronger than the lure of my name on the right office door. "I want to find out if I like teaching," I said apologetically to the director. "So I think I'm going to take a part-time job next year at San Francisco State." I didn't tell him I was also thinking about getting married. I didn't explain that I felt life was waiting, perhaps just across the Bay, and I was afraid I might miss it.

Since the Director of Graduate Studies had once come to Berkeley from the Midwest, did he recall the alluring foreign flavor of the city? Like me, had he perhaps grown up tasting only Scandinavian smorgasbords? Did he love to explore the restaurants of San Francisco? I didn't think I could ask him. I wasn't sure a Director of Graduate Studies was interested in food. When Larry took me to dinner in San Francisco, we sometimes had cheese blintzes at David's, goulash at Des Alpes, flautas with guacamole at a small Mexican restaurant someone in I House had discovered, or snow peas and prawns in a noisy, second-story room jammed above a souvenir shop in Chinatown. I loved it all. As I stabbed with my chopsticks at a slippery bamboo shoot, or smeared sour cream on a blintz, or tried to eavesdrop on a rapid-fire French conversation in Des Alpes, I felt truly cosmopolitan.

To me, San Francisco and Berkeley were a gateway to the world. In Berkeley, in easy walking distance from I House, two tiny theatres, Studio A and Studio B of the Cinema Guild, offered a dedicated repertory of classic and foreign films. Pinned on my wall were the current Studio A and B listings, boasting definitive synopses by Pauline Kael, who had parted from the Cinema Guild so recently that her ghost was still deferentially recalled. With her guidance, I experienced the New Wave, immersed myself in symbolism, shook my head indignantly at important social commentary. I thought I understood Sweden of the 1960s, France of the 1950s, America of the 1940s. I knew, I said happily to myself, what was going on in the world.

Not all my cultural life took place on the screen. Avidly reading the theatre page in the San Francisco *Chronicle* and studying the posters on campus kiosks, I tried to keep up on what was happening "live." Some nights Larry and I drove into the city and sat in cheap seats at the San Francisco Symphony, or stood all through *Don Giovanni,* or squinted at a faraway ballet from the second balcony. As the maestro raised his baton, the curtains parted, and the audience burst into self-satisfied applause, I thought: I am here! Where it's happening! I was convinced art and life were synonymous.

Since I did not have a car, what I saw of San Francisco on my own was limited to where I could go on bus and streetcar. I never ventured very far. So for me San Francisco remained mostly green grass and flower carts, the bustle of Chinatown, and the clanging cable-car ride down to Fisherman's Wharf. I glimpsed the rest of the city — as I had glimpsed the town of Northampton, the suburbs of Boston, and the grimy outskirts of London — only from behind a blurred window. For me, San Francisco was a place where lively, creative men and women lived in flower-decked pastel town houses, drank vintage wines they selected from their favorite Napa Valley wineries, ate quiet suppers in North Beach restaurants I'd never heard of, and sat up late talking about politics and literature.

Things could happen in San Francisco, I was convinced, that might not happen anywhere else. One weekday afternoon Larry and I wandered slowly past the monkeys, elephants, and tigers in Fleishhacker Zoo. This was as close as I would probably ever get to Africa, India, the Himalayas, I thought. When Larry and I came to a cage where a koala bear clung sleepily to a branch, I paused. I had never seen a koala bear before. It looked so soft and fuzzy, like the teddy bear I had loved as a child. Just then a keeper came up to the enclosure, carrying an armful of leafy stalks. Opening the cage, he turned and looked at Larry and me. We were the only visitors in sight. "Would you like to have a closer look?" he asked.

"Oh yes," I said eagerly, and walked inside, carefully moving close to the low branch where the koala still lay, his eyes half-shut. "Pat him if you like," said the keeper. He watched while I reached my hand out tentatively. "Go ahead, don't be afraid. He won't hurt you." To my surprise, the koala was rough, not soft, more like steel wool than the plush of a teddy bear. "Not what you expected, is it?" the keeper said. "Everyone thinks they're all soft and sweet, but they're not."

Driving back to Berkeley that night, my mind kept returning to our afternoon at the zoo. Something had happened there I knew I was going to remember. Was it the astonishment of being invited to enter a locked cage? The keeper had said that the koala ate eucalyptus leaves, which grew well here, but not in many other places; maybe that's why other zoos didn't have them. Was San Francisco the only spot I might ever see a koala again? Or was the rough, wiry feel of the koala's coat an unexpected reality I would never forget?

At my request, Larry took the long route home, so I could see the waves rolling onto Ocean Beach. Once we had driven all the way down to Carmel, just for a day, and I had loved the sweep of the coast, mile after mile of sunlit surf, as the brown and green hills tumbled down to an endless sheet of water. Now when I saw the ocean from the top of a San Francisco hill, or watched its long slow roll onto Ocean Beach, I thought of how far it stretched, south, north, far beyond to the west. In Iowa I had grown up surrounded by space, seeing possibilities reflected in fields and sky. Cloistered at Smith, I had never given up watching for light through the ivy-covered windows. Here at Ocean Beach I was at last free again. If I pushed offshore, and sailed for weeks, I would land somewhere in the Orient; I could almost see Shanghai, Peking, Hong Kong, names jagged as pagodas, echoing to faint temple bells. They waited for me across the water. All I had to do was go.

The sun was setting as Larry and I drove along the beach. I asked him if we could stop for a while. I wanted to watch until all the color had left the sky. "Oh, come on, Susan," he said impatiently. He had been up late in his lab the night before. "It's nice, but it's just a sunset. That's the difference between you and me. As far as I'm concerned, you've seen one sunset, you've really seen them all. I've got other things to do besides sit and stare at the sky."

A few months later I was waiting on the terrace of the student union for Larry to join me for lunch. After a short separation, Larry and I were back together again. I had not thought I was ready to get married, but today I was fairly sure. Today, Larry had suggested, we could go to San Francisco and look at engagement rings. I wondered if I would feel differently about San Francisco now that I was almost engaged.

Behind me at another table, some English graduate students I knew were talking and laughing. I would not be spending much time with them anymore. As I sipped my coffee, hoping Larry would come soon, I caught a glimpse of my friend Josh, who was hurrying across the plaza in the near distance. He was talking animatedly with someone I didn't recognize, waving his hands, his shoulders shaking with emotion. Josh, who was interested in politics, was involved at the moment with Cuba.

Then I saw Larry, passing Josh, whom he didn't like, a few feet away. He greeted Josh without stopping and turned in my direction. Although he couldn't see me yet, I smiled at him. He looked so determined, so purposeful, as he strode through the crowd, carrying a clipboard on which, I knew, dozens of intricate equations would be scribbled like cross-hatching. I didn't understand one of them. I hoped he had had a productive morning in the lab, so he would be in a good mood. I noticed that Josh had disappeared in the crowd. As Larry bounded up the steps two at a time, I admired his lean, graceful body. I stood up to give him a kiss, hoping the graduate students at the table behind me wouldn't notice. Suddenly I remembered Josh's and my conversation in the I House coffee shop earlier that year. "And then what?" he had asked me. I hadn't known. I had looked out the window and gazed longingly at the bright shapes of San Francisco, as though they could tell me. Now, I thought, feeling for a moment the taut muscles of Larry's back, I would be able to give Josh an answer.

ABOUT THE AUTHOR

Susan Toth, author of the successful *Blooming: A Small-Town Girlhood,* was born in 1940 in Ames, Iowa. She attended Smith College, University of California at Berkeley, and University of Minnesota, and, since 1969, has been a member of the English Department at Macalester College. She lives with her daughter Jennifer, on a quiet street in St. Paul, Minnesota.